From *NEVERBOSS*:

0.72

If they were true grades, that would be his GPA.

Jeffrey stood in the bathroom stall and tried to steady his breathing. He felt humiliated. Never, in his whole life, had he received a C. Now they were all C's—at best. Jeffrey knew it was silly, but the grading system got under his skin.

> *How dare they? He thought. I'm a phenomenal leader! I don't just boss people around. I roll up my sleeves and pitch in. I care more than anyone.*

It was arbitrary. They were upset. The grades weren't real.

Jeffrey waited for the gaggle of meeting attendees to pass, and then emerged to wash his face.

> *I'll show them.*

Neverboss is the leadership story of Jeffrey Jackson—a manager suddenly forced to turn around his career, his department... and his company. In the process, he discovers how the best leaders take charge without bossing, and how they unleash lasting cultures of leadership at all levels.

NEVERBOSS

Great Leadership by Letting Go

A Rapid Blueprint for Hands-Off Leadership

KEVIN CRENSHAW
with Laura Shanae Crenshaw

© 2017 Priacta, Inc. All rights reserved worldwide.

Although based on actual events, NEVERBOSS is a novel—a work of fiction to teach leadership and business principles. The circumstances and characters, while based on real situations regularly encountered by clients, businesses, workers, and leaders are fictitious and general and do not represent any particular company, scenario, or individual except where specifically identified. Real stories and experiences not in the public domain have been combined with other stories from similar situations and their identifying information altered beyond recognition. Therefore, any resemblance to any person or company is entirely unintentional except where noted.

Limit of Liability/Disclaimer of Warranty. While the author(s) have used their best efforts and experience in creating this book, they make no representations or warranties regarding accuracy, completeness, or suitability for a particular situation, and they specifically disclaim any implied warranties of merchantability or fitness for any particular purpose. No warranty may be created or extended by sales representatives, websites, or sales materials. The principles taught herein are advisory only, are NOT to be considered legal or medical advice, and may not be suitable for your situation. The reader alone is responsible for their application and the results obtained therefrom. You should consult a professional where appropriate. Neither the publisher nor the author(s) shall be liable for any loss of profit or any other commercial damages, including but not limited to special, incidental, consequential, or other damages.

Websites and other materials referred to herein were current at the time of publication but are subject to change.

NEVERBOSS, LEADERSHIP STEPS, and the relaxed hierarchy symbol are trademarks of Priacta, Inc. HANDS-OFF LEADERSHIP is an "open" trademark of Priacta, Inc. (can be licensed without charge, see handsoffleadership.com). Other trademarks mentioned herein are trademarks or registered trademarks of their respective holders.

Dedicated to

bosses and workers in pain

and aching for excellence.

Based on real events.

Even though the overall plot and characters are fictional, the NEVERBOSS story has been assembled from cases I faced as a turnaround executive and leadership coach, from my personal life experiences, and from public business case studies.

It is our policy to guard confidentiality and always speak well of others. Therefore, we have combined, generalized, and altered stories and identifying details beyond recognition where it matters.

—Kevin Crenshaw, CEO of Priacta, Inc.

CONTENTS

Executive Summary	vii
Leadership is Broken	1
Guinea Pig	5

CULTURE — 11

HANDS-OFF LEADERSHIP
Who Feels the Pain?	13
Who Feels the Reward?	19
Who's Doing the Thinking?	23
Who's Taking the Initiative?	31
Redefining Pride	39
Step Up, Step Beside, Step Away	45

EXCITING MEETINGS
The Rat Trap	55
1-on-1's	71

UNIVERSAL SAFETY
Rules of Engagement	87
Open Floor Policy	97

CLARITY — 105

STRUCTURE
Roles, Supervisors, and Team Leaders	107
Communication	121

AUTHORITY
Give Authority, Not Tasks	129

ACCOUNTABILITY
Loyalty to Purpose, Not Personalities	139

CAPABILITY — 151

COMPETENCE
"How Do You Know?"	153

CAPACITY
Believing the Camel 171

RECRUITING
Moneyball Talent 179

FOCUS 195

MPAs
Most Profitable Activities 197

MULTIPURPOSING
Let Your Dragons Slay Each Other 207

SAYING NO
...To a Thousand Things 213

VISION 223

MISSION
Every Ship Needs a Compass 225

THEMATIC GOAL
The Key to Hyperfocus 235

ACTIVE WAITING STRATEGY
Never Let a Good Crisis Go to Waste 243

RESULTS 253

THE FINISH LINE
How to Avoid Succeeding to Death 255

GIVING CREDIT
Where Hands-Off Leadership Gets Tested 263

Into the Fire 273

Glossary of Tools & Resources 279

EXECUTIVE SUMMARY

We've all heard great stories of empowering leadership—extraordinary bosses who trusted their people and stepped back, with impressive results.

But it's been hard to repeat their success. Every story was unique. Each path forward was uncertain, complicated, or chaotic. If we want to change leadership for good, we need a simple pattern that works for everyone.

Neverboss **solves that problem.** More than a leadership tale, it's a step-by-step blueprint for powerful cultures of freedom and excellence—without chaos, fear, or firing. It's based on actual events, successful turnarounds, and the traits shared by liberated companies worldwide.

Each chapter of *Neverboss* builds on those before it. Each demonstrates a new action or tool that stops the pain of typical management. Relief is almost immediate, so you'll feel confident and excited to move to the next level.

The full transformation happens fast, and it sticks. The *Neverboss* story unfolds over 90 days, but you can do it faster or slower.

At the heart of *Neverboss* is Hands-Off Leadership. It's a new leadership approach, yet it builds on ideas from popular thought leaders like Lencioni, Covey, Marquet, Heath, and Pink. As a result, it feels comfortable and easy to implement. *Neverboss* points to original sources where you can learn more.

Hands-Off Leadership isn't traditional management, Holacracy, or anarchy. *It is firm leadership that gives away power as fast as people can handle it.* It's clearly in charge, but it doesn't dominate. It shares authority, but it never abdicates. It doesn't replace managers—it sets them on a mission to create leaders. With safe boundaries for everyone, bosses stop "bossing," and workers take ownership and initiative. The result is greatness.

HANDS-OFF LEADERSHIP
THE ROADMAP

The CULTURE section of *Neverboss* teaches the basics of Hands-Off Leadership. It forms the foundation of the Hands-Off Leadership Roadmap.

The rest of *Neverboss* teaches the structure that supports Hands-Off Leadership. The right organizational supports are essential. Otherwise, your systems and incentives will reward controlling, punish initiative, and undermine your message.

Executive Summary

> The bottom two Roadmap layers allow autonomy. The next two power mastery. The final two drive purpose/relatedness. These are the three elements of Motivation 3.0 in *Drive: The Surprising Truth about What Motivates Us*, by Dan Pink.

The Roadmap handles typical implementation issues at just the right times. CULTURE creates a foundation of safety, empowerment, and engagement. CLARITY ends confusion and fear. CAPABILITY prevents frustration and exhaustion. FOCUS ensures effectiveness. VISION eliminates futility and missed opportunities. And RESULTS avoids letdown and stagnation.

In the end, your company or team feels new, refreshing, liberated. People love their jobs. They take the initiative instead of waiting to be told. Information and innovation flow freely without distracting anyone. Best of all, your people think and act like leaders at all levels—unleashing cultures of leadership and excellence wherever they go.

I look forward to hearing *your* stories of leadership transformation. Together, one team and one company at a time, let's change the way the world leads.

Highest regards,

Kevin Crenshaw

LEADERSHIP IS BROKEN

"Leadership is broken, and it needs to change."

Edward J. Heart hated being late. But he hated nose-bleed views even more. He hurried to the front of the darkened auditorium and slipped into an open seat.

An energetic speaker paced on the stage.

"We're hardwired for ape-like, power-grabbing social patterns," she continued, "because it worked. In the Dark Ages when information moved slowly, traditional leadership *saved* us. You could either follow the strongest and smartest, or you died. Problem is, workers aren't ignorant anymore. They want to use their brains."

The speaker reached into her pocket and pulled out a cell phone. She held it up.

"Every one of you owns a computer more powerful than any computer in the world 30 years ago. You keep it in your back pocket and sit on it. You drop it in the toilet sometimes."

A ripple of laughter rolled through the crowd.

"Even in the darkest slums, people have smartphones. People can read. Your graveyard-shift, minimum wage janitor knows more than Alexander the Great learned in his entire life."

She paused and held up a finger.

"Think about it. In a different era, that janitor would be a king."

She let the audience chew on that, then hit a clicker in her hand. A graph with average literacy scores over time lit up the wall behind her.

"Our era is people rich. Your people are strong, clever, quick to adapt... and they can no longer be controlled by information monopolies. That's why traditional leadership isn't working. Try to control educated people, and they fight back. That's why you're burned out. That's why your best workers keep quitting."

The woman hit a clicker again. This time, a colorful pyramid graph appeared.

"I'm going to show you how to be a leader among kings. You may need to let go of everything you know about leadership. Forget the charming heroes you've seen in movies. Captain Kirk giving orders from his throne-like chair, looking so cool on the Starship Enterprise? That's not the future. That's the past."

As she moved through her presentation, Edward stewed. He'd seen enough leadership fads come and go. He knew charisma did not equal sound business advice. Still, her theory raised some interesting questions...

After the lecture ended, Edward waited for the usual crowd to dissipate somewhat. When the speaker looked less distracted, he approached and shook her hand.

"Edward Heart, CEO of Heart Manufacturing."

"Alexandra Hamilton," she replied with a firm handshake.

"Like the founding father?" Ed asked, raising an eyebrow.

"Less political and a better shot," she smirked. "It's a pleasure to meet you. What brought you to my keynote?"

"Well... I own a billion-dollar company," Edward said. "I've tried to retire three times, but my company functions horribly without me. The idea of managing less appeals. A lot. I just don't believe it can be done."

Alexandra's eyes twinkled. "It would be my honor to prove you wrong. Hire me to coach your team."

Edward grimaced. "How do I know you can deliver?"

"Give us your worst department. We'll turn it around in three months."

Edward rolled his eyes. "Now you're just exaggerating."

She shrugged. "If you don't see dramatic results in the first 30 days, fire us without pay."

GUINEA PIG

Heart Manufacturing manufactured a lot of things. As a result, they generated a lot of waste. Some of it was hazardous. Not fish-with-three-heads hazardous. Usually.

All the same, Heart wanted to do its eco-friendly duty—and stay compliant with government regulations. So Heart owned a subsidiary called GooCrew whose sole responsibility was to make the hazardous waste disappear. The factories didn't particularly care what happened to the waste, as long as they couldn't get in trouble for it.

Jeffrey Jackson loved his job.

GooCrew was broken up into seven regions. Jeffrey managed one of them all by himself. Unfortunately, Jeffrey's crew recently made a mistake, packing a few shipments of hazardous waste into the wrong types of containers. GooCrew was fined for it. Heart hated fines.

Jeffrey expected that's what this meeting was about.

He checked his watch again. Early. Good.

I'll apologize formally, he thought, *and be in my office in 30 minutes. Piece of cake.*

As the elevator doors closed around him, Jeffrey tugged on his sleeves. The exquisite, hand-tailored suit didn't fit quite right. It never had. But it was by far the nicest he'd ever owned. He straightened his shoulders, wondering if the cufflinks were too much.

Naturally, Jeffrey stopped dead in his tracks when he walked into the conference room and found Edward J. Heart—the owner, the legend—sipping a cup of coffee.

Jeffrey looked around, suddenly starting to sweat. A roomful of faces he vaguely knew eyed him curiously. Jeffrey's supervisor—Mr. Khalil, CEO of GooCrew—stood and greeted him with a handshake.

The meeting went downhill from there.

"Jeffrey, you are extremely valuable to us," Mr. Heart said warmly. "We believe in you and see the makings of a great leader."

"Oh. Thank you." Jeffrey squirmed in his chair, flattered, but unsure where this was going.

"At the same time, we see a few patterns in your management style that do not meet our company's standards."

There's the other shoe, he thought.

"Ah, yes, the storage mix-up." Jeffrey tried to look contrite. "I apologize for—"

"Actually," interrupted Mr. Khalil. "If it were just that one problem, we wouldn't be terribly worried."

Jeffrey's mouth snapped shut.

Mr. Heart nodded. "Your region has been generating an unusual number of complaints. Several assistant managers have quit or requested transfers, citing your management style as their primary complaint. Mr. Khalil, do you still have those complaints?"

Khalil picked up a stack of notecards and read from the one on top.

" 'He's a suffocating micromanager. He ridicules my best work and humiliates anyone who makes a mistake.' "

Khalil switched to another notecard and continued reading.

" 'I feel like a slave. Jeffrey never talks to me except to deliver ultimatums. I feel miserable and lonely all the time. I don't mind taking a demotion if I could just work in a place where people are nice.' "

Jeffrey's eyes widened, but before he could rebut, Khalil drew a third card.

" 'He constantly undermined the instructions I gave my workers. Clearly, you don't need a manager in this position because somehow Mr. Jackson has the time to personally deliver instructions to every employee.' "

Jeffrey felt his face going hot. "Hold on! That's *not* the whole story. Those guys were just mad because I enforce our standards!"

"You're not defective, Mr. Jackson." Mr. Heart smiled warmly. "It's just that there are certain skills that you have yet to develop. We believe you can develop them. In fact, you are *so* important to us that we have hired a personal executive coach for you."

Jeffrey did a double-take.

Mr. Heart smiled and nodded to a sharply dressed woman with bright eyes and a brighter smile. She leaned forward.

"Hi, Jeffrey! I'm Alexandra, and I'll be your coach for the next three months."

Alexandra slid a sheet of paper across the table.

"We don't want to put you in the hot seat for vague reasons," she said. "That wouldn't be fair. Mr. Khalil and I have been observing for a little while. These are the specific areas that need to improve."

Jeffrey looked at the list and scoffed.

"Building relationships with co-workers? Are you serious?"

Mr. Khalil adjusted his glasses with a disapproving frown. "We're not talking about fuzzy, touchy-feely stuff. We're talking about just talking to them. *Listening* to them. Relating to them on some level other than giving orders."

"But these *are* fuzzy, vague requests! How am I supposed to know when I've achieved..." Jeffrey glanced at the sheet, "...focus, for example? Much less prove it?"

"Great question!" Alexandra smiled. "If you turn that sheet over, there's a scorecard on the back. I'll teach you how to use it. You need to score B+ or higher in all these areas. The scores you see now are your current average grades. Scores came from everyone in this room: supervisors, heads of factory, and other people directly impacted by your work."

TURNAROUND SCORECARD

NAME: Jeffrey Jackson

SELF Grade = [/]   BOSS Grade = **D-**

STANDARD: *"An ideal employee in this position..."*	METRICS: *"We will know these standards are met when..."*	
CULTURE Creates leaders instead of followers. Builds relationships with co-workers.	- Workers take initiative - Workers say meetings are exciting and effective	[/] **F**
CLARITY Admits when wrong and allows team members to hold him accountable, regardless of title or rank. Doesn't overrule reasonable decisions made by workers.	- Workers are comfortable speaking up and feel heard - All workers know their areas of responsibility and have authority over them	[/] **D-**
CAPABILITY When a worker is underperforming, trains instead of taking over. Retains and improves employee talent.	- Improve employee turnover by at least 5%	[/] **F**
FOCUS Worker MPAs and KPIs are established. Workers are reporting KPIs.	- Overtime needs to drop to less than 5%	[/] **F**
VISION Responds to sudden threats and golden opportunities. Team works in a unified direction towards a shared master goal.	- Factories serviced on time, never forced to halt operations - Allocates budget carefully and maintains adequate emergency reserves	[/] **C**
RESULTS Team meets commitments and standards. Gives meaningful commendations to workers.	- No fines - Master goal is on target to be met - Workers feel they have received credit for their work	[/] **C**

NOTE: Every Turnaround Scorecard is unique, but uses Standard & Metrics columns. You'll learn how to make your own in the *Competence* chapter, p. 153.

As Jeffrey looked around the room, the last hints of his smirk disappeared. There were a *lot* of people here for a basic intervention.

Mr. Heart spoke. "Jeffrey, let me make this clear for you. Effective immediately, you are on probation. You have three months to improve. We're giving you the best tools available because we *want* you to succeed. But if, in the end, your performance still does not meet our company's standards, we will fire you without hesitation."

Jeffrey almost fell out of his chair.

"Your performance has a *measurable* cost," Mr. Heart continued. "When your crew falls behind schedule picking up hazardous waste, the factories you serve are forced to halt operations. Even a 30-minute delay is extremely expensive. Furthermore, the employee turnover rate in your region is 40% annually, and the workers we're losing are the best ones. Excessive overtime is causing payroll to be wildly over budget. Not to mention violations and fines."

Alexandra looked somber. "Jeffrey, the cost of all these mistakes from the last two quarters has been eight times your annual salary."

Shaken deeply, Jeffrey couldn't bring himself to make eye contact with anyone. Staring at his hands, he nodded to acknowledge he'd heard.

LEVEL ONE:
CULTURE

How to never give another order

WEEK ONE

HANDS-OFF LEADERSHIP

WHO FEELS THE PAIN?

0.72   If they were true grades, that would be his GPA. Jeffrey stood in the bathroom stall and tried to steady his breathing. He felt humiliated. Never, in his whole life, had he received a C. Now they were *all* C's—at best. Jeffrey knew it was silly, but the grading system got under his skin.

How dare they? He thought. *I'm a phenomenal leader! I don't just boss people around. I roll up my sleeves and pitch in. I care more than anyone.*

It was arbitrary. They were upset. The grades weren't real.

Jeffrey waited for the gaggle of meeting attendees to pass, and then emerged to wash his face.

I'll show them.

Within the hour, Jeffrey met with Alexandra again.

"First things first," she said. "You're being transferred to the Northwest region."

"*What!?*" Jeffrey stood, outraged. "That's the *one* region that performs worse than mine!"

"They know," Alexandra replied calmly. "Heart and Khalil think transferring will give you the best chance."

"Best chance to what?"

"To learn interpersonal skills without old grudges getting in the way."

Jeffrey clenched his fists. "No, they *want* to fire me. They don't have the guts to do it to my face."

"Believe me, Jeffrey, if they wanted to fire you, they have plenty of excuse already."

Jeffrey swatted the scorecard with the back of his hand. "These standards are totally unrealistic. Look at this one! *Workers say meetings are exciting and effective.* Are you kidding me?"

Alexandra raised an eyebrow. "Heart and Khalil didn't put that there. I did, and it's going to happen in your first meeting. Khalil will visit us after we've had a week to settle in."

"Wow," Jeffrey snarled. "Thanks for that. Really looking forward to disappointing my boss."

Alexandra straightened her papers. "Are you done feeling bad for yourself? We have work to do."

No, I'm not done, he griped internally. But he sat down anyway.

Alexandra pulled out a notebook and pen. "We have a week till you switch to the Northwest region. I'm excited to help you turn things around, and the first step is to gather good information." She relaxed in her chair, holding her pen loosely. "So tell me your side of the story. How do you feel about your job? What problems have you been facing?"

Jeffrey looked out the window.

"Let me start," Alexandra offered. "Here's what I know about you: You're clever, graduated with honors. You're very young for a regional manager, and you rose here quickly because you do good work. You seem a little overwhelmed by your current role. I also hear you like football."

Jeffrey looked up.

CULTURE - Who Feels the Pain?

Alexandra relaxed, sensing victory was near. "Did you notice that?"

"Notice what?"

"You didn't look up until I mentioned football. Small talk among co-workers isn't all useless, is it?"

Jeffrey wasn't going to let her win. "Not all. Just mostly."

"We'll see. Tell me about the violation you got fined for," she prodded gently.

Jeffrey snorted and sat up. "I can do better than that. I'll show you."

Jeffrey played the security footage.

"You won't believe how ridiculous this is. It's a small problem. I've already taken care of it," he insisted.

Jeffrey pointed to the screen.

"This guy here is called a waste handler. You can see him wandering around like this for hours, moving a barrel or two, then checking his phone, laughing with the other workers. Meanwhile...."

Jeffrey pressed a handful of keys.

A second video appeared of a dozen trucks waiting outside the building, like their own private traffic jam. It was raining.

Alexandra leaned forward. "Oh, that's interesting. How long was it backed up like that?"

"Eh, two hours," Jeffrey admitted grudgingly. "You can see here..."

One of the truckers jumped out of his vehicle and slammed the door. Jeffrey switched back to the other frame. The trucker sloshed through the mud, into the loading bay and appeared to be yelling at the waste handler. Suddenly the workers scurried into action.

Jeffrey paused the video. "*There.* That's the moment. He loads the closest drums onto the truck without carefully checking the labels."

Alexandra leaned on the desk and studied the picture. "What did you do when you found this video?"

"I responded immediately! I called him into my office and chewed him out. I said, 'This fine wouldn't have happened if you weren't neglecting the truckers, playing on your phone, just trying to get trucks out of the way without taking care of them...' "

Alexandra nodded. "Okay, that's definitely a problem. So tell me, when things go wrong, who feels the pain?"

There was big long pause, then Jeffrey said, "I do."

"When you're telling him what's wrong with the video, who's doing the thinking?"

"I am."

"So who feels the ownership of this problem?"

Jeffrey sagged. "I do."

"If he shows up to work each day and you're doing all the thinking, all the feeling, all the owning, there's no incentive for him to step up his game." Alexandra pointed out. "How could you change that?"

Jeffrey stiffened. "I suppose... next time this happens, I could ask *them* to look at the tape and tell me what they see."

"Perfect! You can't be in the bay 24/7, so problems will continue to happen until you unleash their capacity to think. Ownership is the holy grail of business. Everything else depends on it. To measure it, we ask three simple questions. Who feels the pain? Who's doing the thinking? Who's taking the initiative?"

Jeffrey snorted. "Feeling the pain? What's that supposed to mean?"

"Here's an example." Alexandra leaned back in her chair. "Years ago, I moved to New York to attend graduate school. I got an apartment and a roommate. One day, we noticed it was starting to get cold outside, and our apartment was chilly. So I turned the heat on. A couple hours later, our apartment started getting even colder. I turned the thermostat up even more... Then it got *really* cold."

Jeffrey looked at her, puzzled.

OWNERSHIP IS THE HOLY GRAIL OF BUSINESS. TO MEASURE IT, ASK:

WHO FEELS THE PAIN? WHO'S DOING THE THINKING? WHO'S TAKING THE INITIATIVE?

CULTURE – Who Feels the Pain?

Alexandra smirked. "We called the mechanic. He checked our thermostat, went to the furnace room.... Ten minutes later, he came back laughing his head off."

"What was going on?"

Alexandra cast a sidelong glance at Jeffrey.

"Our thermostat was wired to our neighbor's apartment, and *their* thermostat controlled the temperature in *our* apartment."

Jeffrey looked puzzled for a moment. Then it hit him. He couldn't help but laugh.

Alexandra chuckled. "When we felt cold, what's our reaction? Crank it up!"

Jeffrey smiled. "Then they start to feel hot…"

"Exactly! What are they going to do?"

"Turn the thermostat down."

Alexandra nodded. "When I studied physics in college, we called that a broken feedback loop. The person who causes the pain doesn't feel it, and the person who feels the pain doesn't have the power to prevent it."

Jeffrey groaned. "We have a problem like that."

"Really? Tell me about it."

"Every region keeps track of local laws regarding hazardous waste disposal and transportation. Every 6 weeks, we publish any changes. It's a big deal. If the publication is late, *all* the factories we service have to suspend activities until they get the update."

"Woah!"

"It gets better. As part of the process, we have to update a special map. My region is responsible to see that our maps get shipped to the right people. But a *different* department places the order… and the other department keeps messing the order up."

"Can't you just change who's responsible to place the order?"

"I wish." Jeffrey fumed. "The order-placers aren't under my supervision. No matter how often we tell them, beg them, scream at them, the other department keeps messing the order up. *Our* people feel the pain of it. The factory heads call and scream at *us*, not them. It's getting to the point where people want to go over there and punch somebody out."

> **SUMMARY**
>
> - Broken feedback loops cause the pain to bypass the people responsible.
>
> - The three questions that measure personal ownership are: Who feels the pain or reward? Who's doing the thinking? Who takes the initiative?

ACTION: Inspire FEELING by Changing What You Say

As a team, look for broken feedback loops. Divide them into two groups: 1) broken processes where the pain bypasses the person responsible, and 2) broken leadership, where someone is removing the pain by stepping in.

Fixing broken processes is straightforward: just uncross the wires so people feel the consequences and rewards of their own actions.

Fixing broken leadership is also simple: just change the questions we ask. Think of a difficult leadership situation you frequently face. With your team or a co-worker, act out the way it usually happens. Now role play it again, asking the following FEELING questions. How do you feel when you ask these questions?

Who's FEELING?

Why does it matter?
How could this be a problem?
Who does this affect?
What happens if it's not done?
How do you feel about it?
What concerns do you have?
How will it feel when...?

WEEK ONE

HANDS-OFF LEADERSHIP
WHO FEELS THE REWARD?

Jeffrey locked up the security room.

"Would you mind showing me around the bay?" Alexandra asked.

Jeffrey glanced at her clothes and hesitated. "You're not dressed for it. You'd need slip-resistant steel-toe boots, for starters."

"I'll bring them tomorrow."

Jeffrey shrugged. "If you insist. You'll need clothes that cover your body, too. Full sleeves, long pants. Every day, no exceptions. Things get messy around here."

"I like messy." Alexandra smiled.

Jeffrey pocketed his keys. "Back to the video footage... The problem is totally going to happen again—so what then? It's not just that one person. There are lots of lazy people in the loading bay."

Alexandra answered his question carefully. "You need a culture shift where *all* your employees care. How would you create a culture of personal ownership across the entire company?"

Jeffrey barely thought about the question. "We had a cash bonus system once, but it never worked."

Alexandra winced. "I'm not surprised. Research shows that cash only motivates piece workers."

Jeffrey looked confused. "Piece workers?"

"Workers who are paid per piece they assemble, or move, or sell. Like factory workers on an assembly line."

"Okay."

"As soon as their job involves even rudimentary thinking, workers do worse and feel worse when you dangle the cash carrot. Much worse. And most workers these days need to think. And let's face it—do you want workers moving in a mindless fog in any area of your business?"

"Obviously not," Jeffrey said. "I want them to bring their brain to work."

"Then treat them like thought workers. You need to get them to personally identify with their labor. To be intensely proud of their labor, to the point that it feels like part of their identity. And the best way to do that is to give them control. Let them have ideas. Let them experiment. If something is *their* idea, if it's *their* baby, they'll pour their heart and soul into it."

Jeffrey shook his head. "I hate to be a pessimist, but I don't see how that's possible—the pride thing, I mean. We're not the best-paying company, and we're pretty much the sewer rats of the mechanical world. Most people are embarrassed to admit they work here."

"I recently coached a struggling fast food franchise. If they could do it, you can."

Jeffrey stopped dead in his tracks. "You got fast food workers to care?"

"Yes. Not only did they care, at the time there was a political movement to double minimum wage, and people kept trying to recruit our workers. Most of them refused to participate. We taught them to read profit and loss statements, and we treated all them as leaders. When they understood the impacts on sales, jobs, and working environment, they said no."

CULTURE - Who Feels the Reward?

Alexandra smiled at the memory. "I regularly see people—even in stigmatized, menial jobs—bend over backward and take demotions to keep working in environments where they are allowed to own their work."[1]

> People will **BEND OVER BACKWARD** to keep working in environments where they are allowed to own their work

Jeffrey felt grudging respect for Alexandra. Maybe she wasn't a total idiot. Still, hazardous waste was very different from flipping burgers.

"You're on the right train of thought when you bring up rewards," she said. "That's the other half of fixing a feedback loop. It can't just be who feels the pain. Who feels the reward?"

"What reward did you use at the fast food place?" Jeffrey asked.

"We didn't. That's the point," she replied. "The work itself was rewarding to them."

Jeffrey rolled his eyes. "Great propaganda. Really catchy."

Alexandra laughed. "I'm serious. You know what sucks the joy out of something? Being ordered to do it. Being ordered to do it a certain way, by a certain time, and then watching your boss take all the credit."

"The tasks we do aren't up for negotiation," Jeffrey said.

"Right. The opposite of micromanagement isn't anarchy. It's ownership. Being allowed to do it. Being allowed to do it your way. Being trusted to do it, to do it well. Being allowed to decide what that means. Being enabled and supported when things go wrong. And receiving full credit at the end when things thrive."

> The opposite of **MICROMANAGEMENT** isn't anarchy. It's **OWNERSHIP**.

---

[1] The fast food story is based on experiences with an industry-leading franchise group in 2014-2016 in the northwestern United States.

By now they had returned to Jeffrey's office. Someone had left a stack of packing boxes next to Jeffrey's desk. He kicked them into the corner.

"Pride is intoxicating," Alexandra summarized. "There is no trophy, no gift card, no performance bonus in this world that will inspire your workers more than a private rush of adrenaline when *their idea* comes to life."

Jeffrey was still skeptical. "How do you make that happen?"

"You have to stop giving orders. Forever."

> To learn more about inspiring change when change is hard, I highly recommend the book *Switch*, by Chip & Dan Heath. They emphasize three elements of rapid change: Motivate the Heart, Direct the Mind, Clear the Path.

SUMMARY

- The greatest motivator for your workers is feeling personal ownership, accomplishment, and achievement.
- We destroy motivation when we tell people what to do.

ACTION: Measure How Often You Give Orders

Measure your own order-giving for a meeting or a day. Give a 3x5 card to a direct report or co-worker and ask them to make a mark (or jot down what you said) every time they hear you telling, reminding, giving an order, or giving advice instead of asking and listening first. To avoid telling or giving orders, sneak a peek at the feeling, thinking, and initiative questions on p. 18, 29 and 37.

Are you surprised by the results?

WEEK ONE

HANDS-OFF LEADERSHIP
WHO'S DOING THE THINKING?

Jeffrey laughed. "Wait, you're serious? Just stop giving orders? Cold turkey?"

"Cold turkey."

Jeffrey shook his head vehemently. "Nothing will get done."

"There are companies all over who operate this way. Supervisors never give a single order. The workers look around, identify what needs to happen, and they just do it."

Jeffrey was appalled. "There's *no* middle ground? What if I give some orders, but let them do their own thing most of the time?"

Alexandra folded her arms. "When you give orders, what message does that send?"

"...I don't know."

"You're telling them that at any moment, anything that comes out of your mouth can crush whatever they're working on. Does that leave them feeling like they are in control of their life? Do they feel trusted?"

"I don't care!" Jeffrey laughed. "I'm accountable for what happens on my watch! I can't just wait for them to *decide* they like to work."

"Right!" Alexandra agreed. "You need the work done. You need it done correctly. You need it done yesterday. And when hard work, speed, and attention to detail are required, what's going to give you better results? The things *they* care about, or what you're trying to force them to do?"

Jeffrey rolled his eyes. "Look, if you can get them moving, I have no problem not giving orders. I don't care who starts the work, so long as it gets done."

"So you're willing to stop giving orders?"

"Once they're in motion, sure."

Alexandra smiled, unsurprised by his response. "They can't feel motivation if they don't feel ownership. You have to stop giving orders *first*."

"If I stop giving orders, what's the point of me?"

"You get a promotion. You become the builder of leaders who build leaders." Alexandra replied calmly. "Instead of dictating, your job is now to teach, train, coach and support."

Jeffrey scowled.

It wasn't like he had a choice. His job was already going down in flames. If it went poorly, at least he'd have someone to blame. What did he have to lose?

"I'll give you four days," he muttered. "Nothing gets done in the boss' last week anyway."

Alexandra showed up the next day wearing steel-toed boots. To Jeffrey's surprise, they weren't new. They had clearly seen mud, rain, and a lot of walking.

Alexandra caught him staring at her footwear and grinned.

"Farm girl," she explained, kicking one toe against the ground to loosen them a little.

"Are they slip resistant?" he asked.

"I've been in factories before," Alexandra reminded him. "My boots meet all your specs."

Jeffrey handed her a hard hat.

GooCrew's distribution center was an enormous, high-roofed warehouse. Machinery whirred and clanged, chains rattled. Pallet trucks beeped backward. People shouted at each other over the racket.

Jeffrey and Alexandra navigated the maze of pallets, searching for the waste handler responsible for their latest fine.

"The first step," Alexandra explained as they walked, "is to get your workers thinking. We could say, 'Look at the video! Look what you did wrong!' But great leaders use questions to invite thinking."

GREAT LEADERS ASK QUESTIONS TO INVITE FEELING, THINKING, AND ACTION

Jeffrey barely heard her. He pointed to a guy on the other side of the warehouse. "That's him over there."

"Great. Let's think this through before we approach him. We'll role play. I'm you, and you're the waste handler."

After practising the conversation several times with Alexandra, Jeffrey approached his worker. Alexandra shadowed him silently.

"Hey, can I talk with you for a second?" Jeffrey asked.

The waste handler looked up.

Jeffrey tried to remember how Alexandra started. "Did you hear we got fined?" Jeffrey finally asked. "How do you feel about that?"

The waste handler shuffled awkwardly, expecting another round of discipline. He didn't make eye contact. "I dunno. Embarrassed?"

"I felt embarrassed too. What do you think went wrong?"

"I don't know."

"How could you find out?" Jeffrey urged.

The worker paused. "I guess we could look at security footage."

Jeffrey relaxed, relieved that the waste handler suggested it on his own. "Great. Do we need to free you up? What do you need in order to look at that tape?"

"No, it's okay," the waste handler said. "I can find someone to take my spot for a little while." He called out to a coworker. "Hey, Joe! Can you cover me for twenty?"

The coworker gave a thumbs-up. The waste handler turned and started walking to the security room.

"Huh," Jeffrey glanced at Alexandra. "That was easier than I expected."

As Jeffrey went to follow, Alexandra held him back.

"Let's not look over his shoulder," she said. "We've already looked at the tape. The goal isn't to get a perfect answer. It's to kickstart thinking. If he analyzes the tape himself, who's doing the thinking?"

Jeffrey was surprised by the insight. "Oh, fair point."

Alexandra watched the waste handler exit through a door. "Besides, it eliminates pressure. It eliminates embarrassment. Let's see how he steps up."

When the waste handler returned, Alexandra and Jeffrey could see from a distance that he was sagging.

"Do you see that?" Alexandra said excitedly. "Here he comes with his tail between his legs. He's *feeling*! Now we need to build him back up."

"How?"

"Not through praise. Remember—nothing will boost his spirits more than feeling the reward. So let *him* come up with the solution. No guilting. He doesn't need it."

Jeffrey took a deep breath as the waste handler approached. "What did you see?"

The waste handler grimaced. "Well, that was embarrassing. I wasn't paying attention at all. I knew better than to load things that way. I just wasn't thinking. Can't believe I was horsing around and looking at my phone. I didn't realize so many trucks were backed up like that. I feel bad."

"What about the—" Jeffrey started, concerned that he hadn't mentioned the container labels, but Alexandra held up a finger.

"That's okay," she told the manager. "Mistakes happened. And mistakes are good if we learn from them. So what would you like to do differently? What would you recommend?"

The waste handler looked back and forth between Jeffrey and Alexandra for a moment, hesitating. He fiddled with his bushy mustache.

"Well... I think I would like to not talk on my phone," he said. "I think maybe I should leave it in my locker."

Jeffrey looked surprised.

Alexandra grinned. "That's a great start. Anything else?"

"Yeah, I don't want to make truckers wait like that. I'm gonna talk to my team and see what we can do to get them loaded and unloaded faster."

"Wonderful. Thank you for taking the time to look at that tape. We really appreciate it."

The waste handler smiled sheepishly at them. "You're welcome."

Then he went back to work, and the smile lingered on his face.

Alexandra smiled quietly and turned to Jeffrey. "See? Getting to do your own thinking is *satisfying*."

"Hold on!" Jeffrey interrupted, clearly miffed. "You can't just brush it off like nothing happened. It's *not* okay for people to make mistakes in our industry."

"You're right. It's not okay. But they'll happen anyway. If mistakes are punished brutally, your team members will do everything they can to *hide their mistakes—including committing other crimes*. Is that likely to end well in your industry?"

Jeffrey rolled his eyes. "They won't commit other crimes. That's ridiculous."

"No," Alexandra insisted. "That's why we don't administer the death penalty for grand theft auto in this country. If someone can be executed for stealing a car, they'll kill to avoid getting caught."

27

Jeffrey was startled by this insight. "That... makes sense, actually."

Alexandra smiled encouragingly.

"Good. Now put yourself in the shoes of a waste handler," she said. "You're living paycheck to paycheck. Then, like everyone does, you make a mistake. One kind of boss will fire you on the spot. The other will forgive you outright, as long as you're fighting to find a solution." Alexandra raised an eyebrow. "Which one will you hide the mistake from, and which will you ask for help?"

Jeffrey was shocked into silence.

Alexandra leaned against the railing. "Without giving a single order, you have one employee down there who just voluntarily put his phone away. He's paying better attention. Not because you told him to. Because he *wants* to. You tell me. Is he less likely to make that mistake now?"

"Yes," Jeffrey replied reluctantly.

"If you gave him a test about container labels, what questions would he get wrong?"

"Probably none," Jeffrey admitted. "The labels are self-explanatory. He just wasn't paying attention."

"So do you think his performance would have improved more if you had spent your time drilling him on container labels instead?"

Jeffrey hesitated, then looked away. "No, I suppose not."

Alexandra smiled. "That, my friend, is the power of letting your workers do the thinking. Steer the conversation, sure. But don't slap them with the solution. When something is their idea, resistance disappears."

CULTURE - Who's Doing the Thinking?

> **SUMMARY**
>
> - Instead of telling, great leaders ask questions that invite feeling, thinking, and action.
>
> - When people feel, think, and act on their own, they start to become leaders.
>
> - Mistakes are good if we learn from them.

ACTION: Inspire THINKING by Changing What You Say

For the next 24 hours, ask questions to encourage thinking in the people around you. Make a copy of the following "Who's THINKING?" questions and carry it with you. Use these questions when any problem comes up that someone else should own.

Set an alarm on your phone to ask yourself at the end of the day: How did I do at asking these questions? What happened when I did?

A wallet card of this chart is available at NEVERBOSS.com. Clip this card to your security badge at work, facing outward, to encourage FEELING, THINKING, and ACTION in those around you. Try it and see how they respond.

Who's THINKING?

Tell me about it?
What do you see?
Would A or B work better?
What's the standard or procedure?
What do you think?
What are the principles?
What do you recommend?

HANDS-OFF LEADERSHIP
WHO'S TAKING THE INITIATIVE?

For the next few days, Jeffrey and Alexandra wandered through GooCrew's departments. Jeffrey practiced asking questions that invited thinking. He struggled at first, but slowly got the hang of it. As sparks of wakefulness started to appear in the eyes of his workers, Jeffrey couldn't help but be a little proud.

"I think you're ready for the final step," Alexandra said one morning.

Jeffrey brightened. "Oh?"

"This is the single most important step of the whole process. Everything else we'll do," she asserted, "literally everything, was designed to enable and support this one idea."

"So what is it?"

"Initiative."

Jeffrey sat back in his chair. "Expound."

Alexandra stood and paced. "Well, when your workers show up to work, who decides what they work on?"

"It's dictated by the factories. Whatever they need to unload, we have to be ready for it."

"Who approves any deviations from that schedule?"

"Any deviations come to me, but they're rare. If I approve the project, their manager sets the project schedule."

Alexandra wasn't surprised. "We're going to turn that on its head. Instead of taking orders, *they* decide what to work on. If their situation changes, they don't have to wait for permission to switch gears. They just go. They're even allowed to tell you no."

Jeffrey groaned and put his face in his hands. "You're insane."

Alexandra laughed.

Jeffrey scowled. "No, seriously. A bad spill could put me behind bars—and I'm allergic to jail. What checks and balances do you put in place? There are *some* rules, right?"

Alexandra smiled at his joke but took the question seriously. "Yes and no. Rules rarely accomplish great things. They're too rigid. Great businesses run on principles."

Jeffrey gagged. "You mean, like, morals? Endurance, teamwork, all that stuff people put on posters?"

"No, no, no!" Alexandra made a face. "Nothing so trite. Principles aren't vague ideals. They're inescapable truths that guide action. The reason behind any rule."

"Like what?"

"Pretend you're driving a forklift. Which guideline means more to you? OSHA's rule, *You must look in the direction you're moving,* or the phrase *Drive like your two-year-old is somewhere in the factory?*"

Jeffrey's eyes widened. "Okay, that's pretty vivid."

"You still have to obey OSHA," Alexandra acknowledged. "Everyone should know the rules. But never use a rule where a principle will do."

"You're still asking them to do the same thing," Jeffrey argued. "Why does it matter whether we use rules or principles?"

"Because there are many occasions when rules don't match the situation. They defy common sense. Workers who understand principles are armed to act with *confidence* instead of arrogance. They look at the situation. They're *thinking.* When the rule doesn't apply, they are allowed to deliver a different solution. And when the rule *does* apply, they generally do a better job of applying it."

"There's no wiggle room with the government, though," Jeffrey resisted.

Alexandra nodded emphatically. "Right, and you identified a principle there—you're allergic to jail. But not every law is equally important. So if someone *unauthorized* has the ability to prevent a jail-worthy spill, do you want them to take action or obey protocol?"

Jeffrey's eyes widened.

Alexandra smiled, seeing that she'd finally convinced him. "Granted, that's an extreme situation," she said, "but life is bizarre! Sometimes you'll face conflicts like that."

"And my workers will face conflicts like that..." Jeffrey realized.

"Yes. And the more you fixate on *rules*, the faster employees will freeze up when action is needed. Principles give them the confidence they need to respond quickly to threats."

Jeffrey was quiet for a moment.

"Okay," he finally said. "I think I agree with you. But how can you train workers to follow *correct* principles?"

"We'll work later to establish a list of generally accepted principles for GooCrew," Alexandra explained. "When workers know your principles by heart, they can make decisions quickly, knowing with absolute confidence that their actions are aligned with GooCrew's needs."

Jeffrey was still skeptical. "You honestly feel safe setting workers loose to make decisions after you've taught them a few nursery phrases?"

She smiled. "We won't throw them to the wolves all at once. Training workers to make good decisions takes time. We give them authority as fast as they're ready for it, no faster. For now, we just need them to start having their own ideas."

A gaggle of men and women clad in hard hats and orange safety vests filtered over for a meeting. Jeffrey leaned over to Alexandra.

"What good is this if I'm leaving in two days?" he asked quietly. "The next manager will just do things her own way."

"It's good for them," she insisted, nodding to the small crowd. "Never hurts to have thinking workers. But primarily, this is practice for you."

Jeffrey sighed, then turned to face his workers. "Alright team, our dock times are averaging 60 minutes. That's nowhere close to GooCrew standard. Our standard is 20 minutes. Check cargo, unload, reload, drive out. What would it take to get it under 20 minutes?"

The workers looked at each other, confused. "I dunno, boss. What *would* it take?"

"No, I'm asking you." Jeffrey insisted. "You guys are the ones doing this. What are the options? What do you see? What do the people who operate the loading equipment think?"

No one replied. Jeffrey folded his arms.

"Is the standard realistic?" he asked honestly. "Is it possible to always get it under 20 minutes, for *all* our workers, even when there's a crush?"

A worker near the front rubbed a boot against his leg. "Well, maybe."

Jeffrey nodded. "Good. What would it take?

"More workers?"

Jeffrey shook his head. "No, that won't work. You'll get in each other's way."

A young worker scratched her ear. "What if we unload the barrels to the side of the truck, and then sort them after, instead of putting them away immediately?"

"No, I don't want you to do that."

After that, the workers lost interest and Jeffrey couldn't get anything more out of them. Alexandra watched and said nothing. Finally, Jeffrey waved his hand.

"Well, think about it while you work. Let me know if you have any ideas. I'd love to hear them. Meeting dismissed."

When they returned to his office, Jeffrey threw his hard hat on his chair. "I don't understand. Why did they shut down like that?"

CULTURE - Who's Taking the Initiative?

Alexandra took a seat across from his desk. "Principle number one: If you want to shut down thinking, express a strong opinion early. It's good to have ideas in your back pocket, but be prepared to sit on them."

Jeffrey snorted. "But their ideas weren't going to work."

Alexandra raised an eyebrow. "Would they have been an improvement, at least?"

"...Maybe."

"If they have an idea that's 70% as good as your idea, it's a *better* idea, because it's *their* idea."

Jeffrey sighed in agitation. "But we have work to do!"

Alexandra shook her head adamantly. "The goal is *not* the task. The ultimate, overarching, forever goal of an organization is *never* the task. The goal is to create thinking, passionate, self-reliant leaders with initiative. Do that, and the tasks will take care of themselves."

Someone knocked on the doorframe.

Jeffrey and Alexandra looked up. The waste handler they'd confronted a few days earlier popped his head through the doorframe.

> THE GOAL IS TO CREATE **THINKING, PASSIONATE, SELF-RELIANT LEADERS** WITH INITIATIVE **AT ALL LEVELS**

"I was thinking about your question, sir, and I realized..." He took his hard hat off. "There's a bottleneck at the receiving station. We only have one person per shift who's certified to inspect the waste. We always have to wait for them to look at the barrels before we can move 'em."

Jeffrey brightened.

The waste handler shuffled nervously. "Only thing is, the cert's expensive. We've always had to pay outta pocket. But if we even had two workers per shift who could inspect, it would make our lives a lot easier."

"Brilliant! I'll authorize the expense," Jeffrey told him. "I leave in two days, but write down the names of anyone who wants that certification, and I'll get things moving before I leave."

The waste handler's eyes lit up. "I will! Thank you!"

After he left, Alexandra turned to Jeffrey. "How do you feel?"

Jeffrey was caught off guard by the question.

"Less annoyed that I did two minutes ago," he admitted.

"Good. Who's feeling the pain there?"

"He is."

"Who's doing the thinking?"

"Him."

Alexandra lifted an eyebrow. "Who's—"

"—taking the initiative?" Jeffrey interrupted.

Alexandra smiled.

"You win this round," Jeffrey said, rolling his eyes. "Don't let it go to your head."

SUMMARY

- Principles are inescapable truths that guide action.
- Workers armed with principles can take initiative safely.
- The task is not the goal. Your main goal is always to create passionate, self-reliant leaders at all levels of your company.

ACTION: Inspire INITIATIVE by Changing What You Say

As you encourage FEELING and THINKING, start asking questions to inspire INITIATIVE. If they aren't sure how to respond, that's OK, just drop back down to THINKING or FEELING questions temporarily, as needed, or provide clarification or training if that's what holds them back.

CULTURE - Who's Taking the Initiative?

Set a phone alarm for the end of the day to ask yourself:

- How many times did I ask INITIATIVE questions?
- How did people respond?
- How did it feel?

WEEK ONE

Who's Taking INITIATIVE? ☑

What obstacles do you face?
Is anything holding you back?
Do you have a plan?
What do you intend to do?
Tell me about your progress?
What have you done (so far)?
What have you been doing recently?

HANDS-OFF LEADERSHIP
REDEFINING PRIDE

Word spread that Jeffrey was being transferred. Many employees made no secret of their relief. Normally, Jeffrey would have chewed them out for their disrespect. But Alexandra encouraged him to let them express their feelings.

Unfortunately, some of the hard feelings ran deep.

On the last day, Alexandra went outside to take a call. Jeffrey walked into the break room by himself and found everyone giggling.

"What's so funny?" he asked.

People averted their eyes. They munched their sandwiches quietly. Jeffrey snorted and went to get his lunch out of the fridge. Then he stopped. Someone had taped a note to the fridge door. It giant bold letters, it said,

"FLOGGINGS WILL CONTINUE UNTIL MORALE IMPROVES."

Underneath, it was signed with Jeffrey's name. Someone had also drawn a caricature of Jeffrey getting booted out the door.

In a different pen, someone else had scrawled, "Good riddance!"

Ears flaming, Jeffrey tore the note off the fridge.

"How dare you!?" he raged at the roomful of workers. "Do you have any idea what I go through to keep this place running? The long hours, the emergency calls at 2 am? Taking the fall for things when *you guys* screw up?"

Everyone froze. Some stared at Jeffrey with big eyes. Others stared at their coffee mugs.

Jeffrey wadded the paper into a ball and threw it at the wall. "Ungrateful jerks. *Usually,* when a supervisor leaves, people throw a party." Jeffrey stopped, realizing what he was saying. He shook his head. "I mean, they get him a cake and a thank you card. This is *horribly* unprofessional behavior."

Jeffrey quickly grabbed his lunch from the fridge, then slammed the door. "Good luck with your miserable little jobs, you peons."

Then he stalked out.

Alexandra found him in his office, stuffing things in boxes as quickly as he could.

"See?" he huffed. "Give them an inch, and they'll take a mile."

Jeffrey slammed a box down on top of his desk and started stripping his office walls. "So much for crackpot theories about everyone getting along."

Alexandra leaned against one end of his desk while he worked. "That must have hurt tremendously."

"You think?" Jeffrey shot back.

"You haven't made any enemies *this* week, though."

Jeffrey slowed down. He stared at the box he was filling and took a sharp breath. "That's true."

"Do you think this is a reaction to the new way of doing things? Or is it possible that these feelings have been festering for a while?"

Jeffrey sat down heavily in his chair.

"Festering, definitely," he admitted.

"Any idea where it started?"

"Hmm..." Jeffrey swiveled in his chair and looked out the window. "You know... I used to be one of the bay workers. They loved me there. That's why I moved up the ranks so fast. I was a loader, then a shift manager, then a technician. It wasn't until I got promoted to regional manager that the bad blood suddenly flared up. I have no idea why. All I can figure is that they're jealous."

Alexandra pondered his reply.

"Do you enjoy being a manager?" she finally asked.

"Sure!" Jeffrey said, smiling a little. "It's fun to organize teams and plan the day. I love being at the helm, charting a course, and orchestrating people to make it happen. The only frustrating part is that they fight me tooth and nail. It's like trying to herd squirrels."

"Ahhhh..." Alexandra considered his reply. "That's a classic problem I run into with programmers. As a manager, supervisor, or leader of any kind, you have to change where you get your satisfaction from."

"What do you mean?"

"Well, programmers write code. Creative people love *creating*. What happens when you become a super-duper programmer? They turn you into a *manager* of programmers! Now where are they going to get their satisfaction from? From telling *lots* of people how to write code. See the problem yet?"

"Honestly, no."

"The feedback loop is broken," Alexandra explained. "The low-level programmers are also creative people. Where do *they* get their sense of satisfaction from? From what *they* create. So now we have a conflict between the programmers and their manager. Everyone is aching to see their own ideas come to life—in fact, their job satisfaction *depends* on it—but only one side gets to choose what they make."

Jeffrey frowned. "How do you fix it?"

"The *only* solution is for your sense of satisfaction as a leader to come from the success of the other people around you. You get your satisfaction from what *they* accomplish—especially what they accomplish *on their own* through their own initiative. That is your ultimate and highest measure of success."

"But we don't program here."

"This is *just* as true in your industry. Where do you get your satisfaction from?"

"Getting things done."

Alexandra grinned. "As a rancher's daughter, I understand that. It feels wonderful to exert yourself, then look around at the end of the day, see the results of your labor, and know that you've been a force for good in this world."

Jeffrey brightened. "Exactly."

> WHEN YOU BECOME A MANAGER, SUPERVISOR, OR LEADER OF ANY KIND, YOU HAVE TO CHANGE WHERE YOU GET YOUR SATISFACTION FROM

Alexandra raised an eyebrow. "But what about your people downstairs? If they just follow orders all day, most of them go home feeling useless and used. When they look around the bay, do *they* feel a thrill that it's swept and orderly? Not unless *they* were the impetus for it."

Jeffrey rocked backward. "Oh, cripes."

"So from now on," she said, "when we measure leadership on your Turnaround Scorecard, your score is the average of the initiative scores of the people around you."

Jeffrey nodded slowly. "Okay. I guess I can see the value in that."

"Your measure of greatness is how much the people you lead create and do on their own initiative. *That's* why we gave you an F for leadership." Alexandra explained. "Your workers were doing a *great* job of doing what you told them to. That's an F. The standard's higher now."

"Ohhh," Jeffrey relaxed. "Why didn't you say so?"

CULTURE - Redefining Pride

> The book *Freedom, Inc.* by Brian M. Carney and Isaac Getz is an excellent resource that contains detailed case studies of more than a dozen extraordinary companies. Each one liberated its workers by giving them the power to exercise initiative.

WEEK ONE

Jeffrey loaded the last box into his car and shut the trunk. He unlocked his car and was about to get in when he noticed someone running across the parking lot. They were trying to flag him down.

It was the waste handler.

Jeffrey closed the door and walked out to greet him.

"I just wanted to say, sir," the handler breathlessly stammered. "I'm awfully sorry about what happened in the lunch room. That wasn't right."

Jeffrey shrugged, but the manager dug into his vest pocket.

"I just wanted to let you know, sir, that some of us *do* appreciate everything you've done." He pulled out a slightly wrinkled piece of paper that had been folded twice, and handed it to Jeffrey.

It said "thank you" on the front.

The waste handler stuffed his hands in his pockets, a little embarrassed. "It's no Hallmark card, but this is signed by all the people you authorized certification training for. Most bosses would've kicked back on their last week, but you went to bat for us instead."

Jeffrey opened the card, and found it signed by a half dozen people. Jeffrey stared at it for a long moment. Then he tucked it away reverently inside his coat pocket.

"Thank you," Jeffrey said at last. "No one has ever... yeah."

"Aww, it's nothing." The waste handler shook Jeffrey's hand warmly. "Good luck at your next post. They're lucky to have you."

43

> **SUMMARY**
>
> - Instead of feeling satisfaction in their personal achievements, great leaders take pride in what those around them accomplish through their own initiative.

ACTION: Redefine Your Pride

List the aspects of your job that you are proud of. These should be actions you undertake or lead. Now redefine each item in terms of what your team is accomplishing, rather than what you do personally or make your team do. Refocus your satisfaction around seeing them succeed.

Re-read the list. How will it FEEL when they do those things well on their own?

HANDS-OFF LEADERSHIP
STEP UP, STEP BESIDE, STEP AWAY

"You're not flying first class?" Jeffrey teased. He stuffed his carry-on into the overhead bin and sat down next to Alexandra.

"Well, I tried," she said. "But the other customers complained about my fashion sense."

Jeffrey smiled, noticing her scruffy boots and oversized plaid flannel shirt. "Well, you're in good company. I think my sweater is 15 years old. If I'd known we'd be flying together, I would have worn my suit."

Alexandra wrinkled her nose. "That's ridiculous. Airports are automatic casual zones. Your llama sweater looks awesome."

Once they were up in the air, Alexandra read on her tablet. Most of the passengers settled in like professional contortionists and slept. Jeffrey worried.

Eventually, Alexandra set her book down and stared out the window. Glowing cities lit up the darkness. Jeffrey managed to put together in his head what was bothering him. He tapped her arm.

"Do you mind if I ask you a question?" he whispered, careful to not disturb the other passengers.

She turned. "Fire away."

Jeffrey looked away, embarrassed. "I'm nervous about tomorrow."

"Why?"

"New team, different culture. I'm worried I'll come across as weak."

A hint of a smile crept across Alexandra's face. "Why?"

"This region is different than the Gulf. I'm not familiar with some of the waste they handle. Different laws, different everything. There's a lot I don't know. In that context, refusing to give orders can look an awful lot like cowardice. If I start with Hands-Off Leadership, I'm worried they'll roll their eyes, treat me like a bureaucratic necessity, and never listen to me again."

"Ahhhh... Those are good observations. Mind if I show you something?"

"What?"

Alexandra brought her tablet back to life and opened a document. She passed it to Jeffrey.

He studied it carefully. "Step Up, Step Beside, Step Away? What's this?"

"This is how we measure Hands-Off Leadership. Right now, you're on a probationary scorecard. Eventually, you'll graduate to this one. You'll use it weekly to keep from reverting to traditional leadership."

"0 is bad, and 4 is good?"

"They're not good or bad. They're phases." Alexandra tapped on the screen. "Stepping Up is Step 1. That's a vital part of the process. When stepping into a new role, it *is* important to take charge. Show a strong face. Let people know you are 100% in charge."

"Doesn't that go directly against Hands-Off Leadership?"

"No. It's like when you're raising kids. If the parents are timid and permissive, the children don't feel safe. A lot of misbehavior stems from this. When children don't feel secure, they act out to take control of their environment. Workers do the exact same thing. So the foundation of leadership is to take charge. The difference here is that you are taking power so you can give it away."

Jeffrey mused. "I suppose you can't give power away if you don't have any to begin with."

CULTURE – Step Up, Step Beside, Step Away

LEADERSHIP SCORECARD

NAME: _____

MY OVERALL SCORE: _____

WEEK ONE

4 STEP AWAY SUPPORT To Unleash Excellence	Facilitate, Review, Mentor, Advise When Asked
3 STEP BACK COACH To Inspire Ownership	"Who Owns It?" Questions, Focus, eGROW
2 STEP BESIDE TRAIN To Build Capability	Teach Principles, Demonstrate, Certify
1 STEP UP TELL To Ensure Clarity	Decide, Assign, Clarify, Give Authority
0 STEP IN TAKE OVER To Create Stability	Correct, Discipline, Keep The Ship Afloat

"Exactly. Once you establish authority, move to the next step. Make sure you explain that you intend to disperse power. It helps people feel safe, because no one wants to be controlled."

"Got it." Jeffrey glanced at the screen. "So over time, we work our way to Step 4, where we've given away authority completely, and we're totally hands-off?"

"Mmm... Sort of. There will never be a week when you're 100% in Step 4. You'll spend time in different steps with different people, depending on their growth. That's okay. The point of the scorecard is to *know* which step you're acting in and why. Remember the end goal of Stepping Away."

> THE DIFFERENCE IS THAT YOU ARE TAKING POWER SO YOU CAN GIVE IT AWAY

"Why does *Step In* look different?"

"Because you want to avoid it. Stepping In feels like discipline. It's a big slap in the face. You should only do it to prevent a serious accident or fire someone. And you only want to drop to a lower step for specific reasons, like filling training gaps or clarifying when there's confusion. The principle is to use the least power possible so people can act for themselves."

"Okay. So *freedom* is the end goal." Jeffrey started to feel excited. It was starting to make sense.

"Pretty much. To fill it out, we just write down examples of specific moments when you were at each step." Alexandra pulled out a stylus and offered it to Jeffrey. "Want to practice scoring me?"

Jeffrey was surprised. "Score you?"

"Of course."

"But I'm the one on probation."

"So what? In a way, I'm a supervisor over you. But I make mistakes, too. Scoring keeps me from being a hypocrite. Let's see how I stack up."

Jeffrey laughed. "Okay."

"For starters, where do you think I should be right now?"

"Hmm... Somewhere between 1 and 2, I think."

"Good. 2 would be better. I use Step 1 to steady the ship when I do turnarounds and they put me in charge. But for you, I'm in more of an advisory position, so Stepping Beside is more appropriate."

"You used Step 1, Stepping Up, during the intervention meeting, when you delivered the scorecard. You told me I needed to step up and in exactly which ways."

Alexandra considered that. "True. That was corrective action, so it might even fit under Stepping In. But Stepping In usually means taking someone's task away and doing it for them. I wasn't showing you how to do things, just informing you."

"And establishing authority."

"Exactly."

Alexandra typed into the screen for a moment. "Okay," she said, straightening. "What about Stepping Beside?"

"You've been doing that all week."

> USE THE **LEAST POWER POSSIBLE** SO PEOPLE CAN ACT FOR THEMSELVES

"Can you see the difference between Steps 2 and 3?"

He hesitated. "Well..." he said slowly, "if we were flipping hamburgers, I think stepping beside is where you would demonstrate the proper way to cook. And Stepping Back is probably where you let me do it, but you're still watching, asking me questions from time to time to stimulate thinking."

"Good! How is Step 3 different from Step 4?"

Jeffrey smiled, starting to feel like he was getting the hang of it. "Stepping Away sounds like you're satisfied that I can cook a hamburger well enough. You stop watching, but you're still around if *I* want to ask *you* questions."

"Bingo. So when did I demonstrate for you?"

Jeffrey cringed. "Well, there was that one time that I think you Stepped In."

Alexandra looked surprised. "When?"

"When we were talking to the waste handler that first time, after he looked at the security tapes. I was going to ask him about the barrel labels, but you interrupted me to demonstrate inviting thinking."

Alexandra groaned. "Oops, you're right. I *think* in that case it was worth it, but I should have asked to intervene instead of taking over for you."

She wrote that down. "That's the crucial difference between Step 2 and Step 0. One says, 'Do you mind if I show you something?' And the other goes, 'You're doing that wrong. *Yank!* Here's the right way.' "

Jeffrey laughed. "Is it okay for me to say no sometimes?"

Alexandra frowned at Jeffrey like he was crazy. "Of course. Sometimes we're tired, cranky, or busy, and it's just not a good moment for teaching. *Please* say no if you're not in the mood. It's not a question unless you're allowed to honestly answer either direction."

He brightened. "Cool. Thanks."

Alexandra looked back at the scorecard. "So... Step 2, Stepping Beside. Can you think of any examples where I demonstrated for you, but I *asked* first if I could?"

They chatted for a long time. It had been a long week, and there was plenty to laugh and groan about. When the airline stewards came by, Jeffrey bought Alexandra a drink to say thank you. She sipped on it appreciatively.

"Alright, Step 4 is a little different. Instead of writing down the coolest things done by the person being graded, focus on top victories of the people they supervise. Since we're grading me, we'll look at *your* victories."

Jeffrey looked up, surprised. "Mine?"

"Yeah!" She grinned. "The greatest measure of a leader is what the people they lead accomplish on their own initiative. So, that's what we measure."

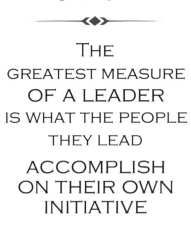

THE GREATEST MEASURE OF A LEADER IS WHAT THE PEOPLE THEY LEAD ACCOMPLISH ON THEIR OWN INITIATIVE

CULTURE - Step Up, Step Beside, Step Away

Jeffrey smiled a little. "What do you think I did well?"

"What do *you* think you did well?" she asked back.

The question caught him off guard, and it took a minute for him to answer. "Well, most of this week we've just been practicing questions," he said. "Helping workers think for themselves and feel the pain. I'm glad for the practice, because every situation is different, so that's been *really* hard to learn. Most of the time when those conversations started, I felt dread over not having the answer." Jeffrey chuckled. "Then I realized, that's the whole point."

"Yes!" Alexandra looked up, delighted by his answer. "Don't own the problem. Give them the problem."

Jeffrey nodded. "So I think that's my first victory: Getting better at asking questions."

"Perfect."

"For the second victory... There was that one moment when we were working with the waste handler. You steered him toward initiating his own solution, but before that, I inspired him to start thinking and feeling."

"Excellent." Alexandra typed his victories beside Step Away on her scorecard.

Jeffrey shrugged. "That's all I can think of right now."

"That's okay. I'm just showing you the general idea." Alexandra held the tablet for Jeffrey to see. "Overall, my average score is 2.3—one point for a Step Up, two points for a Step Beside.... 2.3 is good. That's the right phase for now."

Alexandra tapped the top of the scorecard. "Notice that I'm not taking *credit* for your victories. I just measure them because if you do things of your own initiative and I support you, that means I'm a Step 4 leader. I'm Stepping Away."

Jeffrey thought for a moment. Then he started to smile.

"So.... When that guy came to my office with an idea to certify more workers, and I enabled him without being coached, was that Step 4 leadership for you?"

Alexandra grinned. "*Yes.* And his victory was Step 4 for you."

As Jeffrey watched, she opened a new Leadership Scorecard. "You'll track your scores in here," Alexandra said. She typed '*Bay worker suggested certifications*' at the top, beside Step Away. Then she saved the document and stowed her tablet.

NEVERBOSS – Crenshaw

LEADERSHIP SCORECARD

NAME: _Alexandra Hamilton_

MY OVERALL SCORE: _2.3_

4	**STEP AWAY** SUPPORT To Unleash Excellence	- Jeffrey getting better at asking questions on his own - Jeffrey inspired waste handler to think and feel
3	**STEP BACK** COACH To Inspire Ownership	- Watched while Jeffrey lead group discussion about turnaround times. Discussed improvements afterwards. - Steered the waste handler toward initiating his own solution.
2	**STEP BESIDE** TRAIN To Build Capability	- Introduced Hands-Off Leadership. - Explained principles as appropriate and relevant. Discussed broken feedback loops after lunch disaster. - Introduced Leadership Scorecard (asked first).
1	**STEP UP** TELL To Ensure Clarity	- Intervention, delivered scorecard to Jeff and established my authority.
0	**STEP IN** TAKE OVER To Create Stability	- Interrupted Jeffrey during discussion with shift manager about video.

CULTURE - Step Up, Step Beside, Step Away

It was a small victory, but it felt good. A twinge of hope tickled Jeffrey's thoughts. *Maybe I have been a bad leader*, Jeffrey thought, realizing that the indignation he'd been feeling all week was suddenly gone. For the first time, he could see exactly what he'd been doing wrong. Until now, he hadn't believed he was doing anything wrong at all.

Instead of scaring him, it was a relief. Jeffrey felt an unfamiliar nudge of gratitude. Finally, after years of wielding both greater power and greater intelligence than most of the people he interacted with, here was someone who saw more than he did. Jeffrey wondered how much bigger his world would be before she was done.

Just then, the captain announced they would be landing soon.

"You didn't get to nap or anything," Jeffrey realized suddenly. "I took up the whole plane ride with work things. I'm so sorry."

She just laughed. "Are you kidding? I *love* sharing this stuff. Thank you for asking. Do you feel any better about the meeting tomorrow?"

"Definitely." Jeffrey nodded and stared at his wrists. "You know, it's funny because I'm the boss, not the poor minion getting bossed around. But I feel like I've been wearing shackles, and they're starting to melt away. Is that ridiculous?"

Alexandra leaned back in her seat and closed her eyes. "Whoever said top-down leadership only traps the ones on the bottom?"

SUMMARY

- Great leaders create leaders by giving away power as quickly as people can handle it.

- Once stability is established, shift toward using the least power possible.

- The best measure of your personal leadership is what the people you lead accomplish on their own initiative.

ACTION: Score Your Own Leadership

Where are you at with each of the people you supervise? Use a Leadership Scorecard for each person and jot down your recent interactions with them. Then give yourself an overall score with them. Show them the results and see if they agree. Listen to their feedback and adjust.

All scorecards are available at NEVERBOSS.com, along with other Leadership Steps resources.

ACTION: Use the eGROW Coaching Method

eGROW is simple coaching that works for anyone. Use it the next time (and anytime) you Step Back, review progress, or help someone.

Ask one question at a time. Listen and discuss:

- **E**ncourage: "What are your latest victories?" (Encourage, don't praise. See p. 203.)
- **G**oal: "What is your goal?"
- **R**eality: "What is the current reality?"
- **O**bstacles & Options: "What are the obstacles?" "What are your options?"
- **W**ay Forward: "What do you intend to do?"

Starting now, watch for coaching opportunities. If someone is stuck or you need to discuss their progress, try these steps. Then ask yourself: How did they respond? How did it feel?

WEEK TWO

EXCITING MEETINGS

THE RAT TRAP

GooCrew's Northwest distribution center was old. The main building stank of mildew and cubicles.

Their regional manager, Mr. Vanderman, was on sabbatical for the next three months. Vanderman was uncomfortable letting Jeffrey use his personal desk, so he gave Jeffrey one of the unused offices in their building. When Jeffrey dropped by briefly to drop off his coat, he was greeted by bare walls and a dusty, spartan desk. A floor-to-ceiling window overlooked a gloomy lake. Jeffrey sighed at the skeletal trees. If the weather was going to be so ridiculously cold, couldn't it at least snow?

Jeffrey reported to a conference room on the second floor. As he reached to open the door, he realized it had no doorknob.

"Um..." Jeffrey stared at the hole where a doorknob should have been.

"Good morning," Alexandra said, walking down the hallway.

Jeffrey pointed with a longsuffering grimace. "No doorknobs?"

A cheerful voice called out from inside the room. "That's my doing!"

55

Jeffrey pushed on the door.

The table was cheap. The ceiling was low. The conference room's one cool feature was a large bay window overlooking the loading bay below. A freakishly tall man in a green shirt greeted them with a guarded smile.

Jeffrey tried to size him up. Troublemaker or ally?

"And you are...?" Jeffrey asked.

The green man stood and held out a hand. "Matt, head of HR."

"You dismantled the doorknob?"

"Proudly."

"Why?"

Matt's eyes narrowed. He watched Jeffrey's reaction carefully. "Vanderman gets angry when people leave in the middle of a meeting, even to go to the bathroom. So he started locking the door.[2] For a couple of weeks, I asked nicely for him to stop. He ignored me, so I fixed the problem on my own."

Alexandra started laughing. "*Wow.* I'm adding that one to my list."

Matt turned to her, curious. "What list?"

"Epic meeting fails. I've witnessed meetings in a lot of industries, and the same patterns tend to crop up. Common ones include Death by Slideshow..."

Matt chuckled.

Alexandra listed off a few more. "...Endless Check-Ins, where people try to sound like they've been busy. There's also the Eternal Lecture, where the boss does all the talking."

"Well, now you've heard of the Rat Trap," Matt sighed.

The door swung open again. A woman entered, clinging to a thermos of coffee like her life depended on it.

"Hello," Jeffrey said, holding out his hand.

The woman frowned.

---

[2] Like most stories in this book, this is based on actual events. One company started locking the door because people kept sneaking out of meetings.

CULTURE - The Rat Trap

"I'm Clara," she replied grudgingly, without shaking. "If you want to stay out of jail, leave me alone and follow my memos to the letter. Also, I hate lawyer jokes."

"Noted," Jeffrey replied, feeling some contempt at her prickly attitude.

Jeffrey sat at the head of the table, and Alexandra took a seat next to him.

"Watch carefully," Alexandra said quietly. "Meetings are the best indication of a company's health. Let's see what kind of culture we've been dealt."

MEETINGS ARE THE BEST INDICATION OF A COMPANY'S HEALTH

WEEK TWO

There were only three more team members.

Bob was short, stout, and balding. Despite being head of software, he lacked the usual nerdy characteristics. He was straightforward: starched white shirt, black tie.

Whatever nerdiness Bob lacked, Aaron made up for in droves. Aaron was lanky and talkative. The collar of his polo was decked out with superhero pins. He managed the bay on an interim basis because their previous manager suddenly left without warning. Aaron had been pulled from the ranks to prevent crisis. He was hoping the position would become permanent, but Vanderman had been holding out.

Roxanne, the logistics manager, was the last to show. Her hair was still damp from showering. She was clearly trying hard to look professional, but it wasn't her natural state. She bumped fists with Aaron as she sat down.

Jeffrey felt small. Most of the team seemed cold and wary of him. Jeffrey wondered if they'd been forewarned of his probation status.

Alexandra broke the ice. "You guys are lucky to have Jeffrey Jackson filling in," she said casually as the last team members entered the room. "He's been managing the Gulf region for years."

Jeffrey felt a rush of relief. He wanted a clean slate. Perhaps no one except Alexandra knew the real reasons he was here.

57

Bob eyed Alexandra. "Who are you?"

"I come from a coaching team that specializes in rapid culture change. Heart Manufacturing wants to test run our leadership style. They've selected Jeffrey to champion it. He's learning too, so be patient with him."

Bob blanched. "You're using us as lab rats while our manager is on leave?"

Alexandra laughed. "A little bit, yes. Want to see what it looks like?"

Jeffrey grinned, taking the cue. He stood. "Meetings are miserable when they're slow," he said, "or when they're useless. So starting now, I'm implementing two principles—Agility, to keep things fast, and Buy-In, to guarantee we make decisions. Talk alone is boring. We'll never meet unless there's something to decide."

The team members perked up a little. Jeffrey could see healthy skepticism all over their faces, but they were all listening.

"Early in my career, I believed in listening to everybody," Jeffrey said.

They withered a little and looked away.

Bob snickered. "Now you don't?"

"I took it to the extreme. When I waited for consensus, we had long, confusing meetings. They were painful. Decisions that needed to be made took too long if they happened at all."

A few team members grimaced. The idea clearly resonated.

Jeffrey smiled. "The solution is easy. Perfect consensus is impossible. So instead of asking if you agree to something, we'll ask if you're willing to buy in to it."

"What's that mean?"

"If you can at least 70% agree, then say yes. See what happens." Jeffrey grabbed a marker. "Agility means three things," he said, writing them on the whiteboard.

1. It MUST not be perfect at first.

2. Get it out there quickly, to see what people think about it.

3. Improve it rapidly and obsessively, based on actual feedback.

He capped his marker.

"Agility makes it safe to buy in. If it's not working, we'll gut it and try again. There's nothing more miserable than being forced to build a boat you know will sink."

"What if you see the ship's captain heading toward an iceberg?" Aaron asked.

"Can you 70% agree to steering into an iceberg?" Jeffrey replied.

Aaron laughed. "No."

"Then fight it," Jeffrey answered with a shrug. "We shouldn't demand the mindless obedience of a general going to war. If you see something seriously wrong, be courageous. Be stubborn. But to keep from crippling our entire team, from now on we have a new standard—always give each other a 30% benefit of the doubt. Does that sound fair?"

Intrigued, they nodded.

"Great." Jeffrey reached for his briefcase. "Let's put the principles to use. Did you all bring your laptops, as I requested?"

A painful, awkward silence filled the room. People fiddled with their laptop cases but were afraid to pull them out.

"Vanderman banned laptops at meetings," Roxanne objected.

"Right." Jeffrey quipped. "Your boss also locked you in the room. Do you *want* me to run meetings like he did?"

Resistance evaporated. Everyone booted their laptops eagerly.

Jeffrey slipped on a pair of glasses and logged into his computer. "To start, let's score last week's meeting."

Roxanne blinked in confusion. "You mean our meeting last week with Vanderman?"

Jeffrey nodded. "Yes. On a scale of zero to 100, how exciting was that meeting? How effective was it?"

Matt laughed out loud. "Last week, Vanderman discovered the stolen doorknob."

Clara snickered. "He threw a conniption fit. So yeah, it was actually kind of fun."

AGILITY:

IT MUST NOT BE PERFECT AT FIRST.

RELEASE, GATHER DATA, REVISE.

Jeffrey gathered people's scores of the previous meeting. On average, they rated it 40% for exciting, and a unanimous zero for effectiveness. Because it had been a particularly dismal meeting, they also measured average meetings in the past: 10% exciting, 30% effective.

"Now that we have a baseline, we can start the real meeting." Jeffrey gave everyone a link to a shared online document. He also connected his laptop to the projector screen for everyone to see. In the document, he typed "Check-ins."

"Type in your name," he instructed, "...and the 2-3 most important things you've been working on this week. We're not going to operate like a Dilbert comic strip. I don't want to see every tiny task. Just the pivotal items. This replaces endless check-ins."

Soon cursors started to appear on the screen. Within 90 seconds, the document looked like this:

Check-Ins

Bob – Software

- Fixed compatibility bug for newest version of Windows
- Ongoing tech support

Aaron – Processing

- Purged and reset wastewater treatment system
- Jury-rigged lifting arm (We'll be good for another 6 months, hopefully)
- Installed new incinerator filters

Clara – Legal

- Submitted maps for shipping
- Updated transportation requirements for Zones 12-16, dumping policies for Zone 8

Roxanne – Receiving

- Ordered and shipped maps
- Weekly transportation schedule

Matt – HR

- Prepping for annual hiring (writing job descriptions, taking inventory of who's leaving)
- Internal audit (bacteria and chemical concentration lab tests, mock inspection)

Jeffrey skimmed the list. "Looks great. Okay, that's all for check-ins. Let's move on to burning issues."

"Wait!" Bob, the balding man, raised his hand. "Aren't we going to discuss what people have done?"

"No way." Jeffrey cringed. "That's slow and painful. Just skim the list on your own. If you see something that needs to be discussed, put it on the burning issues list."

The team was stunned. They leaned forward, curious. Jeffrey glanced at Alexandra, who grinned and nodded. He was doing great.

Jeffrey typed in the next heading, "Burning Issues."

"Is there anything that might explode in the next week if we don't address it?" Jeffrey asked. "Or are you stuck and unable to move forward because you're waiting for something? Those are burning issues."

Everyone spent a few minutes throwing items onto the agenda. Then Jeffrey invited everyone to prioritize the list. "Just move things around where you think they should go," he said.

When Alexandra had briefed him on how to run a meeting, Jeffrey worried about letting them move things around willy-nilly. But it seemed to work.

Burning Issues

(Please put your name next to items you add)

- Lifting arm? (Jeffrey)
- Map orders wrong AGAIN (Clara)
- Orders not being fulfilled (Roxanne and Matt)
- Forklift speeds (Matt)
- One of our storage container suppliers is going out of business. (Aaron)

"Aaron, tell us about the lifting arm."

Aaron looked up, the slightest twinge of desperation in his voice. "It needs to be replaced, but Heart keeps turning down our equipment requests."

"Ahhh. We had that problem in the gulf too," Jeffrey empathized. "Is it safe?"

Aaron nodded grudgingly. "Yes. It just gets stuck a lot. We only have a few months of wear left before it gives out, though."

"I'll make some calls today and see if I can add weight to your request."

Aaron relaxed a little. "I'd appreciate that."

Jeffrey turned back to the list. "Okay, Clara, you're having a problem with maps?"

Clara sat up straight in her chair, looking like she wanted to punch someone. "*Yes.* Roxanne, you got our map orders wrong *AGAIN*."

Jeffrey was confused. He looked back and forth between Clara and Roxanne. Then the light dawned on him.

"Wait, *you're* the one who submits those orders?" Jeffrey asked in frustration. "For all the regions? You got *our* orders wrong, too!"

Roxanne glowered at both of them. "You guys have no idea what shipping looks like from our side."

Alexandra spoke up, curious. "Could you show us?"

Jeffrey and Clara looked at her, surprised.

Then Jeffrey shrugged. "Yeah, sure, let's see the process."

Roxanne pursed her lips. She plugged her laptop into the projector so everyone could see, and then booted the ordering process. She went through step by step. Soon another window popped up, saying, "Would you like to autofill this data based on past orders?"

Roxanne clicked "No." The program hiccupped, and another window popped up. "If you leave this window, all your changes will be lost."

Clara groaned in sudden understanding. "Wow, it's *begging* for you to enter the information wrong."

"I tried to tell you!"

Jeffrey looked at the balding man. "Bob, you're head of software, right? Can you fix this?"

Bob shrugged. "Sure. Piece of cake."

"How soon can you have it done?"

"A few days, probably."

Jeffrey lit up. "Really?"

"Finally," Clara sighed in deep relief. "I've been waiting years for this."

Clara and Roxanne made eye contact and smiled sheepishly.

"Well, that was easy," Roxanne said with a quiet laugh.

Jeffrey typed *Decisions Made* into their shared document. Then he added Bob's new task and *Call about lifting arms* for himself.

"What's next?" Jeffrey looked at the Burning Issues list. "Orders not being fulfilled? What's going on there?"

Matt spoke up. "Our internal audit revealed a problem where some of the hazardous waste isn't getting cycled properly. It's sitting in storage too long."

Aaron sighed in bitter frustration. "That is *not* my fault. It's this ridiculous paper system. No matter what I do, shipping tickets keep going missing. This wouldn't be an issue if Bob would just upgrade the stupid system to one that tracks stuff electronically."

Bob harrumphed. "Your workers don't want the upgrade."

"Of course they don't." Aaron griped. "Right now, every barrel of our lovely toxic sludge is tracked on *paper*. So, if someone's feeling lazy and doesn't want to finish their quota, they can just hide their papers in someone else's stack. If we had an electronic system that tracked stats, their names would get flagged."

"The software works exactly as designed," Bob huffed. "It's the people that are broken. You said it yourself—they're lazy."

Aaron spread his arms wide in frustration. "The software you wrote to track inventory is *thirty* years old! In computer years, that's older than Methuselah."

The whole room laughed, even Bob.

Matt chimed in. "He has a point you know. It's getting hard to find programmers that can program in DOS."[3]

---

[3] One client supported millions of customers with systems at least 35 years old. Another firm was using a DOS system with floppy disks in 2015.

Bob grew defensive. "New systems always have bugs and learning curves. We can't afford any mistakes. If our systems went down for even a day, do you know what that would cost our factories? More money than I make in a decade, that's how much."[4]

"Every 18 months, computer processing speed doubles," Aaron insisted. "Our computers are literally twenty generations behind. How much does *that* cost us? You can't ignore that processing power without taking a huge hit in efficiency. Yes, we can keep limping along with Methuselah... or we can take a small risk now for a *massive* improvement in productivity. The check-ins *prove* your workload is way lighter than anyone else's."

"This is a tangent," Bob snorted. "The original question was about cycling the waste faster. Improving the software *might* be *one* solution but it's a resource-intensive one, and would take months to implement. What else could we change?"

"Forklift speeds," Aaron shot back.

Matt jumped into the conversation. He slapped his hand on the table. "Absolutely not!"

Aaron chuckled. "Matt, *you're* the one who put 'forklift speeds' on the Burning Issues list."

"Yes, to insist we turn it down again."

Aaron's hackles rose. "Wait, *seriously?*"

Jeffrey interrupted. "What are your speeds set to right now?"

"Five miles per hour."

Jeffrey cringed and turned to Matt. "You want to turn it down to four?"

"Three."

Aaron groaned in misery. "Shoot me now."

Jeffrey glanced at Aaron, then back to Matt. "Why?"

Matt glowered. Heart Manufacturing's policy is seven miles per hour. Our employees regularly hack the forklifts to increase their speed. Thanks to the change in leadership, Mr. Khalil and

---

[4] In real life, the stakes were much higher. In one firm, their 30-year-old software ran a process so crucial, a mistake could have halted operations at a cost of 6 million dollars every 10 minutes until resolved.

Edward Heart visited us last week. We knew they were coming, so we reset all the forklifts to five. I kid you not, the *next morning*, forklifts were zooming around at full speed in front of Heart. He was furious. When he told me about it, I told him our governors were set to five. He said that's clearly too high."

"Turning it down to three miles per hour is ridiculous," Aaron insisted. "It's not even possible to turn the engine down that low without losing some of the lifting power."

"Oh." Matt looked stumped. "Really?"

"Really."

Matt was conflicted. "Well, what if we put it at four miles per hour?" he offered grudgingly.

Aaron sagged and banged his head on the table in frustration.

Jeffrey shook his head. "You can regulate the speed all you want, Matt, but the lower you set it, the more motivated the drivers are to hack the system."

"If they had it their way, they'd go thirty in there," Matt objected.

"That's because they're feeling the wrong pain," Alexandra interjected. "They need to feel the pain of the *problem*. Right now, they only feel the pain of the *solution* you imposed on them. To you, slowing the forklifts down is a solution. For your workers, slow forklifts are agonizing. Do you honestly expect them to obey with enthusiasm?"

"How could we help them feel the pain?" Jeffrey asked, suddenly curious.

"Well, to start with, what pain do you want them to feel? This isn't about forklift speeds," Alexandra pointed out. "What's the *reason* you want forklifts set so low?"

"Safety," Matt said.

"Are forklift speeds the only way to ensure that?" Alexandra asked, fiddling with her laptop to keep the screen from sleeping. "What if you put the forklift drivers in charge of safety? Don't give them fake power, give them real power. You could say, 'Hey, we know you hate the forklift speed requirements. If you can create a plan that guarantees safety, we'll let you set the speed.' "

Matt looked horrified. "I don't feel comfortable putting them in charge. They underestimate danger."

"How do you know?" Aaron replied hotly. "Are you stereotyping all low-level blue-collars as reckless and half-asleep, or have you personally surveyed every one of them?"

Everyone went silent. Matt, too, was startled by the question.

"If they care," Matt answered slowly, "why do they violate our safety protocols?"

"It's simple mathematics," Aaron said. "You guys want us to meet quota, without overtime. If the forklifts move at seven miles per hour, that's not humanly possible."

"Ohhh." Matt's eyes grew wide.

Aaron folded his arms. "So one way or another, we're breaking regulations. You can have quota, normal payroll, or low speed. Pick any two."

"I like Alexandra's idea," Bob pitched in for the first time. "That's clever. They desperately want to work efficiently. You're giving them freedom if they meet your very basic condition. I think you'd get good results from that."

Matt frowned. "Safety isn't a thing where we can afford trial-and-error. They'll mess up at least once before they take it seriously."

"Honestly, that's possible," Aaron said with a shrug. "But right now, they're driving at 14 miles per hour. I clocked them. And they know how to hack the machines. But if you ask *them* to present a solution, they may *voluntarily* slow down a few notches. A good solution that's followed is worlds better than a perfect answer everyone ignores."

BUY-IN:
IF YOU CAN
70% AGREE,
VOTE YES

Jeffrey grinned. "Let's take a straw poll. Who can 70% agree on letting the drivers propose a solution?"

Aaron, Bob, and Roxanne all raised their hands. Clara and Matt both wavered.

"Alexandra, what do you think?" Clara asked.

"It's not my place to vote," Alexandra said with a smile. "Just here to help."

Clara and Matt looked at each other.

Jeffrey grinned. "Remember guys, as we've all agreed, we practice agility here. If it isn't working out, we *want* to change. Are you comfortable trying this for two or three weeks?"

Clara relaxed. "Okay. Sure."

Matt nodded too. "I guess I'm okay with that. Three weeks is too long, though. Can we revisit the issue in two weeks?"

"Two weeks," Aaron agreed.

"Done." Jeffrey rapped on the table. "Aaron, can you pull all your forklift drivers into a meeting and get them to hash a plan?"

"Of course." Aaron added to the "Decisions Made" section of their shared document.

Decisions Made

- Bob will update map shipping software for Roxanne
- Jeffrey will call about lifting arms
- Aaron will arrange meeting of forklift drivers, where they will propose their own safety solution and try to implement it. Aaron will report back in two weeks.

Aaron made eye contact with Matt. "Did we seriously just agree on forklift speeds? We've been at each other's throats for months."

Matt laughed. "Yes, I think we just agreed. I'm curious to see how it turns out."

Suddenly, Aaron's pocket buzzed and made the sound of Darth Vader breathing. Aaron slipped it from his pocket and glanced at the screen. He winced. "We have a problem downstairs. Massive shipment. Mind if I step out?"

"Did you want to talk about shipping containers?" Jeffrey asked.

"It can wait a week," Aaron said.

"Then I'll put it on next week's Burning Issues list."

"Perfect, thanks."

As Aaron left, Jeffrey looked around the room and reveled in the looks of surprise and disappointment on people's faces. Disappointed to *leave* a meeting? That was a welcome sight.

"But before we go, let's score this meeting. How exciting was it? How effective?"

They posted their scores on the shared document:

Meeting Score

85% exciting
75% effective

Jeffrey packed up his laptop as his new teammates filed out. Soon, it was just him and Alexandra. She stood by the bay window, watching the workers mill around the bay below. Jeffrey came and watched with her.

"Extraordinary, aren't they?" Alexandra whispered.

"You think so?" Jeffrey stared at the workers scurrying below, the forklifts beep-beeping as they moved in reverse.

"I do." She chuckled. "Forklift driving isn't exactly a job people aspire to. It's easy to underestimate them. Who'd have thought they could troubleshoot and disengage a forklift governor? They're a lot smarter than we give them credit for."

"We don't usually trust warehouse workers to understand anything more than a procedure," Jeffrey mused. "We snatch every problem away, like impatient parents, instead of letting them wrestle with it." Jeffrey's eyes softened as he watched his workers. "That's a lot of lost potential. The struggle is where people grow."

Before Alexandra could respond, they heard a scrambling sound at the door.

They turned around to see someone slipping pieces of a doorknob into the door from the other side. One door handle went in, then the door was pushed open a little. Matt stepped through, the other half of the doorknob in one hand, and a screwdriver in the other. He froze when he saw Jeffrey and Alexandra still there.

CULTURE - The Rat Trap

"Oh." Matt seemed a little embarrassed. "Hey."

Jeffrey glanced at the doorknob and raised an eyebrow. "So soon? I thought you'd put up more of a fight."

"You've earned it, for now," Matt shrugged, stifling a smile. "But I still have the screwdriver."

> The concept of real-time meetings is taught by Patrick Lencioni in *Death by Meeting* and *The Advantage*. The *Neverboss* meeting format is highly condensed for focus and speed.

SUMMARY

- Meetings are the best indication of your team/company's health. Meetings are exciting and effective when urgent questions get solved and decisions are made together.

- Use buy-in, not consensus, when making decisions as a team. If you can at least 70% agree, say yes.

- Agility makes buy-in safe.

ACTION: Introduce the New Meeting Style to Your Team

Introduce the new meeting style in your next team meeting. The three parts of Exciting Meetings are:
1. Quick Check-in
2. Burning Issues and Decisions
3. Score the Meeting

The first time you try this meeting format, scores rise to 75% on average. It rises to 85-100% effective and exciting thereafter if you're doing it right.

The team lead helps keep everyone engaged, but doesn't necessarily run the meeting. People introduce their own agenda items. Everyone takes notes together in the same document. This increases ownership, initiative, and engagement.

During the week, new burning issues will arise. Everyone adds these burning issues anytime, directly to the next meeting agenda. This reduces daily interruptions. After your team lead has modeled the first meeting, rotate who moderates each week.

An agenda template is available at NEVERBOSS.com, with full instructions.

EXCITING MEETINGS
1-ON-1'S

Jeffrey left the team meeting floating on clouds.

"The doorknob! He returned the doorknob!" Jeffrey laughed. "Wait till Khalil hears about this."

"It's a great start to the week," Alexandra agreed.

Jeffrey turned the key to open the door of his office. He wasn't sure why he bothered to lock it since there was nothing valuable in the room.

"What's next?" Jeffrey asked eagerly.

"People are about to start acting on their own. However, you still need visibility on what they're doing. Not every tiny detail, but you should know the big picture. That's where the Initiative Scorecard comes in."

Alexandra reached into her laptop bag and handed Jeffrey a sheet of paper.

"You've already seen the Turnaround Scorecard and the Leadership Scorecard," Alexandra reminded him. "This is the third and final scorecard. It measures Initiative. Your employees will each fill this out, and bring it to your 1-on-1 meetings."

NEVERBOSS - Crenshaw

INITIATIVE SCORECARD

NAME: _____

SELF Grade = ☐   BOSS Grade = ☐

A	I did, then reported back PERIODICALLY (as a meeting agenda item, weekly report, etc.)	☐
B	I did, then reported back IMMEDIATELY	☐
B-	I did on my own, but I FAILED TO REPORT back…	
C	I RECOMMENDED we do…	☐
D	I ASKED what to do…	☐
F	I did what I was TOLD to do…	☐

> Stephen R. Covey proposed 7 Levels of Initiative in *The 8th Habit*. They are adapted here to make initiative easier to measure and adopt.

"What 1-on-1 meetings?"

"The ones you're about to schedule," Alexandra replied. "Every week, without fail, you need to meet with each of your direct reports, 1-on-1."

Jeffrey wrinkled his nose. "That sounds overwhelming."

"It shouldn't be. It will save you tons of time. And it should be fun. During these meeting, we'll tackle obstacles together, role play crucial conversations, and review goals. Do *not* miss these meetings. They are your best opportunities for training and accountability."

"I'm afraid I'll ask the same questions every time. 'So, how's work?' 'Good.'" Jeffrey laughed. "What keeps 1-on-1's from getting boring?"

Alexandra smiled. "The same thing that keeps team meetings from being boring. *You aren't running the agenda.* Once Matt or Clara or Bob realize they have a reliable space to talk with you and be heard, they'll start to bring burning issues. Within a week or two, they'll be bursting with things to talk about, and they'll stop interrupting you during the week."

"Fewer interruptions would be nice," Jeffrey admitted. "But I don't believe 1-on-1's will work. In my experience, people clam up. They prefer not to rock the boat. How do you get past that defense long enough to have a real conversation?"

Alexandra nodded, impressed by the question. "The best way is to gather insider data. I need to interview all your team influencers and key stakeholders."

Jeffrey shrugged. "Sure. Go ahead."

"I need to warn you in advance that their replies will be confidential. I won't be able to tell you what was said."

"What?" Jeffrey felt his hackles rise. "Wait, I'm not comfortable with people talking behind my back."

"With good cause. I don't want to start a gossip mill," Alexandra reassured him. "I'm just looking for patterns that are causing pain. As an outsider, I have a rare opportunity to help. When people believe their confidentiality is guaranteed, and I have *no* authority over them—but I potentially have the ear of other people—there's tremendous motivation to spill their guts.[5] Once we know what they need, you can be the champion for it."

Jeffrey relaxed a little. "I guess that's okay."

Alexandra smiled, nodded, and wandered off with a notepad under her arm.

For the next few days, Alexandra floated. Jeffrey saw her talking quietly with people from time to time. Finally, she came back and reported.

"Good news," she said. "You're in no danger of a coup."

Jeffrey rolled his eyes. "What'd you find?"

"I can't tell you because those interviews are confidential, but here are some great questions I think you should ask." She tore a sheet from her notepad and handed it to him.

Jeffrey read through the questions quickly.

"Wow, these are really good," Jeffrey said, surprised. "These will come in handy during my 1-on-1 meetings tomorrow."

"That's the idea." Alexandra smiled. "Good luck."

Jeffrey handed Matt an Initiative Scorecard. Matt peered at it with curiosity. They were meeting in Matt's office. Jeffrey sat in the guest chair while Matt behind his desk.

"I won't be giving orders," Jeffrey explained. "I don't want to tell you what to do all day long. What we measure improves, so I want you to measure the things you accomplish on your own."

---

[5] We call this Delphic Interviewing. It's an allusion to the Oracle of Delphi in Greek mythology, who knew all and saw all. Delphic Interviewing means, "I'm going to interview everybody, but I guarantee their anonymity and confidentiality."

QUESTIONS TO KICKSTART DISCUSSION

> How are you feeling about work lately?
>
> What obstacles are you facing?
>
> What opportunities are we missing?
>
> Do you see anything slipping through the cracks?
>
> What is your role?
>
> What do you feel responsible for?
>
> If you could wave a magic wand and change anything around here, what would it be?
>
> What easy opportunities do you see right now for not much effort?
>
> Is there anything else you feel strongly about?

"Okay, interesting," Matt said. "How do I fill it out?"

"During the week, write down things you do, in whichever box they belong in," Jeffrey replied. "Each week, bring it to our 1-on-1. Based on the spread, you grade yourself from A to F. I'll respond by asking you three quick questions. One – How do you know that's the grade you deserve?"

"Okay..."

"Two – Give me examples where you showed initiative. That's your chance to brag. And three – What areas do you feel you could have done better in?"

Matt tried to wrap his mind around the idea.

"What sorts of things do you want me to show initiative on?"

"Everything," Jeffrey explained. "Don't wait for me to tell you what to do. If something's wrong, fix it. You don't need permission. I don't care *how* you do your job, as long as your work gets done. Beyond that, you have control."

Matt's eyes lit up.

"That would help *so much* working with labor unions." He hesitated. "I mean... how far can I go with this? Can I make small decisions on my own and skip the bureaucracy?"

Jeffrey froze up. Labor unions were serious business. He glanced at Alexandra.

"Principles?" she prompted.

"Oh!" Jeffrey remembered the list of principles he'd been gathering. He flipped through his notepad and then showed the list to Matt.

"Let's talk about principles, starting with common sense. Don't sink the ship. Involve the people who care. If it's the sort of decision where I could go to jail if you're wrong or we might violate a contract, I *obviously* need to be included."

Matt laughed heartily. "Of course."

"But I don't care how long lunch breaks are," Jeffrey said with a shrug, "or when people go on vacation. Do whatever you feel is appropriate for good relationships."

Matt sighed in deep relief. "Wow, this changes everything."

Bob was less receptive.

He peered at Jeffrey in confusion, looking for an ulterior motive. Then he harrumphed and tossed the sheet back on the table.

"*Sure*, that's what they all say. Then when things go wrong, who gets blamed? And when things go *right*? Ha! Who takes the credit?"

Jeffrey nodded. "Unfortunately, that does happen too much in business. Let me explain. My job as a leader is not to whip you like a horse, telling you where to go. My job is to back you up. When you mess up, I promise you won't take the fall for it alone. No more blaming. If there are consequences, we'll face them together."

Bob thought for a moment. When he spoke again, his tone was a little softer but still defensive. "I'll believe it when I see it."

"That's fine," Jeffrey replied, unoffended. "Until then, take this sheet. We'll go over it each week in our 1-on-1's. Write down the things you do on your own. It will create a record that will help me remember to give credit where it's due."

That caught Bob's attention.

Bob glanced at the sheet, then at Jeffrey.

Without another word, Bob took the sheet and left, leaving Jeffrey sitting in Bob's office alone.

Jeffrey met with Clara next.

"In the future," he continued, "you'll fill the Initiative Scorecard out on your own, during the week. But today, we'll do it together."

Clara nodded politely. Jeffrey could tell she was on automatic. She sat straight and took notes, but Jeffrey noticed the notes frequently had nothing to do what they were talking about. Her lawyer brain was itching to get back to work.

"Think back on this week," Jeffrey urged. "Do you have any invisible tasks you're afraid no one ever appreciates?"

Clara froze and looked up from her notepad, interested for the first time. "You're talking about going the extra mile."

"Exactly."

"The things you do because you care. The ones no one sees."

"Yes."

Clara picked the Initiative Scorecard up and set it on top of her notepad. She looked at it thoughtfully for a moment. Then, with surprising ferocity, she started filling in each section. When she finished, she slapped the paper down on the table.

Jeffrey skimmed it, and his eyes grew huge.

"Holy cow!" he exclaimed. "How do you have time for all these things?"

"Long hours," she said with a sigh. "That's what I get for picking a law degree. That was refreshing, though," she added, nodding to the Initiative Scorecard. She looked happier and more alert than Jeffrey had seen her all week. "I feel surprisingly vindicated. Thank you for asking."

"What obstacles are you facing?" Jeffrey asked.

"Paper," Aaron replied without skipping a beat. "This paper tracking system is killing me. Shipping tickets are easy to lose. They get rained on, walked on, used for scratch paper."

Alexandra cocked her head. "Is it bad to the point of being unworkable?" she asked. "Lots of companies use paper systems."

Aaron gave her a sideways look. "Alexandra, this software was written *so* long ago that they assumed anyone who used it would be a programmer. Some of the commands are bizarre. For example, when you try to delete something, it asks if you want to 'supersede this item.' "[6]

Jeffrey rolled in his chair, laughing.

"I think you're dead right," Jeffrey told Aaron. "Maybe I could put some pressure on Bob while I'm here. Get a new software system started."

Aaron shrugged. "No, it's okay, Jeffrey. I've got this. The harder you push Bob, the more he pushes back. But I've learned that it's very hard to say no to a reasonable request 39 times in a row. I've been asking politely, over and over, for months. He'll crack eventually."

Behind Jeffrey, Alexandra started to laugh. "That's a brilliant approach. You know how it'll end, right?"

They turned and looked at her.

She smirked. "One of these days, the software team is going to think it's their idea. *When they do*, bite your tongues and nod your heads."

Aaron looked confused. "Why?"

"It's very important that they think it's their idea," she explained, "because then they own it. If it's their baby, they'll see it through to the end."

"What? No!" Aaron frowned. "I've pushed so hard for this."

"Absolutely," Alexandra said. "Jeffrey will remember that. But can you code that program on your own?"

---

[6] As of 2017, this is the state of software used by some large manufacturers in the United States.

"No," admitted Aaron.

"Ideas are a fickle thing," Alexandra sympathized. "There is a time to claim credit and a time to give credit away. Giving birth to an idea means your heartstrings will always be attached to it. But if someone else wants to take that idea and raise it to maturity, that's a ton of work. That's more work than giving birth. Therefore, credit belongs to the builder, not the architect."

"That seems unnecessary," Aaron said, clearly a little upset. "Everyone's used to seeing the architect's name on things."

"If you insist on taking credit, Aaron, what will happen to Bob's motivation?"

Understanding suddenly hit. Aaron's defensiveness started to melt. "He'd be offended. He'd never finish it."

"Would you rather have software that works or credit for a program that never exists?"

Aaron sagged but smiled. "The software."

> THERE'S NO LIMIT TO WHAT YOU CAN **ACCOMPLISH** IF YOU DON'T CARE WHO GETS THE CREDIT.
>
> — FATHER STRICKLAND, 1863

Alexandra nodded. "Blueprints can't shelter you from rain, and an unwritten software program can't sort your waste. But there's no limit to what you can accomplish if you don't care who gets the credit."

Aaron nodded. "Fair enough."

"In time," Alexandra said, "surrendering credit won't be necessary. People will work with mutual respect, mutual empathy, and mutual purpose. But for now, your humble, persistent approach gets the ball rolling."

Lastly, Jeffrey met with Roxanne.

"Tell me about your department. How do you like your job?"

"It's fine."

Jeffrey could tell from her body language that it wasn't fine. Tense and uncomfortable, she avoided eye contact. It was classic employee misery, and Jeffrey wondered how he could convince Roxanne he was on her side.

"I want to reassure you," Jeffrey said gently, "discussions during 1-on-1's are completely confidential. No one is going to hear what you're saying. Not Vanderman, or Khalil, or anyone. Do you enjoy it here?"

Roxanne hesitated, then gave a short, curt nod. "Honestly, I'm bored."

Jeffrey smiled warmly. "Tell me about that."

She shrugged. "My department was created pretty much because we *had* to be here. But I feel like the red-headed stepchild. We have some very skilled people. It's a little humiliating to take the same calls every six weeks. 'Yes, we'll put that order in for you. No, we didn't mess up your order on purpose.' I studied at MIT, for crying out loud."

She went quiet and looked away.

Jeffrey thought about Alexandra's list of questions, wondering what would help her open up more.

"If you could wave a magic wand and change anything, what would it be?"

"I don't know."

Unoffended but unwilling to let her off easy, Jeffrey nodded. "Would you mind thinking about it, and telling me next week?"

Roxanne paused.

"*Wait.* I *do* know." She scooted her chair forward. "I would like to sell our services to third parties."

Jeffrey gave her a quizzical look. "What do you mean?"

"I get calls *all* the time," she explained. "Factories calling us up, asking if they can hire us. But I've been ordered to say, 'Sorry sir, we're privately owned and only service Heart factories.'"

Roxanne hit her palm against the table. "But I'm the one who *manages* the truckers. I make the schedules and map the routes telling people where to go. I *know* there's space for more pick-ups. We have slow times. Lots of them. Our bay workers get bored, and truckers are upset because they want more hours."

"Oh, wow." Jeffrey reeled.

"I know, right?" Roxanne was getting excited. "GooCrew is a massive drain on Heart Manufacturing's finances. I've seen the financial reports. What if we became cash flow *positive* instead?"

From the corner, Alexandra interrupted tentatively. "Do you mind if I ask a question?"

Jeffrey gestured for her to come closer. "Not at all."

Alexandra turned to Roxanne. "Can you predict the slow times?"

Roxanne sagged. "Well... not yet."

"Why not?" Alexandra asked.

"There's this thing called satellite accumulation," Roxanne explained. "Basically, factories are allowed by law to store a certain amount of waste on site. Once they hit their limit, they have three days to unload it. Some factories are scheduled and we pick up their waste no matter what. For others, we wait until they call, and we'll suddenly find ourselves swamped."

"That's true," Jeffrey remembered, a little disappointed.

Roxanne's eyes lit up again. "I have a hunch. I think those satellite accumulation dumps have a heartbeat too. But it's impossible to track on paper."

Jeffrey and Alexandra's eyes met.

Jeffrey mused. "If we ever convince Bob to develop new shipping software, we could probably run calculations on the data."

Roxanne lit up. "With that information, I bet I could figure it out."

"How much revenue do you think you could make?"

She had a number. It was a good number.

"Great," Jeffrey said. "Put together a quick business case. If you can prove the lull times, I'll make sure you get an opportunity to present your idea to the right people."

Roxanne hesitated. "How do I make a business case?"

"Don't make it fancy," he said. "Answer these simple questions: What's the problem? What's your solution? What are the risks? How much money could it make? And what would the owners have to do to make it happen? Very simple."

"Oh, I can do that!"

"Great. Bring it to our next 1-on-1."

Roxanne nodded. Jeffrey stopped her as she started to gather her things.

"Before you go, Roxanne, I have a question I've been asking everyone..."

"Sure, what is it?"

Jeffrey quickly explained the Leadership Scorecard and showed her what it looked like, as he had shown each of the others.

"Where do you think I am on the leadership steps?" he asked. "I'd love specific examples. Things I did well. Cases where I could have done better. That kind of thing. My goal is to start stepping back as quickly as possible and make Hands-Off Leadership the new status quo."

Roxanne looked surprised. She took a hard look at the sheet.

After Jeffrey met with each of his direct reports, Jeffrey and Alexandra rushed to their meeting with Jeffrey's supervisor, Mr. Khalil. They met in Jeffrey's office, where Mr. Khalil sat in Jeffrey's chair. When Alexandra started explaining 1-on-1's, Khalil frowned.

"You want me to meet with Jeffrey every week?" Khalil asked.

"Yes," Alexandra insisted. "It's absolutely vital."

Mr. Khalil's eyes flicked back and forth, his expression somewhere between brooding and amusement. "I'll be honest with you both. I'm somewhat nervous about this coaching process."

"Why?" Alexandra asked, unoffended.

"There's a lot going on right now. I'm needed in three places at once, and the last thing I can afford to do is retrain someone. If it were my choice, I would have moved you back to a bay position and just hired someone else. I favor a swift and certain hand."

"You didn't want to retrain me?" Jeffrey asked in shock.

"No." Khalil stood and walked to the window. He stared out at the lake. It was raining.

"Be that as it may," he continued without looking at them, "Mr. Heart really wants this. I'm willing to give him his fun and let the clock tick down. Alexandra, as I understand it, the leadership style you preach is hands-off, yes?"

She nodded. "That's correct."

"Then here's what I'm going to do." He flashed her an impish grin. "In the spirit of experimentation, I'm going to give you as much rope as you want. You can build a bridge... or hang yourself with it. I will attend to other matters and simply find out what happens at the end."

Khalil turned and gathered his suit coat, briefcase, and umbrella. "Send any reports to my secretary. I would prefer to only be contacted if there's an emergency."

Alexandra looked at him carefully. "Okay... You don't want to give *any* input along the way?"

"Surprise me," he said with a smile.

Then he left.

Jeffrey was shaken by the interaction, but when he turned to Alexandra, she was smirking.

Jeffrey panicked a little. "Are we still going to be able to do this?"

"Absolutely."

"But you said weekly meetings with him were vital."

"They are if he doesn't want to be blindsided at the end," she laughed. "But plenty of people implement Hands-Off Leadership from the middle of their organization, without any support from above."

With that, she clicked her pen and sat down in a chair next to Jeffrey.

"I guess you'll be reporting to me. Let's get started." She pulled out a scoresheet. "Time for our weekly grade. Let's talk about Initiative. How do you feel you're doing?"

"I think I'm at a B, at least!"

Alexandra pulled out copies of the other team member's scorecards. "Well, let's find out."

Together, they averaged all the scores. On his Turnaround Scorecard, Jeffrey's leadership score had risen from an F to a D.

Jeffrey sagged.

Alexandra smiled encouragingly. "You should feel great about that. It takes a while for people to honestly believe it's okay for them to act on their own. Years of conditioning need to be undone. This is a really good start."

Jeffrey smiled tentatively. "Thanks."

She switched to the Leadership Scorecard. "Where are you at on the leadership steps?"

"I'm Stepping Up," Jeffrey said confidently. "Showing a strong presence, teaching principles. I'm already Stepping Beside and Stepping Back a little—training, encouraging people to take initiative and letting them do so. And we're laying the foundation to Step Away in the future."

"Bravo!" Alexandra said. "That was perfect. Now for the next section."

"Top Victories?"

"Yup. Of all the things your workers have accomplished on their own this week, what three things are you proudest of?"

Jeffrey thought hard. "Man, that's hard. People have gotten a LOT done this week."

Jeffrey racked his brain. "I think Roxanne gets first place for her business idea."

"Agreed. That was amazing. What else?"

"Um... Aaron requested we let the forklift safety crew rearrange temporary storage. I liked the idea, even if asking was technically a C on Initiative."

"Well, when clarification is needed, asking is important. Do you think he brought you into the decision at the right time?"

Jeffrey thought about it. "It could go either way. I wouldn't have minded if he'd gone ahead. At the same time, shifting things can be a safety issue."

"Do you trust him to make safe decisions in the bay area?"

"So far, yes," he replied.

Jeffrey breathed in. He looked around the cold, dreary room. The walls were blank, and only one lightbulb was installed. Jeffrey shuddered involuntarily.

"What are you thinking about?" Alexandra asked, curious.

"It feels deliberate," Jeffrey said slowly. "The cold, bare desk. The stark, barely functional furniture. They're taking away all the safety nets and training wheels. The message is clear. No one above will swoop in for a rescue. If I can't cut it on my own... That'll be it. They aren't invested in me."

"They hired me," Alexandra insisted.

Jeffrey gave her a sad, longwise glance. "Let's be honest, though. You're here because they wanted to test run your services. They would have hired you anyway. I'm just the guinea pig. They'll let you fail, too. There's no help coming from above."

Jeffrey touched the breast pocket of his suit jacket. A piece of paper crinkled inside. He drew comfort from the wrinkled thank-you.

"You know what, though?" Jeffrey realized. "I think it's going to be okay."

SUMMARY

- You can measure personal initiative. Use the Initiative Scorecard for weekly reporting and discussion.

- Weekly 1-on-1's are your best training opportunities, and they reduce interruptions. 1-on-1's should include burning issues, brainstorming, and coaching.

- Letting others take credit allows them to feel ownership and ensures better results.

ACTION: Introduce Initiative Scorecards

Introduce Initiative Scorecards to your direct reports. (If you're not a supervisor, start using one yourself and show it to your boss to get their buy-in.) Review them weekly in your 1-on-1's.

ACTION: Schedule 1-on-1's

Schedule 1-on-1 meetings with each of your direct reports. Create shared agenda documents for each employee. Use the questions and guidelines in this chapter to run your meetings.

UNIVERSAL SAFETY

RULES OF ENGAGEMENT

WEEK THREE

The next Monday, Jeffrey asked to have a special meeting. No one complained. People showed up early, eager, toting laptops. They were bright-eyed and ready for battle.

Jeffrey invited people to do check-ins again. It took 90 seconds. But then the meeting went a little differently.

Jeffrey smiled mischievously. "Today, instead of talking about burning issues, we're having a special meeting to discuss elephants. Alexandra will explain the Rules of Engagement. Then we want you to put the biggest, nastiest issues you can think of on the list. Sore spots, things you've been feeling ignored on, things you're afraid to talk about."

An awkward pause followed. People glanced at each other.

"Well, we could talk about Methuselah," Aaron said.

Bob rolled his eyes. "You mean my software? We aired that out last week."

Aaron glanced at Bob. "Yeah, but we didn't make a decision."

Jeffrey drummed his fingers on the table. "That's definitely an option. Add it to the list. What other elephants are lurking?"

87

Clara tentatively raised her hand. "Can we talk about eco-friendly ethics?"

Aaron rolled his eyes and groaned bitterly. "Don't even get us started."

Jeffrey grinned. "Sounds like there's conflict there. That's *exactly* where we should start."

Aaron grimaced and typed in "Eco-ethics."

Alexandra looked around. "Hey, is Aaron the only one taking notes? If only one person takes notes, only one person remembers what happened."

Jeffrey quickly opened his computer. The rest of the room followed suit. "Alexandra, go ahead and explain the rules of engagement."

Alexandra stood. "It's really easy." On the board, she wrote,

> *MUTUAL EMPATHY*
>
> *MUTUAL RESPECT*
>
> *MUTUAL PURPOSE*

"Let's skip empathy for a second and start with mutual respect." Alexandra capped her marker. "When I was in fourth grade, my teacher gave us a riddle. She said, 'Pretend someone built a house on a hill with no windows and no doors.' Then she held up an enormous bag of candy and said, 'Whoever can think of the most reasons why someone might do that gets all this candy.' "

Bob snickered. "Good idea. Give the smartest kid diabetes."

"Oh, I was very motivated," Alexandra laughed. "I came up with 89 different reasons."

"Wow, seriously?"

Alexandra nodded. "*And I lost.*"[7]

Surprise rippled through the room.

"The point is this," she said. "There are *loads* of *good* reasons why people might do things. Reasons you never dreamed of. Never

---

[7] The House on the Hill story is true and was life-changing for me personally.

CULTURE - Rules of Engagement

assume someone is just being stubborn or stupid. Never reach a negative conclusion without carefully clarifying, because people always do things for *good* reasons. That's mutual respect."

Aaron shuffled in his seat. "That's nice, but it has *nothing* to do with our industry."

Matt chuckled darkly. "It *totally* does. I'll give you a prime example: Saddam Hussein."

Alexandra folded her arms. "Now I'm curious."

Matt leaned forward. "Saddam bragged that he had weapons of mass destruction. We threatened war unless they destroyed them. Anthrax, too. We knew they had it, and destroyed some, but 1800 gallons were missing. One of the inspectors grappling with the case said, 'Mustard gas is not marmalade. You are supposed to know what you did with it.' "

MUTUAL RESPECT:
PEOPLE DO THINGS FOR
GOOD REASONS

Everyone chuckled. Matt allowed himself a brief smile.

"We pressed Iraq like crazy for proof that all their weapons had been destroyed. One of Iraq's chief weapons scientists assured us all the anthrax was gone. But she refused to provide evidence, so we went to war."

Matt let that sink in. "Many people died. We destabilized the region. After we'd taken power away from Saddam, we *still* couldn't find the anthrax. You know what happened to it?"

"They never had it?" Jeffrey assumed.

"Oh, they totally did. And it had been destroyed. But nobody considered the possibility that she might have destroyed it somewhere Saddam wouldn't be happy about. She was *afraid* to tell us because she knew he'd retaliate against her personally."

Alexandra gasped. "Oh no... Where did she destroy it?"

"Right next to one of his palaces."

Jaws dropped.

89

Matt looked at Aaron pointedly. "We deal with volatile substances all day long. Fear is a huge motivator. We often overlook it. When someone is acting erratic, we should ask, 'Gee, are they afraid of something?' It's amazing how often that's a factor."

"Absolutely," Alexandra agreed. "Start by making it safe for them to tell the truth. And it's easy. You just say, 'I'm *certain* you have a good reason for what's going on here. Tell me about it.' "

You can't reach the mind until you calm the heart

"What about when they're angry?" Roxanne asked timidly. "You can't even start a conversation because they won't listen."

"Good point," Alexandra said. "In practice, Empathy comes first. You can't reach the mind until you calm the heart."

"So..." Bob squinted at the board. "How is Respect different from Empathy?"

"Another great question," Alexandra said. "Mutual respect acknowledges the logic behind someone's argument. Mutual empathy acknowledges that their feelings have equal value."

Bob sagged. "That doesn't change what needs to be said."

"Right! But *how* you say things is as important as *what* you say. For example, I can deliver the message, 'You're fired.' That's data. But if I'm laughing while I say it, what does that tell you?"

Bob frowned. "Okay, I see your point. But... I *hate* it when people beat around the bush. It's so inefficient."

Alexandra nodded. "I know, right? Luckily, there are three very simple, very fast things you can do to put people at ease."

"What?"

"Just ask yourself, am I being kind? Am I being gentle? Am I being generous?"

"That's it?"

"That's it. When you need to approach a hard conversation with someone, be kind with your words. Be gentle with your tone. And be generous in your offering. Even when firing someone, you can look around and say, 'Well, Joe is an atrocious programmer, but is there a different position we could offer him? Maybe he'd make a great admin.' Even if it's a downgrade, many people will take it. Everyone will appreciate the offer."

"Huh." Bob seemed mollified. "Okay. Thanks for explaining."

"No problem." Alexandra glanced at the clock. "I'll keep this last one short. Mutual purpose is easy. When things get heated, remember what goal you have in common."

Bob rolled his eyes. "Like a mission statement for the company?"

Alexandra shook her head. "Not usually. Mutual purpose isn't something you craft in advance. It always revolves around some specific issue. Last week Aaron and Bob were butting heads over how to track our inventory. Aaron favored high visibility, and Bob favored simplicity, but both of you want to make sure we don't mess things up."

"*Yes*," Aaron said.

"Absolutely!" Bob agreed emphatically.

They paused and looked at each other. Aaron raised an eyebrow.

"Careful," Aaron joked, "If you start agreeing, you might see eye to eye with me on this. Then you'd have a lot of work to do."

Bob couldn't help but laugh. Resistance was still palpable, but as everybody watched, they could feel it starting to slip. Alexandra paused, giving them opportunity to talk, but neither of them seemed inclined to push the issue at the moment. So she continued.

"So does mutual purpose make sense?" she asked. "In general, you start the discussion, listen, and then look for what you have in common. Once we see where the conflict is, we can look for the mutual purpose."

They were nodding their heads. Nobody commented, but the idea made sense.

Other resources for creating safety and making debates productive are *Crucial Conversations* by Switzer et al. and LetsKeepItCivil.org.

"Cool." Alexandra grinned mischievously. "You guys ready? I'd like to set you loose for a heated discussion. Let's roll the elephants out. Do you mind if I play referee and interrupt when you step out of bounds?"

Everyone agreed.

"Perfect." Alexandra smiled and turned to Clara. "Tell us about eco-ethics."

Clara stood, glancing nervously around the room. "GooCrew is good about following the law. But we're not always concerned about ethics."

"Can you be more specific?" Jeffrey asked.

"Yes. I feel like one of our major dumping sites is too close to humans. It's in a poverty zone, and we use it because it's convenient. I'd like to propose an alternative destination."

Jeffrey nodded. "I like this idea. Where's the conflict?"

Roxane leaned forward. "She's suggested this before. The problem, sir, is that the landfill she wants to use is both more expensive and *much* farther away."

"Time out!" Alexandra said. Everyone stopped and looked at her.

"Your points are fair," Alexandra reassured Roxanne. "Can you include mutual respect or mutual purpose, though? Without those, your data can feel like a personal attack."

Roxanne thought for a moment, then rephrased. "I'm sure Clara has good reasons. She knows this proposal is expensive. I'm certain there's some benefit. But we have to justify the expense."

"Exactly." Aaron huffed. "If we're going to be throwing money around, there are pieces of equipment in the bay area that desperately need replacing, more than we need eco-ethics. I feel like I'm working with arthritic dinosaurs. We need to get our priorities straight."

"Time out..."

Aaron turned a longsuffering eye to Alexandra.

"You need mutual purpose," Alexandra clarified. "It's not your needs versus Clara's. Can you find common ground? How do you balance money and eco-ethics?"

CULTURE - Rules of Engagement

"Profit comes first," Jeffrey said immediately. "I mean, GooCrew is a cash-negative subsidiary, but Heart Manufacturing has to profit or die. Our budget is fixed."

"Mmm...." Alexandra grinned at Jeffrey. "*Mutual* purpose. Or empathy. I'm not feeling it yet."

Jeffrey turned to Clara. "I like baby seals as much as the next guy. Let's keep the Earth clean. I'm happy to authorize the expense if it fits within our working budget."

"Errrr." Alexandra made a buzzer sound. "Try again, less sarcasm."

Jeffrey rolled his eyes, but he paused and thought hard this time. "Lately, businesses everywhere have been finding that being environmentally responsible can be profitable. Maybe we're fretting over pennies. Do you have numbers for us?"

"Awesome." Alexandra looked pleased.

Wordlessly, Clara opened a spreadsheet. She switched the projector to display her screen so everyone could see.

Jeffrey flinched. "*Oh.* You want to divert 20% of our dumping? For twice the dumping fee? There's no *way* we can afford that."

"The word *can't* is the enemy of innovation," Alexandra chided. "Instead of saying it can't be done, try, 'We can if...'"

Roxanne raised her hand. "Jeffrey, what about the idea I had? That would generate extra cash."

Jeffrey hesitated. "Well, I love your idea. But the principle there is 'don't count your chickens before they've hatched.' We shouldn't spend dollars before we have them."

Roxanne looked disappointed. "Ah. Touché."

Jeffrey turned to Matt. "You're the guy who has to soothe the public if something explodes. What do you think?"

Matt wavered.

"I think I'm opposed to the idea. What we have is good enough. I seriously doubt anyone would put dump sites close enough to cause problems for humans."

Clara turned bright red. "This is my *job*. I know where the dump sites are. I understand the legal ramifications of what we carry. Exactly how dangerous it is, exactly what containers it belongs in, exactly how long those containers last, and exactly what happens if something fails. That's what you hired me for, Matt. Just because some ignorant politician thought Hooverville was a great place for a dump site doesn't mean *I* do."

Jeffrey butted in. "Are these quantifiable risks or hypothetical ones? I mean, are we *actually* leaking stuff into the groundwater, or just at risk of doing so in 50 years?"

Suddenly, Clara stood up, her face flushed with anger. Tears starting streaming down her cheeks. She pushed her chair in firmly and left the room.

Everyone sat stunned for a moment. Then Roxanne jumped up, about to chase after Clara.

Jeffrey waved her back. "No, that was my bad. Let me fix it."

When Jeffrey stepped outside, Clara was pacing in the little-used end of the hall. She looked livid. And mortified.

When she heard the door click, she looked up and noticed Jeffrey.

She instantly scowled and turned away.

Jeffrey almost turned around and let her have her space. But he couldn't leave without apologizing, or it would set the tone for their relationship for the next three months.

> TO HANDLE YOURSELF, USE YOUR HEAD; TO HANDLE
> # OTHERS,
> USE YOUR
> # HEART.
> —ELEANOR ROOSEVELT

Jeffrey put himself in her shoes for a moment. He'd rather be shot than have anyone's pity.

"You know something really unfair about business culture?" he asked slowly. "Something I hate?"

The question surprised Clara. She shot him an annoyed, confused look and didn't respond.

Jeffrey put his hands in his pockets and leaned against the wall. "When men show emotion at work,

CULTURE - Rules of Engagement

it's seen as strength—he's passionate about something. When a woman shows emotion, it's seen as weakness—she's out of control."

Astonishment rippled across Clara's face.

"It's a vicious double-standard," Jeffrey said. "Respectful emotion is *always* strength. Emotion means you're bringing your heart and soul to work. Emotion means you're paying attention. No one should feel small for doing that."

When Jeffrey and Clara rejoined the meeting, Clara's eyes were still red, but she was smiling and confident. Her teammates rallied around her, concerned.

"Are you okay?" Matt asked. "Did we push too hard?"

Clara laughed confidently and shook her head. "No, you guys are okay. I just have strong feelings about this!"

Aaron smiled guiltily and pulled out a chair for her. "I think we're not quite getting the picture. Take as much time as you need. What sort of impact is our dumping having on local life?"

> **SUMMARY**
>
> - Universal Safety requires mutual empathy, mutual respect, and mutual purpose. When these are present, teams can engage well on tough issues.
>
> - You can't reach the mind until you calm the heart. (Mutual empathy.)
>
> - People do things for good reasons. (Mutual respect.)
>
> - Find common ground. (Mutual purpose.)
>
> - Listen to outliers. People expressing strong emotions usually have important information.

WEEK THREE

ACTION: Tackle an Elephant

Pick a big, nasty issue your team hates talking about. Introduce your team to the Rules of Engagement and ask for buy-in to adopt them as your new standard. Then work through the impasse together. If things get heated, focus on slowing the conversation down and hold each other to mutual empathy, mutual respect, and mutual purpose until they become second nature.

Don't be afraid. You now have the tools to do it: buy-in, agility, and the rules of engagement. Remember to be kind, gentle, and generous with your teammates.

WEEK THREE

UNIVERSAL SAFETY

OPEN FLOOR POLICY

Matt knocked on Jeffrey's doorway and leaned in. "Sorry, do you mind if I borrow Alexandra for a moment?" Jeffrey and Alexandra looked up from a chart.

"Rough day?" Jeffrey asked.

Matt growled and closed the door. He flopped down in a chair.

"Ever wish you could go back and beg your younger self to pick a different career?" Matt rubbed his forehead. "I picked HR because I love peace. Now I spend every day in the *dead center* of corporate drama. I should have been a mortician."

Jeffrey leaned back in his chair, laughing. Alexandra smirked and set down her pen.

Matt looked at her sheepishly. "Can I get your advice on something?"

"Sure. What's up?"

"The culture among bay workers is atrocious. Backbiting, gossip, undermining, cutting each other down. Every two hours, someone storms into my office and vents. Then I have to talk to the person they're upset with. I'm falling *massively* behind in my other duties, and I'm running out of patience."

Alexandra chuckled. "Let me guess. Your company has an open door policy, which means people bring complaints to you, and you promise their confidentiality."

Matt nodded. "Of course."

"That's your problem."

Matt did a double-take. "What do you mean?"

"Open door policies were created because conflict is uncomfortable. Businesses wanted to make sure no one lingered in an unsafe situation because they were afraid to speak up."

"Right."

"It's a good starting place for extreme cases like sexual harassment. But for everything else, it's a mistake. If I can pass my complaints on to you, and *you'll* confront someone for me, why on earth would I bother to do it myself?"

Matt hesitated.

Alexandra smiled gently. "That's how you get bogged down with things you instinctively know aren't your responsibility. But there's *another* problem."

"What?"

"Pretend you're coming to confront me about something."

"Okay. Alexandra, I received a complaint. Someone's upset at you about something you did last week."

"Great, I'd love to talk with them," Alexandra said cheerfully. "Who's upset?"

"I can't tell you."

"There it is." Alexandra chuckled. "The moment you say that, suddenly *anyone* in the office might be upset with me. Anyone could have turned me in. So it suddenly feels like *everyone* might be upset with me. That devastates team trust."

Matt grew defensive. "Usually, people are trying to be nice. They are afraid if they confront a co-worker, it will damage their relationship permanently."

"Absolutely. People aren't good at conflict. But it's worse to confront someone through the grapevine. It creates a hos-

CULTURE – Open Floor Policy

tile environment and gives the other person no chance to explain themselves."

Matt frowned. "So what should I do?"

"Replace your open door policy with an Open Floor Policy. It works like this: Someone comes into your office angry. They're upset. You listen. Reflect empathy, ask questions, and coach them on ways they might approach the other person. But here's the thing... *You must not do anything about it* unless they may be in danger."

"Nothing at all?"

"Correct. Let the person who's venting know that you *will not* confront the other person for them. It's *their* job to do so. Tell them, 'If you don't feel safe, no problem. I'm happy to come with you to ensure you don't get beaten up, and we will resolve it together. Do you feel comfortable going to him first to see if he can resolve it with you?' "

"What if she isn't willing to confront the other person?"

"Then you don't either. But most of the time people say, 'Okay, I'll give it a shot.' They know you'll back them up if necessary. That gives them the courage to try. Plus, when they vented at you, you armed them with ways to explain how they're feeling, ideas for compromise, and good questions to ask. Most people avoid conflict because they don't know how to ask for what they want. If you get that conversation started in their head, they'll usually follow through."

Alexandra snapped her fingers and turned to Jeffrey. "I almost forgot. When managers confront a team member, there's a temptation to chastise everyone together in a group meeting, without calling anyone specific out. That's not acceptable either. The person you're upset with always knows who you're referring to, so it feels like public humiliation. And again, it doesn't give them a chance to communicate back."

"Gotcha," Jeffrey said. "Thanks for letting me know."

Matt fiddled with his tie. "Interesting. I think I agree. What's the best way to implement a culture change like that?"

Alexandra smirked. "What do you think would be the best way?"

Matt groaned and smiled. "You want me to do the thinking. Okay. I'd probably update the employee handbook to say, 'This is our new conflict resolution process.' And because no one reads emails about employee handbooks, we should also have quick meetings to announce it. Two meetings. One for the bay workers, one for the office staff."

Alexandra shrugged. "Sounds like a plan."

Matt glanced at Jeffrey. "Any objections, boss?"

Jeffrey grinned and shook his head. "Go for it."

After Matt left, Jeffrey sat tapping a finger against his face.

Alexandra looked at him, curious. "What are you thinking about?"

"There's just something... doesn't quite..." Jeffrey suddenly snapped his fingers and sat up straight. "I know what it is! Your confidential interviews. That's a total contradiction of the Open Floor Policy. It's hypocritical for you to go on a gossip circle, then tell us not to. No offense."

Alexandra chuckled. "I like that you're making connections. If you think about it, though, it doesn't violate the open floor policy at all."

"Why not?"

"After those meetings, did I confront you about *anything* on their behalf?"

"No..." he said quietly. "I guess you didn't."

"What *did* I do?"

"You suggested questions I could ask to find the same information."

"Does that inhibit conversation between the right parties, or help it flow?"

Jeffrey groaned. "Okay... You win."

Alexandra smiled. "And here's the most important part. Did those conversations leave you feeling unsafe in any way?"

Jeffrey laughed. "Nervous, definitely. But I didn't feel like my reputation was in jeopardy. I knew I'd get to help in the end."

"That's the goal."

CULTURE - Open Floor Policy

> **SUMMARY**
>
> - An Open Floor Policy helps create universal safety and reinforces personal initiative. It replaces traditional open door policies, which rarely work well.

ACTION: Add the Open Floor Policy to Your Company Handbook[8]

Introduce the Open Floor Policy to your team. Reinforce the Open Floor Policy by adding it to your company handbook. If you don't have a company handbook, you need one. It's essential for CLARITY. See NEVERBOSS.com for a sample you can download as a starting point.

Here is the Open Floor Policy in a simplified form:

> *When you have an issue with someone, you have the option to talk with your manager about it first. They will advise but not act on what you say. Then go directly to the person you're struggling with to try to resolve the issue.*
>
> *If you don't feel safe or can't reach a resolution, then take it (back) to your manager. The three of you will resolve it together or escalate it to the next manager.*

SPECIAL SITUATION: Bullying

Bullying is emotional harassment that doesn't always rise to the *legal* definition of harassment, but it's still serious.

One subtle, damaging kind of bullying is "repeated, unwarranted accusations against another worker that put them at risk of their job." When this happens, it can derail your Open Floor Policy if you're not prepared.

---

[8] You may need to review this Open Floor Policy with HR and your legal experts first, since this book cannot give legal advice, and local laws vary.

However, if you add this definition of bullying to your harassment policy, the solution is simple. Take every accusation 100% seriously. Start with the Open Floor Policy. When you need to become involved, document everything. Write down what the findings were, what action was taken. Then you keep *permanent, written* score. At the end, was it warranted, unwarranted, or undetermined? After someone has filed 3-4 unwarranted accusations in a row, remind them gently:

> *"Everyone has the right to be safe here. You may have noticed this updated policy in our handbook. Bullying includes repeated unsubstantiated complaints against others. In the future, let's make sure your concerns can be substantiated. Otherwise it's going to look like you're bullying Joe."*

If you don't have a written bullying policy, add one to your handbook. A sample bullying policy is available at NEVERBOSS.com.

LEADERSHIP SCORECARD

NAME: Jeffrey Jackson

MY OVERALL SCORE: 2.1

WEEK THREE

4	**STEP AWAY** SUPPORT To Unleash Excellence	- Bay worker suggested certifications - Roxanne's business idea - Aaron's request to rearrange temporary storage
3	**STEP BACK** COACH To Inspire Ownership	- Allowed worker to look at tape by himself - Asked questions during 1-on-1s - Apologized to Clara during Universal Safety meeting
2	**STEP BESIDE** TRAIN To Build Capability	- Teaching exciting meetings - Teaching universal safety
1	**STEP UP** TELL To Ensure Clarity	- Established authority as manager - Established new team meeting format - Established universal safety - Established weekly 1-1s
0	**STEP IN** TAKE OVER To Create Stability	- Shut down worker thinking during meeting (should have Stepped Back) - Outburst in lunchroom (I tore down poster instead of leaving it up to them)

103

LEVEL TWO:
CLARITY

Where you fit and why you matter

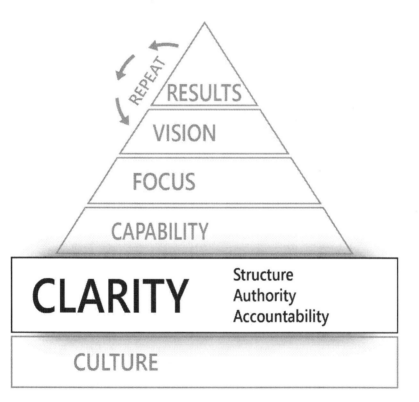

STRUCTURE

ROLES, SUPERVISORS, AND TEAM LEADERS

WEEK THREE

Over the clang and chatter of the bay, one sound rose loudest. Two people were screaming at each other.

Jeffrey had been inspecting the bay area with Alexandra when the yelling started. They could hear it clear across the warehouse. Alexandra jumped in surprise.

Jeffrey growled in frustration. "You know what? I put up with this at my last region. Not here." He stomped down the aisles towards the melee.

Alexandra was horrified. "Do fights break out among bay workers often?"

Jeffrey laughed dryly. "Not the bay workers. I bet you anything, when we round this corner, you're going to see two men in suits."

Sure enough. The taller one wore glasses. The other was built like a tank. A short tank. They weren't throwing punches, but they shouted at each other like the world was ending. Jeffrey pulled them apart.

"What is this, kindergarten?"[9]

They both gave him scathing glares.

"Who are you?" said Mr. Glasses.

"The regional manager."

The Tank snorted. "Where's Vanderman?"

"On sabbatical. I'm Jeffrey Jackson. I assume you're from the factories we service? How can I help?"

The Tank started to raise his voice again. "Your workers won't process my shipment correctly!"

Jeffrey glanced at the shift manager, who cowered in the background. She pursed her lips and looked extremely frustrated.

"What's your name?"

"...Nia, sir."

He turned back to the factory heads. "I'm sure Nia has a very good reason," Jeffrey said calmly. "Have you asked her?"

Nia looked relieved. "I was trying to tell them the hang-up is at the incinerator today," she said. "I *can't* help them."

Mr. Glasses balled his hands into fists. "That's not the real problem," he said, scowling at the other man. "His standards are outrageous. He comes in here *every* week and slows processing to a dead stop. I keep telling your workers to cut the red tape, but they're too afraid of him."

"I see. Here's the thing..." Jeffrey replied. "*Neither* of you should be bossing my workers around. You're not in charge here. I am. If you don't like what's happening, by all means, bring me into a meeting. Rake me over the coals. Ask me the tough questions. But *you will not give orders to my workers.* You can't do that. You're welcome to ask questions, discuss, listen. But if you have requests, you come to me."

"You're just janitors," the Tank sneered. "We outrank you."

Jeffrey gave him a scathing glare. "This is *my* warehouse. These are *my* workers. If something spilled or went wrong, *I* could go to jail for it. Don't you dare tell me how to process anything. If you contin-

---

[9] Again, based on actual events. Power struggles are common—and workers suffer, even in public—when zones and authority are unclear.

CLARITY - Roles, Supervisors, and Team Leaders

ue to harass my workers, I will have security escort you politely to the front gate."

"I'm a factory head," Glasses fumed.

"Yeah, so are the other nine," Jeffrey replied. "You all come in here issuing ultimatums, assuming you're the most important person here. Meanwhile, my workers are getting mauled to death by the ten-headed monster. No more ultimatums. If you make requests politely, we will consider your opinion."

"Mr. Khalil will hear about this!"

"I hope so," Jeffrey replied brightly. "But I have a feeling he'll trust me on this one. Now, can you play nice, or do I need to call security?"

The factory heads scowled at each other, then turned to go.

The moment they disappeared around the corner, Jeffrey groaned and slumped down on a bench. "Ugh, I can't believe I just yelled at them."

Alexandra sat down next to him. "What you did was perfect. Don't let anyone boss your team around. You *must* stand up for your workers' right to exercise initiative. Meddling is common, but it will confuse and cripple your workers. Your *job* is to hold back the onslaught of all the people above you."

Jeffrey perked up a little. "You think so?"

"Absolutely, with one caveat..."

"What?"

"You don't want to shut down that flow of communication. They have data, you know. We can't operate without their data."

Jeffrey's eyes widened, and he exhaled heavily. "Shoot, you're right."

Alexandra smiled. "They're stakeholders. Don't let them take over. But *do* hear them out."

Jeffrey chased down the factory heads before they left the building.

"Gentlemen... I'm sorry I yelled at you. Your input is extremely important, and we want to make sure your needs are met."

This was clearly not the greeting they were expecting. They stared at Jeffrey in confusion, but they were listening.

"You're feeling frustration, and you're concerned," Jeffrey empathized. "I understand. It's no secret that this GooCrew region has been dragging its feet in the mud. We're slow as molasses. Nobody blames you for getting upset. But—you'll never be able to micro-manage this floor."

Glasses chuckled. "I guess that's true. I already have my hands full with one factory."

"Let's go talk to Nia together," Jeffrey proposed, "in a quieter place where we can talk without shouting."

Jeffrey refereed the conversation to make sure both sides were feeling safe and listened to.

The factories had two complaints. First, they hadn't been getting paperwork back. They needed proof that all waste was properly disposed of. Second, sometimes the bay got backed up so badly that truckers were late picking up shipments—or worse, unable to accept additional waste, which meant the factories had to hold onto it.

The bay workers' primary complaint was that each factory had different standards for waste processing and paperwork. It was too hard to keep track of all the customizations, Nia argued.

Finally, Alexandra raised a hand. "This process you guys are fighting over... What's it called?"

"It's literally the whole disposal process," Nia sighed. "From taking things off the trucks to sending paperwork back."

"Every project, process, or task needs a single point of accountability," Alexandra explained. "The disposal process is suffering because it has no owner."

"Well, there are a *lot* of people affected by this process," Glasses pointed out. "If you just install a mini-dictator over it, you're going to get terrible results."

"Exactly," Alexandra said. "So don't install a dictator. You need one *point* of accountability. That point doesn't have to be a single person. Create a team."

Jeffrey was surprised by the idea. "A team to do what?"

"To synchronize factory requirements to a single flow and reduce processing time," Alexandra answered.

Glasses laughed. "That's a lovely idea, but there isn't a department under our control that has that kind of power."

"Teams aren't limited to departments," Alexandra said with a smile. "*Cross-departmental teams* can be created around processes, projects, or major burning issues. What you need here is a process team. Gather diplomats for each kind of stakeholder—factory heads, workers, lab techs. Put them in one room together. Give them the power to compromise. Choose one flow for everybody."

Tank and Glasses looked at each other and shifted uncomfortably.

"Each factory produces different products." Glasses reminded them. "Therefore, different byproducts. Each industry has unique tax breaks if our waste is handled in extra-ecofriendly ways. We're just trying to protect those tax breaks."

"We care, too," Nia replied. "And we're all operating under the same government regulations. There's a lot of overlap with your byproducts. *Everyone* sends paint and aerosol cans, for example. I believe we can find a process that meets everyone's needs. As long as we're legal and you can't get in trouble, can you leave convenient bonuses like tax breaks up to us? We know they're worth crazy amounts of money. But they're not always cost effective to earn. Those specialty processes are exactly what back us up."

Glasses glanced at Mr. Tank, then back at Nia. "I don't think you understand the kind of money we're talking about."

Nia held his gaze. "Are the tax breaks anywhere close to the cost of halting production when we're late picking up waste?"

Tank was stalemated. "That's an excellent point. I don't know."

"Bring the numbers," Nia suggested. "Let's compare."

Glasses turned to Alexandra. "So... pretend we wanted a process team. Who has the power to put together a team like that?"

"Anyone who cares."

"Anyone?"

"Anyone."

"Well, *I* care," Nia said.

They all looked at her.

"I mean it," she insisted. "When can I start?"

ANYONE
CAN START A TEAM.

JUST GATHER THE ZONE OWNER, STAKEHOLDERS, EXPERTS,

AND ANYONE ELSE WHO WANTS TO BE A
CHAMPION.

"You're welcome to form teams whenever you see a problem that needs attention," Alexandra answered, "as long as you're not neglecting your zone. If the problem is actively preventing you from completing the work in your zone, you don't need to wait. Just find a good stopping point."

"Hey, don't forget us!" Tank said. "We want to be on that team."

Nia nodded.

Alexandra pulled a card from her jacket pocket and gave it to Nia. "Here, use this to choose members for your process team. Every team needs to include stakeholders, zone owners, subject matter experts, and anyone else who wants to be a champion."

Nia blinked. "Come again? In English?"

Alexandra laughed at herself. "Sorry. Who is affected by this problem, or might care if you changed the process?"

"The factory heads," Nia replied. "Workers in the bay, supervisors, Aaron, and probably the forklift guys."

Alexandra nodded. "Those are your stakeholders. Anyone who cares is a stakeholder. You need representatives from each of those groups on your team."

LEADERSHIP ROLES

(ZONE) OWNER	Owns the vision and has success/fail responsibility for the zone. Has final decision-making power when buy-in and agility aren't enough.
TEAM LEAD	Owns the team zone. Responsible for team progress and culture. Manages team roles and meetings. Holds 1-on-1s as applicable. Default owner of all unassigned team zones and processes.
STAKEHOLDERS	Advocate for significant groups affected by the process or team. Bring important perspectives and needs to team discussions.
CHAMPIONS	Take what the team decides and win buy-in from the rest of the organization
SUBJECT MATTER EXPERTS (SMEs)	Gurus or aspiring experts with key knowledge for good decision-making.

Nia smiled, looking excited. "Alright. I'll take care of it. Can we use the conference room tomorrow afternoon?"

Everyone sat down. Jeffrey noticed in a heartbeat that all the suits were on one side of the table. The bay workers sat on the other... scruffy, dressed in orange, looking rather sheepish.

Jeffrey laughed. "*Nope*. This isn't going to work. First of all, on this team, who has seniority?"

All the bay workers looked at the suits.

"Wrong," He said flatly. "Nobody has seniority. This is a process team. On *this* team, you're all equals. The bay workers have frontline knowledge. And the factory heads understand the big picture. We need *both* perspectives... So... Let's not sit all blue collars on one side and white collars on the other. Let's mix it up."

Everyone stood awkwardly. After a minute of musical chairs, they were intermingled. The bay workers seemed to sit a little taller, which made Jeffrey smile.

Jeffrey scrutinized the team. "Anytime we create a project or process, we need a single point of accountability. So we need a team lead. Nia?"

Nia smiled but shook her head.

Jeffrey nodded in understanding. "That's totally fine. Any other volunteers?"

Two of the factory heads raised their hands confidently.

At the back, one of the bay workers tentatively raised his hand, too. Of all the people in the room, he might have been the scruffiest. Covered with black grease, blue jeans ripped. He wore a wedding ring so cheap his finger was stained green from copper hiding beneath the flaking gold.

Jeffrey didn't know him, but he knew from his uniform that he was the absolute bottom of the totem pole. Still, the man's eyes danced with sheepish hope.

Jeffrey pointed to him. "You. What's your name?"

Astonished, the worker straightened his shoulders. "Hans," he replied.

"Hans, are you willing to own this process of synchronizing factory standards, and to be accountable when it succeeds or falls short?"

"I'd love to!"

Jeffrey turned to the other team members. "All in favor?"

The factory heads responded with surprised approval. The decision was unanimous.

CLARITY - Roles, Supervisors, and Team Leaders

Jeffrey gave them a two-minute run-down on how to run a safe and effective meeting. It turned out that Aaron had already changed weekly meetings with everyone in the bay. They were familiar with the structure, so Jeffrey let Hans take the lead.

They started the meeting by collecting burning issues. To visualize the problems better, Nia started drawing a map of the bay floor on the whiteboard.

That's when a key issue came up.

"What do you mean you don't know your primary duty?" asked Tank in shock.

"Well, we float around, helping each other out," Hans said. "Some days I run the incinerator, sometimes I sort dry stuff. And especially since Mr. Jackson came, there's been more collaboration than ever."

"No offense, but we came down here yesterday because you've been *less* efficient," Tank replied. "Whatever you're doing isn't working."

Jeffrey thought for a moment, then turned to Alexandra. "What do you think?"

"The real issue here is stewardship," she replied. "It's time to set boundaries on your workers' initiative."

Nia looked alarmed. "Wait... Aaron *just* gave us power to start acting more on our own. You want to take it away again?"

"No," Alexandra chuckled. "It's just a matter of focus. Once people start to care, they'll start accidentally abandoning their posts. Happens every time. To prevent that, people need to know exactly what their zones are."

"Zones?" Hans asked.

"Areas of active responsibility. Think of a checkout lane at the grocery store. What is a cashier responsible for?"

"To check things out," Jeffrey answered.

"If you are a customer trying to check out, and the cashier is doing *anything* other than helping you leave, how do you feel?"

Jeffrey laughed. "Annoyed."

"So that's their zone. They need to be there, helping customers check out, or things will fall apart. We need to define your worker's zones so they are *that* simple."

115

"What if people have multiple zones?"

"They will. But if I'm the cashier in checkout 5 and checkout 3 is slowing down, should I go over to help?"

"No."

"Right," Alexandra said. "I can't go to checkout 3 without abandoning my post. Sometimes I may have other responsibilities, like cleaning up a spill nearby. But you only have one *primary* responsibility at a time."

"Wait, the last thing I want around here are silos or turf wars," Jeffrey objected.

Alexandra shuddered. "Me, too. Charting zones actually helps. Most turf wars start because people aren't clear about their zones. They think they only have one zone, so they don't help out. Or the roles are unclear in shared zones, so people argue."

Nia was intrigued. "So what happens when you share a zone?"

"It's like this process team. You can have multiple stakeholders, and SMEs, and champions—but only one owner. You all share the process zone, but Hans is responsible for it. Does that make sense?"

"Works for me," said Jeffrey. "How do we define these zones?"

Alexandra pulled out her laptop and pulled up a blank page. "With a shared online document."

"Can you show us an example?"

"Yeah. Let's start with me." Alexandra typed her name into the document. "My job title is Coach. And my primary responsibility is to train Jeffrey." She added these to the chart. "Within this zone, I serve as a Subject Matter Expert, also called an SME."

Alexandra Hamilton - Coach
Zones: Train Jeffrey (SME)

"Jeff, what team are you and I both a part of?" Alexandra asked.

"Team? Uh, the Regional Management team, I guess."

"Great. So we'll make a big heading... And we'll add you. What's your primary responsibility?"

"To keep things running," Jeffrey replied.

"Good guess, but it's broader than that."

CLARITY - Roles, Supervisors, and Team Leaders

"Er... Fix and prevent emergencies?"

Alexandra smiled and shook her head. "That's something you could do by rolling up your sleeves and stepping in, taking over for your workers. But that's not *really* your job."

Jeffrey hesitated. "Then I'm not sure."

"What have we been spending all month doing?"

Jeffrey laughed as understanding hit him. "Leading."

"What does that make your zone?"

Jeffrey responded with conviction. "I own Hands-Off Leadership. My primary responsibility is to make sure this culture keeps working. I'm here to turn my workers into leaders, and remove whatever barriers keep them from excelling."

Alexandra lit up. "Yes! That's *exactly* right."

REGIONAL MANAGEMENT TEAM
Jeffrey Jackson - Regional Manager (Team Leader)
Zone: Hands-Off Leadership culture for Northwest Region (Owner)

Alexandra pointed to the screen. "Do you notice how I'm not just saying *what* Jeffrey does, but also defining *where* he does it? My action is training. But am I training everybody?"

"No," Jeffrey said. "You're primarily training me."

"Good. And you own the Hands-Off Leadership culture, but do you own it for *all* of GooCrew?"

"No, just this region."

"Excellent. Now, Jeffrey is responsible for way more than Hands-Off Leadership. It can all be summarized into one idea: Jeff, you're a team leader. As a team leader, you are the default owner of everything in this region until it's owned by someone else. Basically, your job is to own everything your people can't... until they can."

Several people nodded, following along on their computers.

> THE LEADER'S JOB IS TO OWN EVERYTHING THEIR PEOPLE CAN'T... UNTIL THEY CAN

WEEK THREE

"Perfect," Alexandra continued. "After you set up the Zone Chart for this team, throw down names of GooCrew's other departments, and share this document with everyone. Ask every worker to put themselves on this list, define their zones, and specify their roles within each zone."

"Even the workers on the floor?" Hans asked

"Especially the workers on the floor."

Hans shook his head. "That's a great idea for office people, but it won't work in the warehouse. Laptops would get trashed down there."

"Good point! You don't need laptops. Edit the document with phone apps. Or use a whiteboard. Zone Charts don't need to be on-line—they just need to be public and easy for everyone to change."

Hans nodded. "Okay."

When you outline your teams, don't just put the obvious members on the team roster. Teams include everyone who ought to be part of the discussion."

"Like who?"

"Stakeholders. Stakeholders are those affected by your decisions. Broadly speaking, it's anyone who cares."

Jeffrey rocked in surprise. "Why so broad?"

"Because anyone who cares has a reason they care. We need their perspective. We need to make sure we're meeting their needs."

Nia shifted uncomfortably. "I feel like that leaves the door open for busy bodies. Anyone can say, 'Wait, I care about this!' and bottleneck progress."

"That's a fair concern," Alexandra replied. "It doesn't happen, though. We don't give stakeholders equal power."

"So how much power *are* we giving them?"

"The power of influence. The number one thing that kills companies is developing a product without asking what people want. If you get buy-in from large accounts before the product is created, it eliminates resistance to change. When people help design, they're happier to adopt."

CLARITY - Roles, Supervisors, and Team Leaders

Hans smiled. "And they look forward to the change instead of getting clotheslined by it."

"Yup. That's how you prevent turf wars. All stakeholders get a say, but the decision ultimately rests with the team."

By the end of the meeting, they'd made major headway. They would need more meetings, but the process team had found a rhythm. Jeffrey trusted that they would be self-sufficient from then on.

Jeffrey checked in with the factory heads before they left. "Thanks for coming back, gentlemen. We appreciate your feedback. How do you feel now?"

Glasses looked around the room at the other process team members. "Well, we still have a long way to go, but I feel like I have allies now. I always worried that they wouldn't follow through. Now I have confidence that they care. I know they have the power to act, and I know who to ask if it's not working."

SUMMARY

- Great leaders prevent outside bossing but encourage others to talk with and influence their teams.

- Process teams can be created anytime, by anyone.

- Zones are areas of active responsibility.

- Well-defined zones and roles prevent silos and turf wars and help everyone pull loads together effectively.

- Zone Charts replace or support traditional org charts. They are more flexible, collaborative descriptions of the current structure of your organization.

ACTION: Create Your Own Zone Chart

Using a shared document that anyone can edit simultaneously (like a Google Doc), create a Zone Chart for your organization. No fancy graphics. This is NOT a flow chart either. Flow charts are too inflexible. Just use text. Don't try to make it perfect at first—you want "progress, not perfection."

Start listing the key teams in your organization. Ask everyone to add themselves to it with their job descriptions as zones and roles. Include process and project teams (see p. 111). When listing teams, don't just list the team members. List their zones, and list Owners, Team Leads, Stakeholders, Champions, and SMEs—including outside resources. That way people know their zones, roles, and support system.

See the sample Zone Chart at NEVERBOSS.com for more instructions and answers to common questions.

STRUCTURE

COMMUNICATION

WEEK FOUR

J effrey's office was often a center of activity and conversation, but this morning was particularly bad.

Alexandra walked up to Jeffrey's doorway and found four other people waiting to talk. She waited her turn politely, observing the conversations. When it was finally her turn, she sat down in one of his chairs and smirked.

"You do realize 45 minutes of human time were just wasted," she said. "You're officially a bottleneck."

"Well, they're lining up because they don't know how else to get ahold of me," Jeffrey huffed, glancing warily at the doorway, afraid someone else might come through it.

"No, they know they can email you. They just don't trust you'll get back to them in time. Out of curiosity, what does your email inbox look like?"

Jeffrey grimaced and pulled it open. He slid his laptop across the desk.

Alexandra peered at his screen. "Yup, that's impressive. 1500 unread... We've been here, what, three weeks? Hey, two more just bounced in."

She slid the laptop back. "I'll bet a third of those emails are duplicates. When people don't hear back, they ask the same thing over and over—especially if they have nowhere else to go. Your inbox is a Goo-Crew Twitter stream."

Jeffrey grunted. "If you have any suggestions..."

"Great leadership requires great communication. Right now everything goes through your inbox," she pointed out. "It's like having all radio stations on one channel. You can't hear anything that way. You need to put communication on different channels, with different frequencies, so you can tune into what you need when you need it."

Alexandra pulled out her phone, pulled up an email template and forwarded it to Jeffrey. "Here's the list of communication channels I recommend, and how to make them work well."

> GREAT LEADERSHIP REQUIRES GREAT COMMUNICATION

Jeffrey pulled the file up on his laptop. He rubbed his eye wearily. "Help me understand what I'm looking at."

Alexandra slid off her chair and walked around so she could look over Jeffrey's shoulder. "The goal is to get the right information to the right people, at the right time, in the right way. Share knowledge, but don't overwhelm. Discuss, but don't distract. But that only works if everyone agrees on the purpose for each channel."

"Great," Jeffrey said dryly. "So now instead of having all my communication in one place, it's spread out in *eight* places."

"This isn't that different from what you already do," she replied. "You already have a phone, email, an office where people visit you, and the meeting agendas. The biggest difference is that quick questions move to instant messaging, where you can give quick answers at your convenience. And critical knowledge moves to public documents so that anyone can comment and edit."

CLARITY – Communication

CHANNELS OF COMMUNICATION

WEEK FOUR

Less Urgent ↑ ↓ More Urgent

	You Will Hear Back In	Good For
Shared Documents	Whenever	Shared collaborative knowledge. Company standards, processes. Edit, comment in each document.
All Hands Meeting	Quarterly - or - As Needed	New thematic goals or directions. Everyone at once. All levels of company.
Burning Issue in Next Meeting Agenda	Next Scheduled Meeting	Discussions and decisions with all stakeholders. "Report Back Periodically."
Email	Hours - to - Days	Assignments. Use other channels to free this up.
Instant Message (Skype)	Minutes - to - Hours	Short replies/discussion, not assignments. Answer when able. Turn alerts OFF.
Texting	Minutes - to - an Hour	Personal or group chat.
Phone Call	Right Now - or - Voicemail	Interruptions and issues that need more discussion. Leave a message if they are busy.
Video Chat	Right Now if Available	Face-to-face discussions. More Invasive. Saves a trip down the hall.
Office Visit	RIGHT NOW	Emergencies, sensitive or crucial conversations. Very urgent matters.

123

Jeffrey hesitated. "Well, video makes me nervous, too. I don't want people just calling me up in the middle of the day. That's worse than an office interruption. It's on my screen."

"So establish video chat etiquette. You don't have to answer. Before starting a call, they should shoot you a message first and say, 'Hey, can I just chat with you on video for a second?' "

"But everyone I ever talk with is in this building."

"Doesn't matter. Use it anyway. It saves you time walking to their office. You won't get interrupted by other people along the way. In my experience with other organizations, this is a huge boost to everyone's productivity. Video is better because you can decide when to allow that interruption."

Jeffrey tapped his screen, moving windows around. "I *do* like using the team meeting agendas. I've definitely noticed a drop in certain types of interruptions."

"Yes, that's one of the best channels," Alexandra agreed. "That only works because your meetings are now happening every week without fail."

"Even so," Jeffrey frowned. "I don't know if the team is going to like this..."

Alexandra chuckled. "In my experience, what happens is almost a mutiny. People *will* resist. They're resisting for good reasons. Great leaders ask for buy-in. Ask them to try it for a couple of weeks and see what happens."

"They'll feel a little cornered," Jeffrey objected. "They'll try to be good team players, but it will frustrate them."

"Of course. I don't blame them. Technology is annoying. It's always vibrating, making noises, interrupting them. Every time they get a new notification, a rush of anxiety hits. It's terrible. So they're right. It'll never work. And that's not how you're supposed to use it. For everyone to have a good experience, everyone needs to turn all alerts off."

Jeffrey raised an eyebrow. "How does that help? I'll forget people."

Alexandra shook her head. "If people *know* your notifications are off and know approximately when you'll get back to them, they won't mind. The principle is, *People are okay with 'not now' if they know when.*"

"Yeah, but *I* won't feel any better," Jeffrey resisted. "I'll either be constantly checking it or constantly afraid I'm ignoring something important."

Alexandra folded her arms. "Not only are you allowed to ignore it, you're *required* to ignore it. You're only allowed to look at it when you have a little time on your hands."

Jeffrey slouched in his chair, grumpy and unconvinced.

Alexandra pulled out her phone. "Here, I'll make this easy."

She dialed a number and turned speakerphone on. It rang a few times. Then...

"Alex?"

"Hey, Ben!"

"*Alex!* Wow, it's so great to hear from you!"

She laughed.

"Is there anything I can do for you?" he asked cheerfully.

"Yes. I have a coaching victim here. I think I've scared him. Remember that time I told you to implement communication channels, and you screamed and cried and didn't want to do it?"

The man on the other side laughed heartily. "You poor soul. That was a rough week for us."

"Yes. Yes, it was. How do you feel about it now?"

Ben breathed a huge sigh of relief. "I can't imagine living any other way. It's a permanent part of our company now."

"How much benefit did you see?"

"Email bloat plummeted. Literally two-thirds of incoming email just stopped. Office interruptions all but disappeared. Urgent questions got the attention they deserved. Somehow, I suddenly had enough time for everyone."

> PEOPLE ARE OKAY WITH 'NOT NOW' IF THEY KNOW WHEN.
>
> — DAVE CRENSHAW, THE MYTH OF MULTITASKING

"Do you have any recommendations for making it a good experience?"

"*Yes.* Remember to turn off the notifications. All of them."

"Oh, you're an advocate of that now?" Alexandra teased.

Ben sighed. "Rub it in. You were right."

They laughed.

"Also," Ben added, "um, resident victim, what's your name?"

"Call me Jeffrey," he laughed.

"Jeffrey! Don't be shy about customizing the system. Start with Alexandra's setup, and when you realize something isn't working, tweak it. My teammates kept sending me tasks through text, and it drove me crazy. I vetoed that and things got better."

Jeffrey laughed. "Got it."

"Get my contact information from Alex. You're welcome to chat me up if you have questions." His voice turned mischievous. "I also have some great blackmail on Alex."

Alexandra cocked her head, confused. "Do you?"

"The bonus birthday party?"

Alexandra gasped. "I did *not* lie to you. You heard me wrong!"

Ben chuckled. "Anyway, I need to run. Alex, can I call you again later? I could use your advice on something."

"Absolutely. Thanks for your help."

"No problem. Good luck, Jeffrey."

Alexandra hung up the phone.

Jeffrey immediately grinned at her. "Bonus birthday?"

Alexandra rolled her eyes, a little embarrassed. "They threw a surprise birthday for me. Invited the whole executive team. It was a *huge* surprise because they totally had the wrong date." She shook her head. "They threw another party for me two months later. Never let me live it down."

Jeffrey busted up laughing. "That's amazing."

"Just goes to show," she muttered, "if you have sensitive information people might remember wrong, send it through a written channel."

SUMMARY

- Hands-Off Leadership depends on excellent communication, which means that information is shared freely, without overwhelm or distraction.

- Excellent communication gets the right information to the right people, at the right time, in the right way.

- Filter discussions and data using different channels for messages of different urgency.

- Flex meeting agendas are excellent communication channels that reduce interruptions.

ACTION: Clarify Company Communication Channels

Introduce the Communication Channels to your team. Announcing in-person is important since they may have fears. Be sure to listen with mutual empathy, mutual respect, and then establish mutual purpose. The dialog in this chapter can guide you.

An editable Communication Channel chart is available for download at NEVERBOSS.com. We strongly recommend dispersing those charts along with setup instructions.

AUTHORITY

GIVE AUTHORITY, NOT TASKS

WEEK FIVE

One morning as Jeffrey unlocked his office, he noticed Alexandra walking briskly down the hallway.

"There you are!" she said.

Jeffrey turned around. "What's up?"

"The process team is stuck. They have an important decision to make, but they're evenly divided and can't get buy-in. They finally cried uncle and asked for my help. I'm going to coach you instead and send you to resolve the dispute."

Jeffrey removed his key. "Cool. What are they gridlocked about?"

"Doesn't matter. The principle is this: When a team reaches an impasse, it's *very* frustrating to have nothing decided, so great leaders Step Up and make the call. You can say, 'You know what? It's time to make a decision. It looks to me like X is the best direction we can take right now. Who can buy in?' "

"What if the leader has a personal agenda?" Jeffrey frowned in distress. "We've been trying to prevent heavy-handed decisions. People will abuse this power."

"If you're constantly overriding your teams, there's a problem. This power is *absolutely* vital to prevent blockages. But it's like a taser. You'll rarely use it."

Jeffrey was quiet for a second.

"I'm afraid *I'll* misuse the power," he confessed. "It's so close to how I used to do things."

Alexandra stared at Jeffrey with a degree of pride.

"That temptation will never go away," she said softly. "Your Leadership Scorecard will keep you in line. Just remember that the goal is not the task. It's creating leaders. Instead of plowing forward to get the task done, slow down. Listen, and invest in these people."

Jeffrey walked into the conference room.

He was immediately bombarded. Team members immediately started appealing to Jeffrey, trying to convince him to take their side. The factory heads and bay workers were clearly butting heads. Hans looked frazzled.

Jeffrey raised his hands and laughed. "No, you don't understand. *I'm* not going to make the decision."

They reeled. "You're not?"

"Nope." Jeffrey turned to Hans. "Hans, you are Owner of this process, because you lead this team. As someone who fills that role, you have the responsibility to make a decision if your team is in gridlock."

His eyes widened. "But I thought we were doing Hands-Off Leadership."

"This *is* Hands-Off Leadership. Have you done everything you can to encourage buy-in?"

"Yes."

"Has everyone had a chance to express their opinion, and do they feel listened to?"

"I think so." Hans looked around the table. His team members nodded.

"Yes, we feel heard," Glasses said with a groan, obviously sick of the debate. "We keep repeating the same arguments."

CLARITY - Give Authority, Not Tasks

Jeffrey turned back to Hans. "Is this decision time-critical?"

Hans nodded. "It really is."

"Then at this point, what could you do as a leader to best serve your team? Do they need more listening? Or do they need to move forward?"

"Move forward."

Jeffrey nodded. "Brilliant. Now, before you make your decision, may I show you some cool things I just learned about good decision-making?"

Hans was curious. He gestured for Jeffrey to take the floor.

Jeffrey reached into his pocket and pulled out a stack of laminated cards. He started passing them out. "These are presents from Alexandra. Take a look."

The workers picked them up and eyed them curiously.

"These are the 5 Levels of Decision Quality," Jeffrey explained. "Everyone makes stupid choices sometimes, including me. This card will help you be mindful of *why* you're making a choice. I'll explain each level, and then we'll put together a list of guiding principles. These principles will steer you towards decisions that are aligned with GooCrew's values and needs. Once you know how to make good choices, I can Step Back, and you will have much more freedom over your work. Sound good?"

The workers listened attentively.

"Level 1 – Gut Feeling," Jeffrey began. "Turns out, this isn't a bad way to make some decisions. There's a region of the brain designed to take incomplete data and respond. When a car is coming at you at 70 miles per hour, you rely on that. It's a lot better than we give it credit for. But it's still just intuition."

"Next," Jeffrey continued, "we have Reasons. This is better than Gut Instinct. At least you're thinking. But you can do anything for a good reason. Terrorists have good *reasons*, in their minds, for what they're doing. Reasons alone justify nothing. You are accountable to each other. If you see a teammate deciding something based on reasons, call them on it."

Glasses and Tank were leaning their heads together, quietly whispering.

"Level 3," Jeffrey continued. "Here's where choices start to grow a little backbone. Likely Results. Good, we're thinking ahead now. What's the likely impact of this decision or policy? What might go wrong? If it doesn't work, what will happen? If it *does* work, what will happen? Are we prepared for either outcome?"

"Level 4 – Principles. The question to ask here is easy. What principles apply in this situation?"

Tank raised his hand. "Can you explain what you mean by principles?"

"Principles serve as guardrails and guides," Jeffrey replied. "They are time-tested truths that inspire action. General guidelines for behavior, with space for common sense. They help us make snap judgments based on what worked well in the past. Usually, they also help us sort between several confusing options, highlighting one clear winner."

"Can you give us some examples?" Hans asked.

"Sure." He grabbed a marker and started writing on the whiteboard.

Progress, not perfection.

Jeffrey pointed to it. "This principle reminds us to make small changes and test them early. It keeps us from wasting time on a bad

CLARITY - Give Authority, Not Tasks

direction. It also reminds us that something doesn't have to be perfect to be functional."

Jeffrey invited them to suggest principles they knew. It took a few minutes for them to warm up to the idea, but they started to get the hang of it. He collected their ideas.

> *The dullest pencil is better than the sharpest memory.*
> *What we measure improves.*
> *Chase three rabbits, catch none of them.*
> *Manage risk, don't eliminate it.*

An older fellow with a big beard spoke up. "When you hit rapids, give everyone an oar. It might not help, but it'll sure make 'em feel better."

Everyone laughed. Jeffrey added to the list.

> *When you hit rapids, give everyone an oar.*

"So that's the general idea," Jeffery said. "Correct principles outrank likely outcomes because principles have a long, proven track record of good outcomes." Jeffrey capped his marker. "Tonight I'll create a shared document with our favorite principles, and email you all the link. Add to it whenever you please."

Jeffrey glanced at his card. Just one level left.

"Level 5 – Actual Results. This is the golden zone. It's not always possible, but get as close as possible. Has anyone attempted what we're about to do? Has anyone tried anything *like* it? What happened? Actual Data means we can prove on paper how something is going to turn out before we start. This can also mean we've done a test run and identified a pattern."

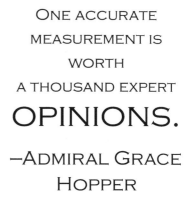

ONE ACCURATE MEASUREMENT IS WORTH A THOUSAND EXPERT OPINIONS.

—ADMIRAL GRACE HOPPER

Jeffrey tossed the marker back to the team lead.

Jeffrey raised a finger. "One last point... and this is crucial. When the decision is made, team members need to support it *as if it had been their idea.*"

Glasses folded his arms. "But what if it's the wrong choice?"

"Agility makes it safe. Remember: it must not be perfect at first, and you'll improve rapidly based on Actual Results."

"That's all. Now if I remember correctly, you had a decision to make. Want to try these methods while I watch?"

"Yes!" Hans took his place at the front of the room again, standing with greater confidence this time. "Okay, so we're deciding whether to color-code incoming waste or update the numerical system. After listening to your arguments, I think the numerical system is the way to go."

The factory heads high-fived. Nia and the forklift operator groaned and sagged.

"I hate numbers," Nia sighed, discouraged. "Even when I'm at the top of my game they're hard to remember and time-consuming to match."

"Ditto," the forklift guy agreed. "And I'll still have to get out of my forklift *every* time to read the packaging."

"Those sound like Reasons Why," Tank pointed out, looking at his card. "But color categories aren't specific enough, so the Likely Result is a lot of mistakes."

"We're already making mistakes," Nia shot back, discouraged. "If we change the numbers, the Likely Result is more mistakes."

Hans hesitated.

"Ah. We're missing a Principle," Jeffrey realized out loud. "Hans, can I have that marker for a second?"

Hans tossed back it to him. Jeffrey added to the whiteboard:

Mistakes are okay if we learn from them.

CLARITY - Give Authority, Not Tasks

"Mistakes are unavoidable," Jeffrey acknowledged. "You don't have to be perfect. Just don't be reckless. Here are some strategies for managing risk."

Jeffrey made a separate list:

1. Limit the scope by doing a small test run.
2. If you don't understand it, it's dangerous.
3. Never put more than 40% of your eggs in one basket.
4. Implement a stop-loss point.

"Stop-loss?" Hans asked.

"It's a stock market term," Jeffrey explained. "When you buy stock, you can set it up so that if its value drops below a certain point, it automatically goes up for sale."

"Gotcha." As Hans studied the list, the fatigued look in his eyes disappeared, and he started to smile. "I like the first one. We can do a small test run of the new process with one delivery from each factory, to see if it meets everyone's needs."

Tank brightened. "Now *that* is something I can buy into."

"I think a number-based system falls under the Principle of *if you don't understand it, it's dangerous*," the forklift operator worried. "Even though the numbers have meaning, they're not obvious. If you're tired or sick or new, it's too easy to mix things up."

Suddenly, Glasses looked up.

"Color-blind workers!" he blurted out, remembering. "We *know* from experience that they make mistakes with color. Actual Results."

Hans frowned and turned to Jeffrey. "Mr. Jackson, what do you think?"

"Well... it looks like colors are vetoed by Actual Results. Principles and Likely Results look bad for a number system," Jeffrey coached. "Is there a third option?"

"What if we used shapes?" Nia asked.

The team froze and looked at her.

"Shapes?" Hans asked.

135

"Circle, square, triangle, star," she explained. "There are more basic shapes than colors. We wouldn't have to worry about color-blindness, but it would still be easy to sort."

"We still have more than 50 categories," Glasses pointed out.

Hans thought for a moment. "You could put a number in the middle. One through nine. Would that give us enough categories?"

Suddenly, the whole team got excited.

"If we had six basic shapes with a single number inside, you could sort into the different processing zones by shape," Tank realized. "Then those zones could use the numbers to break it down into disposal process."

Hans turned to the forklift operator. "If we made the stickers big and bold, do you think you could read them from inside your cage?"

"Absolutely!"

Hans nodded. "We need someone to make the label. Someone who will design everything and order new ones."

Nia raised her hand. "I'll do it."

"Great. When can we have new labels in hand?"

"I'll email a design tomorrow for everyone to review."

"Perfect. Thanks, Nia." Hans turned to the team. "Once we have labels, we'll need Champions to get people used to them. Let's pick someone for each section..."

Jeffrey watched for a few more minutes, but it looked like the team had found a winner. The roadblock was gone. People were all standing up, talking animatedly. They'd found common ground. Hans listened brilliantly and was asking great questions.

Jeffrey realized suddenly that he wasn't needed. With a bittersweet pang in his stomach, Jeffrey flashed Hans a double-thumbs up. Then he left.

CLARITY - Give Authority, Not Tasks

> **SUMMARY**
>
> - Teams should not be allowed to deadlock. When everyone has been heard and buy-in encouraged—and especially when the need is urgent—a decision must be made.
>
> - Zone owners have final decision-making responsibility. Team Leaders are the default owners of all unassigned team zones and processes.
>
> - When a decision is made, great teams support it as if it had been their idea. Agility makes this safe.
>
> - There are five levels of decision quality. The best choices focus on outcomes, principles, and data.
>
> - Principles are *not* rules. They are time-tested truths that inspire and guide action.

WEEK FIVE

ACTION: Add Guardrails for Safe, Effective Decisions

Decision Quality: In your next meeting, distribute Decision Quality charts and discuss how to make the best decisions. Consider giving everyone plastic wallet cards to carry or attach to their security badges as they master this skill.

Principles: Every organization needs a master list of principles. Start creating yours in a shared, collaborative document. Invite everyone in the organization to use that document and update it.

Wallet cards and a Guiding Principles template are available at NEVERBOSS.com.

ACTION: Divest the Power to Decide

Give more authority (power to decide and act on their own) to your teams and owners. The goal is to push authority to the people closest to the information, so they can act quickly and intelligently.

In your next meeting, clarify that zone owners have the power to "make the call" for their zones —or team leaders if a zone is unassigned. Ask your team where they are feeling stuck and want the authority to make decisions so they can improve workflow. Update the Zone Chart to make owners and team leaders clear.

ACCOUNTABILITY
LOYALTY TO PURPOSE, NOT PERSONALITIES

WEEK FIVE

Ever since Aaron joked about the shipping software being as old as Methuselah, the programming department had taken the nickname as a matter of pride. The programmers reminded everyone that "Methuselah" was so brilliant it had filled their needs for decades. They only issued small updates.

Aaron continued to banter with the programmers about their crotchety old program and bided his time.

―――――◆―――――

One day, Jeffrey visited Bob's office for their weekly 1-on-1. They were about to begin when Bob got a call from a shipping manager from one of their factories. She spoke with icy, forced calm.

"Your shipping software just deleted all the files on my hard drive."

Bob was unimpressed. "What? How?"

"I was hoping you could tell me," she replied.

Bob tried not to laugh. "Ma'am, that's not possible. Methuselah *can't* delete. There's no code in our program that could possibly delete all the files on your hard drive."

Bob paused. Jeffrey could hear the woman on the other side getting angry.

Bob gave Jeffrey a long-suffering look as he responded.

"Yes, ma'am, I hear you," he told her. "But a dozen factories have been using this software for thirty years, and you're the first person ever to complain. I'm not saying you're wrong. I'm just saying the odds are so outrageously small that—"

Bob paused to listen for a moment and then rolled his eyes. "Look, there's nothing I can do. It's some sort of a user error or operating system error. I'm really sorry. Do you have a backup? You should always use backups."

After the lady hung up, Bob stood, laughing.

"Is everything okay?" Jeffrey asked, concerned. "Are you *sure* Methuselah didn't break her computer?"

"Positive," Bob shot back. "Methuselah works like accounting software. It's impossible to delete records."

Jeffrey relaxed. "Gotcha. That's reasonable to ignore, then."

Bob walked into the next room, where a giant whiteboard listed out software development plans. In the corner of the whiteboard, a special space was reserved for client quotes of epic stupidity. Bob picked up a marker and called out to his programmers.

"Guys, I just got the stupid tech request of the day. You're not going to believe this..."

Two days later, Aaron came upstairs from the bay area and entered the software department. Even though he was agitated, he politely approached the nearest programmer—a young man who seemed to be unoccupied.

"Excuse me. We have a problem downstairs."

The programmer was in the middle of a game of Tetris, but he hit space to pause it.

"What's up?"

"I think the last software update you issued fried our computer."

The programmer lifted a skeptical eyebrow. "Fried it?"

"Wiped it. Whatever," Aaron said, frowning. "You need to take a look, please."

CLARITY - Loyalty to Purpose, Not Personalities

"Do you have the most recent antivirus updates?" the programmer asked.

"This is *not* a virus."

"Of course it's not." The programmer turned back to his computer and resumed his game.

Aaron was flabbergasted. "Dude, are you even listening to me?"

"Nope. I'm on break. I don't have to listen to anyone for..." The programmer glanced at the clock on the wall. "...twelve minutes."

Aaron reached over and hit the spacebar. "This is *your* team's fault. We just lost two months of data."

"You're not my boss. I'm not accountable to you."

"I may not be your boss, but I'm a stakeholder. So yes, you are accountable to me."

"Okay, stakeholder," sighed the programmer, turning his chair to face Aaron. "Here are the facts. Methuselah is specifically designed to not delete records. Ever."

Aaron shook his head. "You need to look again."

The programmer started to grow angry. "Come on, man. Are you ever going to let this go? You're on our case *all* the time about this software. *Now* you're seeing things that aren't even there. You *want* there to be something wrong with Methuselah. Stop blaming us every time you do something stupid!"

"I'm not demanding an upgrade right now," Aaron spat back. "I'm just upset because we lost a *ton* of work downstairs, and you won't give me the time of day. I was forced to install the update, and within five minutes the whole computer suddenly started wiping files."

"Correlation doesn't prove causation," the programmer quipped.

Aaron stomped off, livid.

The programmer shook his head and returned to his game of Tetris.

The third time, Jeffrey got the call. He was feverishly writing a massive, mind-numbing report due in two hours. When his phone rang, he answered on speakerphone.

"Jeffrey Jackson, Regional Manager speaking," he said, continuing to type.

The voice on the other line was less perky.

"Congratulations. GooCrew's software just formatted my hard drive."

Jeffrey smirked, remembering Bob's conversation from a few days before. "No, sir, that's not possible. Methuselah *can't* delete files."

"Oh yeah? Hit these keys on *your* computer."[10]

The man on the phone listed off a string of computer commands.

Jeffrey froze. Gingerly, he pulled his hands away from his keyboard.

"Okay, you have my undivided attention." Jeffrey grabbed his cellphone and a notepad. Then he stood, making a beeline for Bob's office. "Tell me exactly what happened."

An hour later, a very humbled Bob reported back to Jeffrey. Jeffrey brought Alexandra along.

"We issued a minor update last week," Bob explained. "One of the bug fixes was designed to erase the last item queried. Which *should* have been a temporary file. But under exactly the wrong circumstances it pulled up the entire computer directory instead. So... that's what got erased."

Alexandra listened somberly. "Wow. How much data was lost?"

Jeffrey grimaced. "He told us his work files were backed up. But he lost all his personal files and photographs."

Bob exhaled. "Can you imagine if it had grabbed one of the network directories instead of his personal files? I feel terrible, but I'm grateful too. That could have been a very, very expensive mistake."

Jeffrey shook his head. "Maybe it *was* an expensive mistake. We don't know what the first victim lost."

"Spilled milk," Bob grunted. "Sad, but someone has to experience the bug before we can see it. I'll issue an update as soon as possible."

"The sooner the better," Jeffrey agreed. "I'd like to forget about this whole nightmare and move on."

---

[10] This entire scenario is based on a true story of a catastrophic bug in a software program used by millions of people.

CLARITY - Loyalty to Purpose, Not Personalities

"*Hold on,*" Alexandra interrupted, aghast. "Don't just paint over this embarrassment and run away. The problem here wasn't that the software was flawed. Mistakes are inevitable. The problem was that when you first became aware of the problem, you ignored it—both of you. You *shamed* your stakeholders and co-workers for failing to use backups."

Jeffrey and Bob were stunned silent by the rebuke.

Alexandra faced Jeffrey. "What are the principles here?"

After a moment, Jeffrey gathered his courage and swallowed his pride.

"If you don't understand it, it's dangerous," he said. "You're right. We need to pay attention to the outliers and not ignore people because we think we know better. Those outliers are an early warning system."

Jeffrey stopped, wondering how he could undo the damage to partner and employee trust. "Coach, what would you recommend at this point?"

"Ignoring outliers is *your* bad habit," Alexandra replied. "How do *you* want to break it?"

> PAY ATTENTION TO OUTLIERS.
>
> # THEY ARE YOUR
>
> EARLY WARNING SYSTEM.

Jeffrey called the entire IT department together.

"Guys, we made a painful, embarrassing mistake this week," he said, clearing his throat awkwardly. "From now on, *everyone* is accountable to *every* team member, regardless of rank or title."

Then Jeffrey reached into his pocket, pulled out his wallet, and withdrew a stack of five dollar bills. He held them up.

"To prove I mean it, I'll go first... I will give a five-dollar bill to anyone who catches me failing to live up to the standards of this organization. If I'm forgetting to be accountable, or Stepping In when I shouldn't, call me on it."

Bob's jaw dropped.

Jeffrey made eye contact with several of them. "Simple as that. I'm going to repeat this announcement in every department. Let me know if you have any questions."

With that, Jeffrey left.

Bob's workers started to disperse, but he held up a hand.

"Wait a second, guys. Come back." Bob stared at the door Jeffrey had just left through. After a moment of introspection, Bob moved to the software department's shared whiteboard. He picked up an eraser.

"I think it's time to retire the stupid tech request of the day," Bob announced half-heartedly.

His team groaned in disappointment.

"No, it was funny, I agree," Bob said. "But at what cost? At *whose* cost? We're accountable to *everyone* in this company."

The first five-dollar bill went to the process team leader.

Within hours of repeating his announcement in every department, Jeffrey and Alexandra encountered the process team in the hallway.

"Hey," Jeffrey called to them. "How's it going?"

Hans grinned. "Good! We just finalized our new traffic plan for the bay."

"Cool. Can I see?"

With a knowing glance to one of the team members, Hans handed a few sheets of paper to Jeffrey.

Jeffrey flipped through it and quickly blanched. "You want to *rearrange* the bay? No, no, no... You can't do it this way."

Hans tried to conceal a smirk. "Wait, you're not Stepping In, are you?"

Jeffrey froze. "Uhhh, you're right, I'm not." Jeffrey felt his anxiety rise a little, but he pulled out his wallet and handed a five to Hans. "Ignore what I just said."

The entire process team lit up with excitement and pride.

Jeffrey glanced at the papers in his hand, still cringing. "Let me rephrase this. As a stakeholder, I have some concerns. This isn't my favorite solution. I *do* trust you, but—"

CLARITY – Loyalty to Purpose, Not Personalities

"Hey boss, *you* put me in this zone," Hans replied. "Let me own this."

Jeffrey hesitated.

Yeah, I put him in charge, Jeffrey thought to himself, eyeing Hans, *but maybe that was a mistake. I don't know anything about this guy. Does he really have the expertise to pull this off?*

Alexandra interjected gently. "Jeffrey, were you a part of these discussions? Were you privy to the analysis and agonizing and compromises made?"

Jeffrey paused. "...No."

"So how sure are you that this isn't a brilliant solution?"

Jeffrey sagged and laughed.

"Touché." He turned quietly to Alexandra. "I'm uncomfortable just letting this go because it could mess things up, but I don't want to Step In. What should I do?"

"You gave them the Decision Quality cards, right?"

"Yes."

"Then ask them why they made this decision. What level are they at?"

Hans overheard the question. "We are on the level of Likely Results. We see potential risk with a speed limit of 12 mph. We've managed it by separating foot traffic from forklifts." Hans pointed to the map. "It only impacts this area. We don't have enough information to verify our choice yet. We'd like to do a test run and check it again in a week."

Jeffrey handed the papers back to Hans. "Are you okay keeping the scope small and making sure it works before we commit the whole floor?"

Hans grinned. "We're counting on it."

Jeffrey nodded. "Great. Proceed."

Jeffrey's attitude was infectious. His workers were quick to correct him. He even noticed them holding each other accountable... but it was frustrating to realize how often he still gave orders by accident. By Friday morning, Jeffrey had given out far more money than he was comfortable with.

Friday afternoon, that investment paid for itself forever.

The programmer who had spurned Aaron sat at his desk, staring at a five-dollar bill in his hands. He'd caught Jeffrey giving a minor order, but instead of feeling victorious, the money made him feel guilty. It was his break time again, and his game of Tetris called less seductively than usual.

Finally, the programmer slipped from his cubicle and slunk down to the bay. He found Aaron without much trouble. Aaron was sitting in front of a dusty old computer, entering data from a massive stack of paper.

The programmer tapped him on the shoulder. "Can I talk to you for a sec?"

Aaron looked up from a stack of shipping tickets. When he recognized the programmer, his eyes went cold and wary.

The programmer held out a five-dollar bill. "I'm sorry for laughing at you the other day. Even if I had been right, my response was unkind and immature."

"Oh." Aaron blinked at the five. His eyes registered surprise, but also fatigue. After a moment, Aaron grudgingly took it. "Okay. Thanks for apologizing."

The response was far less enthusiastic than the programmer expected. He felt a small rush of offense, until Aaron set the money down next to the shipping tickets and went back to punching in data.

That was an awfully big stack of tickets.

"Are those the two months' worth of data you lost?" the programmer realized.

Aaron looked up, startled by the question. "Um... yeah. We have backups of everything else, but the most recent data has to be re-entered."

"Let me see."

Perplexed, Aaron stood and allowed the programmer to sit down. The programmer referenced the sheets and stared at the screen.

"Doesn't look too hard," the programmer commented after a moment. "Let me enter them. I'm sure you have more important things to do."

CLARITY – Loyalty to Purpose, Not Personalities

Aaron's eyes widened, and the programmer saw the look of surprise and gratitude that had been missing before. "Wait, you'd do that?"

The programmer shrugged and started entering data.

Aaron reeled. "Wow. Thank you. I really appreciate it."

―――――<◆>―――――

That evening as things were winding down, Aaron and Jeffrey were discussing the new floor layout when Bob approached.

"Good, I was hoping to talk to both of you," Bob said brightly.

"What's up?" Jeffrey asked.

"My team has an idea." Bob grinned. "One of my programmers came to me and pointed out how bulky and inefficient a paper tracking system is. There's a lot of opportunity for mistakes. So, we were thinking, maybe we could build a new system. Not just something for tracking barrels, but a system that synchronizes with factories and tracks barrels before we even pick them up. They could send pickup notifications electronically instead of calling. We could send disposal verifications automatically instead of mailing them. Everything could be automated and electronic. Not just internally, but communicating with the factories. Wouldn't that be cool? What do you guys think?"

Aaron blinked.

Jeffrey and Aaron glanced at each other from the corners of their eyes. It was just like Alexandra predicted. Bob honestly thought the idea was his. With their very best poker faces, Aaron and Jeffrey bit their tongues and nodded.

"Huh," Aaron said. "That sounds promising."

"Maybe we should assemble a team," Bob added eagerly. "Can you pick some workers? This would replace Methuselah. The transition might be hard for you guys, so you should help design the specs."

"I'm sure we can work something out," Aaron replied.

> **SUMMARY**
>
> - In great companies, everyone is accountable to everyone else, regardless of title or position. The shared principles you listed earlier are standards people can hold each other to.
> - When managers stay accountable to the workers and each other, it inspires more initiative and builds leaders.
> - When someone wants to take ownership of an idea you championed, *let them*. The more they feel an idea is theirs, the more driven they are to make it happen.

ACTION: Implement Daily Intents

For good accountability, you need transparency and good communication without overload. Daily Intents does this. It's a simple morning check-in to sync up, sharing plans and results as a team.

Use a group on your instant messaging (IM) channel (see p. 123). Use a texting group if IM isn't possible for this team. Do NOT use email; it has the wrong response time.

Check in around the same time each morning. Plus or minus 30 minutes is OK.

Each person shares, in very few words:

- Their top 3 intents for the day
- WINS since last check-in
- Things they are stuck on

All discussion about these items should take place on a different channel, so you don't clutter the intents channel.

It's essential to have every team member on a single shared channel—and other teams on separate channels. You'll learn from each other and remind each other to participate without overload.

CLARITY – Loyalty to Purpose, Not Personalities

OPTIONAL ACTION: Make Yourself Accountable

Make yourself accountable like Jeffrey did with the $5 bills. (See p. 143.) Example is powerful.

NEVERBOSS – Crenshaw

LEADERSHIP SCORECARD

NAME: _Jeffrey Jackson_

MY OVERALL SCORE: _2.5_

4	**STEP AWAY** SUPPORT To Unleash Excellence	- Supported Nia in forming team - Programmers holding themselves accountable - Aaron allowing Bob to run with Methuselah
3	**STEP BACK** COACH To Inspire Ownership	- Stepped Back and coached Hans through the process of making a decision
2	**STEP BESIDE** TRAIN To Build Capability	- Demonstrate first process meeting for Hans - Trained process team on Decision Quality - Set example of Accountability by offering $5 bills - Certifying bay floor design with Hans - Taught need for communication channels and asked for buy-in
1	**STEP UP** TELL To Ensure Clarity	- Intervened in fight - Defined zones with team and workers
0	**STEP IN** TAKE OVER To Create Stability	

LEVEL THREE:
CAPABILITY

Knowing we can deliver

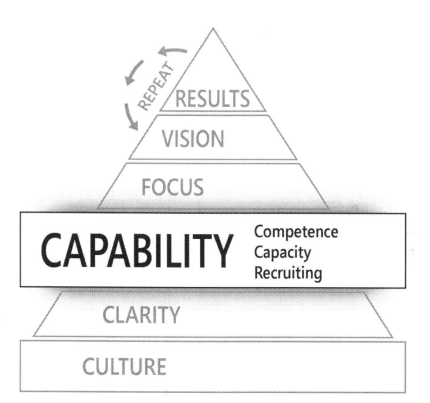

COMPETENCE
"HOW DO YOU KNOW?"

WEEK SIX

Jeffrey was depressed. Alexandra showed up for their weekly 1-on-1, cheerful as ever. They went over Jeffrey's Turnaround Scorecard. There were still multiple C's.

She was saying something about training workers. It was all Jeffrey could do to sit up in his chair. His eyes kept wandering to the bay window. Thick layers of old, dirty snow slumped against hills. Sleepy ducks waddled extra-awkwardly around the edge of the lake. Occasionally they poked at the frozen surface, looking for water.

Finally, Alexandra stopped.

"Something seems different today," she said. "Tell me what you're thinking."

For the first time all morning, Jeffrey looked her in the face.

"Honestly... I'm concerned," he admitted grudgingly. "The region I used to work at now has a new permanent manager, and they love him. My chances of ever going back are zero, and I know I can't stay here. Vanderman comes back soon. I'm just wondering what good this is. I'm wondering if I even want to stay at GooCrew anymore."

He looked back out the bay window. "Now that the adrenaline is wearing off from convincing Bob to digitize our shipping process... I'm realizing we're halfway done, and I have very little to show for it."

"Ahhh, I can see why you'd be nervous," Alexandra said. "I have good news. You've been making great progress. You *do* have to have a B+ or higher, but they *do* have another position for you."

Jeffrey's head snapped up. "They do?"

"Yes. The head of the Nebraska region is anxious to retire and needs a replacement. Or there's another position in Florida. They're giving you your choice of these two areas. In fact, they don't *want* to send you back to your old region. They want to give you a fresh start."

Jeffrey's spirits rose. He knew immediately which he'd want; he was sick and tired of snow.

As fast as hope came, Jeffrey felt himself trying to crush it. There were so many unknown variables. Most days, the Turnaround Scorecard daunted him. Change was slow, and they only had six weeks left. But... thinking of Florida gave him a goal to shoot for, at least.

"Speaking of fresh starts..." Alexandra dug around in her briefcase until she found a slip of yellow paper. She handed it to Jeffrey.

"What's this?" he asked.

"About a week ago, I asked the department heads to quietly gather the names of underperformers."

Jeffrey skimmed the list. "Okay," he said with a shrug. "Let's replace them."

"Woah," Alexandra chuckled. "Who said anything about replacing? We didn't do that to *you*. Think! What would a mass layoff do to morale? To mutual respect, mutual purpose, mutual empathy?"

Jeffrey nodded, suddenly embarrassed by his suggestion. "Then what are we going to do with them?"

"Assess their skill level. There are three main reasons passionate workers underperform: They're suppressed, undertrained, or overwhelmed. We can't know if we're giving someone too much work until we verify they have the necessary skills, so that's the first step. Anything they're missing, we'll put it on a scorecard and give them a chance to learn."

CAPABILITY – "How Do You Know?"

Jeffrey nodded. "Like that intervention you did with me?"

"The intervention we're still doing? Yes."

A shadow crossed Jeffrey's face. "I have a selfish question…"

"Shoot."

"Why didn't you suggest this earlier? I'm painfully aware that management needs to see results. After training someone, it takes time for us to start seeing the benefit. It would have been nice to start this ball rolling a month ago."

"I thought of that, but can you assess how well people are filling their roles before you've defined their roles in the first place?"

Jeffrey hesitated. "No, I suppose not."

"This is the natural progression of Hands-Off Leadership. We now have structure in place. People know what their responsibilities are. Next, we want to finish giving authority, but it's unwise to step away if they lack the skills to complete the work safely and efficiently."

"Absolutely," Jeffrey agreed, feeling a sudden wave of panic. "So… why have we already started dispersing authority?"

Alexandra laughed. "Great question! Did you know that when someone has a heart attack, most people are afraid to administer CPR?"

"Why?"

"They're afraid they'll do it wrong."

"Ahhh…" Jeffrey's face fell. "That makes sense. I'd probably hesitate too."

"Here's the thing… Even if you're not trained, doing *something* is better than nothing. CPR poorly done still improves someone's chance of survival."

"So we're giving out authority so people are poised to jump into action in case of an emergency."

"Exactly. It's like the story of that boy who noticed a leak in the dike, so he put his finger in it until help arrived. Is it the best fix? No. Does he have the authority to make a permanent repair? No. Should the kid have even been playing near the dike? Probably not."

Jeffrey laughed. "But he's still more qualified to respond to the problem than all the experts who aren't there."

"Exactly. So here's the principle: *Ability is authority.* You see a hole? Are you *capable* of plugging it? You're qualified."

Just then, someone knocked on the door to Jeffrey's office. Jeffrey flipped the list of names face down on his desk. "Come in."

A heavily freckled redhead with a bright smile stepped in, holding his hat respectfully. His uniform tag said, "Fitzherbert."

"Good morning, sir. I just came to ask..." Fitzherbert laughed awkwardly. "Well, to ask for a raise, sir. I've been working here five years, which is longer than most. I figured it's past time for a raise, and maybe this is one of those places where I'm supposed to ask."

Jeffrey looked at him, perplexed. The name sounded so familiar....

Then it occurred to Jeffrey. He lifted the edge of the sheet on his desk and snuck a glance at it. "*Arnold* Fitzherbert?"

Arnold brightened. "Yessir."

Jeffrey was flabbergasted by the request. "Um... No. I'm sorry. I can't give you a raise right now."

"Oh." Arnold's face fell. He stood there for a moment, frozen to the floor. Then he put his hat back on. "I'm sorry to bother you. I'll just go back to work, then."

Arnold left quickly and closed the door behind him.

Jeffrey turned to Alexandra, expecting a shared laugh. But the look of disappointment on her face killed the mirth in his throat.

"What's wrong?" he said. "You're mad."

"Mmm." Alexandra stood, and walked to the window. She stared out across the lake pensively. "May I tell you a story?"

"I'm listening," Jeffrey replied sincerely.

Alexandra nodded her thanks. "I had a close friend who worked at a non-profit. She sacrificed to work there... spent hundreds of unpaid hours and thousands of dollars to make herself a more valuable employee. But she wasn't being promoted, and no one would tell her why."

"That's frustrating."

"Yes, it is," Alexandra agreed. "Even though they were a wonderful company that helped thousands of people, they had a major

CAPABILITY - "How Do You Know?"

problem. In some roles their employee turnover rate was 90% every four months. *90 percent.*"[11]

Jeffrey's jaw dropped. "That's an *outrageous* waste."

Alexandra smiled painfully and nodded. "Even when every other person with equal experience had been promoted—and many people less experienced—she kept getting denied. *No one would tell her why.* Eventually, she burned out and left, feeling hurt and untrusted."

Alexandra looked Jeffrey in the eyes. "Here's the point. Never, *ever* turn an eager employee down cold when they ask for a promotion. *Never.* If you have an employee who is falling short in some way, give them hope. Say, 'yes, we'll promote you when...' Use the scorecard if you need to. It's not a punishment. I promise you, it may chafe a little at first, but it will be a relief to them."

Jeffrey shifted uncomfortably in his seat. "I don't know... I'm still chafing over the intervention you did with me, honestly."

"Of course. Imagine, though, how you'd have felt if we fired you instead."

Stunned, Jeffrey opened his mouth, searching for the right words. Finally, he sighed. "I'm sorry. You're right. It's just an awkward situation. I don't know what to tell Arnold."

"Then let's role play it," Alexandra said. "You play Arnold, and I'll be you."

"Okay." Jeffrey grinned. "I'd love this promotion. Do you think I qualify?"

"I'm so glad you asked. I would love for you to get that promotion. You will be ready when..." Alexandra looked at Jeffrey. "...and then you lay out precise standards."

"How?"

"Be specific. If it were my friend, I'd say, 'You seem to struggle with depression. Sometimes sadness clouds your judgment and

> **NEVER EVER** TURN DOWN AN EAGER EMPLOYEE WHEN THEY ASK FOR A PROMOTION. INSTEAD, SHOW THEM THE PATH TO **VICTORY.**

---

[11] These are real metrics for a real company. Not a client. As of 2016, their employee turnover rates had not improved.

makes you focus too much on yourself. This impacts your ability to perform your job. How do you feel about that?' "

Jeffrey raised an eyebrow. "That's why she wasn't getting promoted?"

"It was," Alexandra confided. "But her depression was treatable. If the nonprofit had been candid, she would have sought help years earlier."

"That's too bad," Jeffrey said.

"That's preventable," Alexandra emphasized, leaning forward. "No matter what the problem is, the next step is to work *together* to decide *specific metrics* that measure and celebrate the criteria you're concerned about. So, Arnold, you will be ready for that promotion when… A, B, C. We will know you've reached those criteria when… X, Y, Z. Every week, let's go over this in our weekly 1-on-1 so we can track your progress and reward you when you've reached that level. I'm so excited for you. I believe you can do this."

"Huh. That's actually a sensitive approach."

"That's the goal. And it's effective. Even though you're discussing a difficult topic, the employee now knows *exactly what's wrong.* He finally has an assurance that what he wants is possible, and you've laid a clear path for reaching it. It won't necessarily be easy. But Arnold's been here five years. Do you imagine for a minute that an employee *this* loyal would look at the scorecard, say 'That's not worth it,' and throw in the towel?"

Jeffrey smiled and shook his head. "No."

"Of course not." Alexandra agreed.

Jeffrey pulled out his phone and dialed someone. It rang a few times. "Hey, Aaron? Would you mind sending Arnold Fitzherbert back up to my office? He was here just a minute ago, and I owe him an apology."

"Invite his supervisor, too," Alexandra suggested. "They should be part of this conversation."

CAPABILITY – "How Do You Know?"

Arnold Fitzherbert sat in front of Jeffrey's desk, stunned. He breathed heavily, trying to keep from crying, and chose his words carefully.

"I see..." Fitzherbert said. "I appreciate you letting me know that you're unhappy with my work. Um... I really *do* want that raise. My wife just got laid off, so I either need a raise here or a second job. I'm happy to make whatever changes you require, sir. What would qualify me for that raise?"

Alexandra pulled out a blank sheet of paper. "What exactly is your role?"

"I'm a forklift operator, ma'am."

Alexandra looked at Arnold's supervisor, who stood at the back of the room. "What are the exact job requirements of a forklift operator?"

"To operate the forklifts safely," the supervisor said. "To move cargo efficiently and put it in the right place. They need to maintain their equipment and treat the cargo gently."

Jeffrey wrote these down on a scorecard and handed it to Arnold. "Please grade yourself on each of these items. How well do *you* think you're doing?"

Arnold did this very quickly. He ranked himself highest on safety and equipment maintenance. Trying to be fair, he gave himself a C on moving cargo efficiently. This was his lowest grade.

"Tell me about this C," Jeffrey said.

Arnold grew embarrassed. "Well, if you're comparing me to other forklift drivers... The other drivers hack the speed setting on their lifts, sir. I try to obey the rules, so they'll always be a couple miles faster per hour than me."

"Is that still a problem?" Jeffrey asked. "I thought you guys were working with the process team to find a better speed."

"They're still working out the kinks, sir," Arnold said with a shrug. "Anyway, I'm also not the best stacker. And there have been a few times when I put barrels in the wrong place."

The supervisor chuckled. "Don't worry about that. Other people misplace things just as often. You're just the only one who fesses up to it."

NEVERBOSS - Crenshaw

TURNAROUND SCORECARD

NAME: _Arnold Fitzherbert_

SELF Grade = [B]   BOSS Grade = [ ]

STANDARD: *"An ideal employee in this position..."*	METRICS: *Arnold Fitzherbert will be ready for a 15% raise when:*	
SAFETY Operate forklifts safely.		[B+]
EFFICIENCY Move cargo efficiently and put it in the right place.		[C]
MAINTENANCE Maintain equipment and treat the cargo gently.		[A]

Arnold brightened a little at this comment.

Jeffrey smiled too. Alexandra had been right. There were plenty of good things about this worker. He was glad she'd encouraged him to take a closer look.

"Why did you rate yourself so high on safety?" Jeffrey asked.

CAPABILITY - "How Do You Know?"

"I stop 100% at the stop signs in the bay." He said with pride. "I never use my cell phone while I'm on the forklift. I always wear earplugs and safety glasses. I always look over my shoulder when backing up. I've never had a safety accident."

"Cool. How do you feel about your work overall?"

"I thought I was an excellent employee. I'm never late. I take honest lunch breaks, and I turn in my equipment checklist every day." Arnold sagged. "Honestly, I don't understand why I'm in trouble."

Jeffrey took notes on Arnold's column of the scorecard. Then he handed it to Arnold's supervisor. "Would you please rate Arnold on each of these items?"

Arnold's supervisor started filling out the other boxes. He took longer than Arnold, agonizing a little over each grade. He eventually handed it back. "I think that's the honest truth."

Arnold looked at the sheet and wilted. Jeffrey felt awful for him. He remembered that feeling vividly.

He put a hand on Arnold's shoulder.

"Arnold, *it's okay*," he said. "*You're* okay. You obviously care a lot about your work. These grades aren't permanent. They aren't even on your record. It's just a quick, informal comparison so you can see what we see."

Arnold took courage from this. He turned to his supervisor. "How is *safety* a problem? I'm *way* more careful around pedestrians than the other drivers!"

"I'm not worried about you hurting someone else," the supervisor responded just as forcefully. "I'm worried about you maiming yourself!"

Arnold reeled. "Wha... Really?"

The supervisor nodded emphatically. "You don't keep your hands and legs inside the cage. You let your leg dangle all the time. Sometimes you drive with your head outside the cage so you can get a better view. Makes me cringe *every* time. One of these days, you're going to lose a leg. Or worse."

"*Oh.*" Arnold sat stunned for a minute. He thought long and hard. "Um... I don't always put my head out. I only do that when I can't see. Those lifting arms block my view."

WEEK SIX

161

NEVERBOSS – Crenshaw

TURNAROUND SCORECARD

NAME: _Arnold Fitzherbert_

SELF Grade = ⌈B⌉   BOSS Grade = ⌈D-⌉

STANDARD: *"An ideal employee in this position..."*	METRICS: *Arnold Fitzherbert will be ready for a 15% raise when:*	
SAFETY Operate forklifts safely.	**Safety** – All body parts must remain within the cage at all times. No violations for 6 weeks.	⌈B+⌉ ⌈F⌉
	Spatial Awareness – Also able to stack high, awkward loads while maintaining at least 2 feet clearance from all walls, ducts, and other barriers. Able to navigate the entire floor carrying highest load without incident.	
EFFICIENCY Move cargo efficiently and put it in the right place.	**Efficiency** – Pulls up to pallets in one smooth operation. No stopping, side-shifting, or excessive maneuvering.	⌈C⌉ ⌈D⌉
	Precision – Able to stack and unstack the annoying 30x32" containers in straight lines, variation no more than 4 inches, while keeping all body parts inside the safety cage.	
MAINTENANCE Maintain equipment and treat the cargo gently.	**Maintenance** – Love the batteries. All the batteries are happy. (3 weeks of maintenance records demonstrating that batteries have been rotated, recharged, and watered at the end of every shift.)	⌈A⌉ ⌈F⌉

NOTE: Every Turnaround Scorecard is unique, but uses the same grid. Focus on the specific skills and habits your employee needs to excel in their position. All scorecard templates are available at NEVERBOSS.com.

    The supervisor folded his arms. "*No one* can see the edges of the smaller boxes, Arnold. Experienced forklift drivers learn to estimate

CAPABILITY - "How Do You Know?"

it. Putting your head outside the cage puts you in serious danger. It's not an acceptable solution."

Arnold bit his lower lip. He swallowed his pride and nodded. "Well... I'm happy to learn. Would you mind showing me how *you* navigate forklifts when your view is blocked?"

"Sure," the supervisor responded with a smile.

Arnold looked back at the sheet. "Why the D for moving cargo? I know I'm not amazing... but I do *not* deserve a grade that low."

"Your steering is too jerky, and you have poor spatial awareness," the supervisor explained. "You overshoot when lifting, undershoot when stacking. You need to be aware of how tall your load is and how high you're carrying it."

"Those are tiny details, though. I don't believe that causes Goo-Crew serious enough problems to warrant a D."

"What about that time that you tore a hole in the air ducts?" the supervisor reminded him.

Arnold winced.

Jeffrey looked up, shocked. "Wait, *what* happened?"

"I backed into a low-hanging pipe a few months ago," Arnold admitted grudgingly. "I forgot about that."

Arnold looked at the sheet in a last-ditch attempt to redeem his honor. "What about the F for maintenance? That's just... cruel. It feels like you're ignoring all my hard work. What about my maintenance sheets?"

"Okay.... Now we get to the meat of this conversation." The supervisor sat down across from Arnold. "You've been destroying our batteries. It's driving *everyone* crazy."

Arnold looked confused. "Wait... what?"

"You leave your battery in your forklift at least once a week. You're supposed to charge it at the end of every shift. Whoever comes in on the night shift gets a battery that's near empty. They've gotten in the habit of charging them for 10 minutes before taking them for a ride, in case they're unlucky enough to get yours. But that devastates the battery capacity."

Arnold blinked. "Wow, I'm sorry. I'm usually in a hurry to pick up my daughter from school. I guess I've been forgetting. I had no idea everyone was upset. Why didn't you tell me?"

WEEK SIX

163

The supervisor shuffled, embarrassed. "We weren't sure at first who was doing it..." He rushed past the question. "That's not the only problem, though. Not only have you been forgetting to charge your battery, you haven't been watering them either."

"We're supposed to water our batteries?" Arnold asked in astonishment.

"Yes!"

"Like... how often? Every 6 months or...?"

"No! Every day!"

Arnold was shocked. "Seriously? I didn't know that was part of my job. Why isn't it on the maintenance sheet?"

The supervisor blinked. "It's not?"

Arnold laughed. "Sir, I turn in my maintenance sheet every day, come hell or highwater. If it were on the sheet, I would have done it."

"Wow, that's embarrassing." The supervisor borrowed a pen from Jeffrey's desk and scribbled a note on his hand to fix the sheet.

Jeffrey grinned at Arnold. "How do you feel now?"

Arnold gave a shy smile. "Hopeful again. I was so confused when you turned me down. Thank you for calling me back and telling me why."

"We're not quite done," Alexandra said. "The last step is to choose specific metrics." She turned to the supervisor. "What would your dream forklift operator look like? At what point would *you* recommend a raise?"

Over the next few minutes, Arnold and the supervisor found metrics that seemed fair to both of them.

For a great book on developing personal competence, I recommend *So Good They Can't Ignore You*, by Cal Newport. Pay special attention to the chapters on deliberate practice and career capital. These two principles will make it easier to develop and certify skills.

CAPABILITY - "How Do You Know?"

After they left, Jeffrey turned to Alexandra. "Wasn't that weird how the things Arnold thought he was best at were actually the biggest problems?"

Alexandra smiled. "That happens almost every time."

"Seriously?"

"Yes. Novices tend to overrate their ability. When they're just starting to get good at something, they know it all."[12]

Jeffrey leaned back in his chair. "Ha! I've seen that on ski slopes. It's never experts on black diamond trails who get hauled away by the ski patrol. It's the intermediate ones trying to hotdog it down the hill."

Alexandra groaned. "It's true... Experts don't see clearly either, though. Have you ever heard of Michelangelo's tantrum?"

Jeffrey shook his head. "What? No."

"It's a great story. When he was 72, Michelangelo started a massive sculpture that meant a lot to him personally. Worked on it for eight years. But one day, he got so frustrated that he took a hammer and started hacking it to pieces."

Jeffrey's jaw dropped. "Seriously?"

Alexandra nodded. "Because he knew *so much* about stone, he could see a thousand imperfections. He was so overwhelmed with a sense of inadequacy that he thought the whole thing was unsalvageable. Fortunately, a friend was visiting and stopped him. He said, 'Look, even if *you* don't want it, *I do*,' and offered to buy it on the spot."[13]

Alexandra smiled. "That's why experts underestimate their abilities. It's not false modesty. The expert genuinely sees what is missing, and it irks them. The novice will *overrate* their abilities because they're oblivious. Be careful, or you'll accidentally punish expert employees because they self-report low, while you reward the least competent ones."

---

[12] This is called the Dunning-Kruger Effect.
[13] The statue mentioned is called *The Florence Pieta.* Michelangelo carved himself into the scene. After his friend purchased the statue, the broken pieces were reattached. The statue was never completed, so we can see the exact state of the art when Michelangelo had his breakdown.

Jeffrey paused for a moment. He slid his own assessment sheet closer and looked at it, suddenly wondering how much he overestimated himself. It was a painful question.

Finally, he looked up. "Okay, so how do we get a realistic assessment of skill level?"

Alexandra made eye contact, quietly acknowledging his dilemma. "Great question, and it reminds me: It's time to add a very important skill to your toolbox."

"What?"

"Certifying. This tool comes from leadership maverick David Marquet. Marquet was a nuclear submarine captain who wanted to give power to his sailors instead of giving orders. But submarines are dangerous. Small mistakes can kill everyone on board. Marquet balanced precision and freedom using the principle of certifying. So when workers wanted to do something, Marquet stopped running down a checklist. 'Have you checked all the dials? Is everyone below deck? Is the hatch secured?' Instead, ask: "Are we ready? *How do you know?*"

"Aha!" Jeffrey laughed. "I love that question. Then they're doing the thinking. And they'll be mortified if it doesn't work. They'll feel the pain."

"Precisely," Alexandra said. "Certifying lets you let go without dissolving into chaos. Whatever happens, you're still informed. You still have opportunities to influence, train—even Step In—before things go horribly wrong."

"You know..." Jeffrey felt a sudden wave of relief. "This whole time you've been talking about giving away power, and in the back of my head, I've had this nagging fear. Giving your workers freedom is a beautiful theory, but leaders are in all kinds of dangerous situations."

"Absolutely," Alexandra acknowledged.

"GooCrew handles hazardous waste. Minor missteps could cost someone time behind bars," Jeffrey explained. "If Heart pursued an unprofitable project, it could cost thousands of jobs. And for small business owners, mistakes could mean personal bankruptcy. The stakes are never small, and when you're sailing through reefs, you

CAPABILITY - "How Do You Know?"

want the person with the most experience at the helm. The thought of handing out power like fairy dust—you can fly, and *you* can fly—"

Alexandra started to laugh.

"—and then handcuffing myself," Jeffrey continued, "Not being allowed to intervene... That scares me to death!"

"With good cause," Alexandra assured him. "As a leader, it's wildly irresponsible to give full power until you've ensured that your workers are competent. That's step one: Do widespread training to help everyone get up to speed. Step two, certifying, is your ongoing opportunity as a leader to verify they are using that training."

"And once they've demonstrated their competence, I give my approval," Jeffrey agreed.

"No, not quite," Alexandra smiled. "There is a *huge* difference between 'approving' and what we recommend. It's tempting for both the leader and the workers to assume that certifying with your captain means they are asking for the captain's *approval.* They're not. The captain is mostly a stupidity filter. You're saying, 'I'm about to do this. If I'm horribly mistaken, stop me.' Then, *even if the captain has a better idea*—if the teammate has certified everything and managed risk with good principles and data—the captain should buy-in."

Jeffrey's eyes grew big. "If I can 70% agree... If their idea is 70% as good as mine... because the goal isn't the task. The goal is to create leaders."

"*Yes,*" Alexandra confirmed.

"I'm starting to see how all these principles fit together," Jeffrey mused.

"In summary," Alexandra said, "For Hands-Off Leadership to truly work, the leader can't just *give authority*. We want workers to *take initiative*. Otherwise, the leader still has a subtle stranglehold. Your team will feel it, and they'll shut down."

"That's going to be hard for me," Jeffrey realized. "It'll be hard to remember to buy-in when I have the power to veto. But I'll try."

Alexandra grinned. "When you do, initiative-based leadership will work whether the company is massive or tiny. As Marquet proved, it even works in war, or in nuclear power plants. When you

WEEK SIX

167

certify, have daily check-ins, and hold your weekly meetings, the leader never loses visibility."

> To read more about David Marquet's remarkable turnaround of the Navy's worst-performing submarine, we highly recommend his book, *Turn the Ship Around!*, endorsed by Stephen Covey.

SUMMARY

- Passionate workers underperform when they are suppressed, undertrained, or overwhelmed.

- Never turn down an eager employee when they ask for a promotion. Create a plan together instead, using a Turnaround Scorecard.

- Novices tend to overrate their abilities, and experts tend to underrate their work. Mutual discussion reveals their true skills.

- To assess competence quickly, invite people to certify. Don't remind or grill them. Just ask, "How do you know?" Move to more specific questions if you see gaps.

- Hands-Off Leadership works in organizations of all sizes and almost any industry.

ACTION: Use the Turnaround Scorecard to Help Someone Change

If someone is struggling, identify exactly what's wrong and talk with them about it. Use a customized Turnaround Scorecard with specific metrics, and review weekly.

CAPABILITY – "How Do You Know?"

ACTION: Introduce "Certifying" to Your Team

Introduce "certifying" in your next meetings with each team or manager. (Add this now as a Burning Issue to your next meeting agenda.) In these meetings, role play actual situations so they see and understand how certifying feels. Explain that we often certify as issues come up during the workday instead of in formal meetings.

Certifying measures competence. Instead of telling or grilling people, we ask "Are we ready?" "How do we/you know?" and "How sure are you?" Their answers show their skill level. Be sure to make "I don't know" a safe answer. Certifying lets us Step Back once we're confident in their CAPABILITY.

ACTION: Use Certifying to Update Training Plans— or Step Back

In your next 1-on-1's, certify skills in areas where you or they are unsure. Start with a scorecard like Arnold's. List specific areas. *However, this is NOT a Turnaround Scorecard.* It's just review. Let them choose areas first, then you add to the list.

If they score high, congratulate them and let them know you'll be Stepping Back or Stepping Away in that area. If improvement is needed, ask: "What would you like to do to improve? What's the next step?" Let them think, plan, and help set metrics. Then add a future 1-1 agenda item to follow up together.

CAPACITY

BELIEVING THE CAMEL

WEEK SIX

J effrey had seen many things. But he'd never seen a worker run into his office sopping wet.

"Mr. Jackson," he called breathlessly. "Come quick! The bay is flooding."

Jeffrey and Alexandra jumped to their feet.

The bay was in chaos. Hundreds of gallons churned across the floor. They could hear the steady hiss of a broken pipe before they even saw it. Supervisors in the bay area scurried frantically, cutting power to machinery and shouting at workers to evacuate the building.

Jeffrey pulled yellow rubber slip-ons over his boots. Alexandra followed suit. Grabbing goggles and gloves, they hurried to the center of the action.

"Geez," Alexandra said, covering her nose. "It smells like something died."

"Is this the pump for the wastewater treatment unit?" Jeffrey asked in horror.

A maintenance engineer crouched under the machine, poking around with a flashlight, avoiding the water splashing down.

"No, it's a cooling line for the incinerator," he said.

"Why does the water smell so bad?" Jeffrey insisted.

The engineer shrugged. "It's from the lake. Have you been outside? The water's nasty."

Come to think of it, the water did smell strongly of fish. Jeffrey relaxed a little. "What happened?"

"The pipe corroded."

Jeffrey's jaw dropped. "That should *never* happen. Why haven't you been maintaining this?"

The engineer sagged. "It's a weird size. I haven't had time to track down the part."

"What else are you doing? I don't see why it's so hard."

"All kinds of equipment in this stupid bay is breaking down," the engineer shot back. "I have to maintain *all* the machines, alone, as a salaried employee, on a shoestring budget. Compared to everything else, the water lines have been really low priority!"

"Fine, then I'll do it."

With a stormy face, Jeffrey slipped his suit jacket off and tossed it aside. He rolled up the sleeves of his crisp white shirt and knelt in the putrid water under the pump, pushing the engineer out of the way.

Alexandra tried to interrupt. "Woah, Jeffrey, I think—"

"Stay out of this!" Jeffrey yelled. "You're a shrink, not an engineer."

Alexandra's eyes widened in surprise and hurt.

The worker glared at Jeffrey. "Are *you*?"

"*Yes*, actually." Jeffrey spat back. "Cornell University, *summa cum laude*. Followed by an MBA. Now go shut off the water flow."

"I tried," the engineer replied, embarrassed. "The valve is stuck."

"Then find another one!" Jeffrey yelled.

The engineer scowled and ran off.

Jeffrey slipped his fingers behind the pump and started feeling along the pipes for the break. From the corner of his eye, Jeffrey noticed Alexandra walk away. He felt a wave of anger. He knew he shouldn't have pushed the engineer out of the way, but there just wasn't time. He couldn't believe Alexandra was sulking about it.

There's the problem.

The pipe had burst open. Jeffrey could feel a short, wide crack. He'd never seen pipe corroded so thin. He took one of his rubber gloves and wrapped it around the casting, twisting the glove like a twist-tie to create a tight seal. The leak stopped.

Then he heard a sharp metallic popping sound and water started to gush again a few feet away.

Cripes! Jeffrey thought as a rush of shock and frustration hit. *There's a second break?*

Wherever it was, it wasn't within reach.

Suddenly, Alexandra appeared at his side with a wad of towels. She squatted in the water alongside him.

"What other tools do you need?" she asked quietly.

Jeffrey stared at her in surprise. She met his gaze without a trace of resentment. Just waiting, ready to help.

Jeffrey gratefully took one of the towels and wrapped it around the gloved pipe.

"Could you hold that? I need to find the other break."

She immediately slid in and took his place. Jeffrey grabbed the other towels.

They held the gushing back for a few minutes. Finally, the water cut off. Jeffrey stepped back and removed his goggles.

"There's a shower in the women's locker room," he told Alexandra in a softer voice. "Clean yourself up immediately. Rinse for 15 minutes, just to be safe. I'll send someone with a spare uniform."

They met back up in the break room. Jeffrey had scrounged up the gym clothes from his car. Alexandra wore an orange coverall, the same kind the bay workers used. Her hair was sopping wet. The room was packed with bay workers waiting for the all-clear.

When Jeffrey arrived, they burst into applause.

Jeffrey looked at Alexandra, confused. "What did I do?"

She smiled. "You rolled up your sleeves. They'd never seen someone jump in a graywater shower wearing Giorgio Armani."

Jeffrey flushed with pride.

"Also," Alexandra added, "They think we're going to have superpowers."

"Ooooh! Do we get nicknames?"

Alexandra grinned mischievously. "I'm Whisper. They're still deciding on your name. Best one I've heard so far is Fishstick."

Jeffrey laughed. "That water was vile. We're *both* going to smell like fish for a week."

He sat down in the chair across from Alexandra, and then stared across the room, thinking. "It's strange those pipes were so corroded..."

Alexandra smiled, then stared at her coffee mug. "Jeff?"

"Yeah?"

"As much as I admire your willingness to get your hands dirty..."

"...I shouldn't have pushed that engineer out of the way."

Alexandra nodded.

"Why'd you help me?" Jeffrey asked.

She shrugged. "The damage was done, and you weren't in a mood to listen. I figured help now, talk later."

Jeffrey scowled. "I'm kind of upset this even happened, to be honest. I can't believe our engineer would be so irresponsible and ignore a pipe long enough for a break like this. I hoped getting employees to care would prevent these sorts of disasters."

"It does. But caring alone isn't enough."

"What do you mean?"

"There's an element of Hands-Off Leadership we haven't addressed yet: Capacity. To prevent disasters, you start with workers who care, but then you *also* need to narrow their responsibilities down to realistic levels. It doesn't matter how much your employee cares if they're spread too thin. You'll still have accidents. Big ones."

Jeffrey huffed. "Well, we can't tell him, 'Don't worry about maintaining the machines on the right. Just keep the left half in working order...' "

CAPABILITY - Believing The Camel

"Well, this isn't just a problem with that one employee. It's your whole company. One of the issues you're supposed to tackle is excessive overtime, right? The majority of those hours are clocked by assistants in the legal department."

Jeffrey grunted in frustration. "I *still* can't get them to cut back. Clara knows they aren't authorized to stay late."

"Right, but their workload isn't flexible," Alexandra pointed out. "If they miss their publishing deadline, there is a big, nasty train wreck on the other side. You're not requiring overtime directly. But they have too much to do. There's no hope of completing it if they don't stay late. Same with this engineer. His zone is too big."

"We can't afford a second engineer."

"Can you afford today's disaster? I'm no expert, but I imagine that will be an expensive repair."

Jeffrey winced. "Good point."

"Penny-pinching by overworking employees is an expensive way to run a business. Not just because of overtime. When your only engineer gets tired, he won't think straight, and things slip through the cracks."

"I hear pain in your voice," Jeffrey mused. "You care a lot about this, don't you?"

Alexandra sighed. "I once worked for a Silicon Valley CEO who was a dynamo of ideas. A visionary, idea-generator personality. He came to our meetings with three new ideas every week, and he assigned them all. Soon, he had us working 60-70 hours. Sometimes we were given assignments that moved us *off* projects we'd spent 60-70 hours on the previous week."

Jeffrey raised his eyebrows. "*Ouch.*"

"Yeah," Alexandra said, her voice still flinching at the memory. "When we showed up to team meetings, he'd ask for a report. Then we'd say, 'It's not done.' And he'd go, 'Why? What's the problem? Why is this taking so

WHEN IT LOOKS LIKE **LAZINESS,** IT'S USUALLY **EXHAUSTION**

WEEK SIX

long?' He would even reach a point where he'd say, 'Fine. I'll do it myself.' What's wrong with that picture?"

"It was his fault you weren't done. He was being unrealistic."

She shook her head. "It's not just that. Jumping in to finish a task when you're frustrated is manipulation. You're calling them lazy. You're saying, 'If you just tried harder, you could do this. Look at me. I'm busy too, and *I* can do it.' That's Stepping In. That's Step Zero. That's an F."

Jeffrey huffed. "Well, I *can* do it better. Honestly, I haven't been impressed with that guy's work. When we showed up, he was just standing there, with his eyes glazed over, watching everything leak out."

"When it looks like laziness, it's usually exhaustion. And your first indication that something is wrong here is your engineer complaining about being a salaried employee."

Jeffrey grimaced. "I'm not convinced we need another person. I think that engineer just works slow."

Alexandra's eye narrowed.

WHEN A LOYAL CAMEL STARTS TO COMPLAIN, BELIEVE IT

"That's a vicious assumption," she chided. "Once you begin to have an empowered organization, where people feel ownership, they care about the company, you see them showing initiative, and they want great things to happen... *Why in the world* would you assume they're lying about how much they can handle?"

Jeffrey frowned. "Are we sure he's competent? Maybe he needs retraining."

"Good question. We already assessed Competence, though. Anyone who needs retraining is already getting it. Any residual shortcomings mean the worker is simply overwhelmed."

Jeffrey winced, still agonizing over the budget. "Could we maybe just give him a raise? Make him hourly again, so he feels better about the overtime?"

CAPABILITY - Believing The Camel

Alexandra gave Jeffrey a sidelong look.

"Humans only have 168 hours in a week. You only have claim on 40 of them. Don't kill off the employees you love. You know that old saying about the straw that breaks the camel's back?"

"Yeah."

"When a loyal camel starts to complain, believe it. When well-trained workers start crying uncle, they either need less to do, more time to do it, or more people. Make sure you support their choice."

Jeffery couldn't help but smile. "They get to pick?"

"If at all possible. At very least, don't choose without them. Remember, great leaders don't give orders. They help workers find and apply their own solutions."

Jeffrey nodded and stood up from his chair. "Well, we can't give him less to do. The equipment won't change. But maybe there are things we could do to slow down the deterioration. Give him more time. Or maybe he has a friend who needs a job…"

"You owe that guy five dollars." Alexandra teased.

Jeffrey chuckled and reached into his wallet. He pulled out a five and gave it to Alexandra.

"I owe you, too. I'm sorry for shutting you down."

SUMMARY

- Stepping In when we feel anxious or frustrated hurts employee ownership. Avoid damage by asking yourself, "Do I really need to take over? What's the least power I can use to resolve this?"

- When it looks like laziness, it's usually exhaustion.

- When loyal workers say they have too much work, listen. They either need less to do, more time to do it, or more hands.

ACTION: Unburden Your Team

Add a burning issue to your next team meetings to ask team members where they're overloaded. Make it safe to say "I have too much." Point out that being overloaded results in feelings of exhaustion or missing important tasks.

Then decide together what they would like to do about it:

- Do less
- Allocate more time
- Get more people (shift assignments around, hire)

Supervisors: It's not reasonable to expect crazy hours. Anything over 50 hours is too much. Some studies show that people get *less* done, not more, if they work more than 50 hours on a regular basis.

Workers: Speak up. If you're getting whiplash from being dragged around on too many projects, say so. Until *somebody* says something, the problem will continue.

SPECIAL SITUATION: Very Small Businesses

Small businesses are especially needy. Slowing down or adding more full-time workers may seem impossible. If so, laser-sharp focus and part-time talent are good bets for boosting capacity. Pay special attention to the chapters on Focus and Moneyball Talent.

RECRUITING
MONEYBALL TALENT

WEEK SIX

"We need to hire another maintenance engineer," Jeffrey said as he pulled up a chair.

Matt glanced at Tickerman. "What, this one isn't good enough for you?"

The engineer laughed half-heartedly. "I'm just stretched too thin. I need an assistant, or we're in trouble."

Jeffrey, Alexandra, and Tickerman had reconvened in the HR office after they'd been given a medical okay. They wore an odd assortment of clothes. Jeffrey smiled at how strange the image would look to an outsider: a brawny man listening attentively to three ragamuffins.

Matt frowned. "You think we might have another accident?"

"Of course. Have you seen the list of repairs I'm behind on?"

"How soon?"

Tickerman sighed. "I don't know... Maybe we'll be fine for a couple of months. But something could break next week. I can't promise anything."

"Could we pay you overtime to get up to speed?"

"I'm salaried," Tickerman said bitterly.

"Hmm..." Matt narrowed his eyes and spun around to his computer. He typed a few things in, then winced. "That's what I thought. We don't have the budget for another engineer."

Tickerman cringed. "Well, if I quit, will you have the budget for it?"

They all laughed. Tickerman didn't.

"Wait," Matt said with sudden surprise. "You don't really intend to quit, do you?"

"Well, not exactly, but... guys... I can't keep going like this!" Tickerman looked around the room, desperation in his eyes. "How much overtime do you want? Last week I spent 78 hours here. You want 90? 100? I'm exhausted!"

Alexandra spoke up. "How much money *is* in the budget?"

"We can spare $23,000."

Jeffrey whistled. "You're right. We'll never find a decent engineer at that rate."

Tickerman looked like he was ready to cry. "I will take a pay cut if necessary. I would gladly give up $6,000 annually to get an extra 20 hours to myself each week."

They all stared at Tickerman in shock.

"We're not going to demote you!" Jeffrey said, appalled.

Alexandra jumped in. "But he has a great idea. What about hiring a part-time employee?"

Matt shook his head. "People this skilled don't work part-time."

"Lots of great people *want* part-time work," Alexandra insisted.

Jeffrey glanced at his phone. "Can we trust you to draft the job description, Matt? We need someone next week, if possible."

"Hold it," Matt said in frustration. "You can't just saddle me with an impossible job description and walk out. You guys do this to me all the time!"

"What else can I do?" Jeffrey shot back. "We need an engineer. Cash is tight everywhere. Those constraints are fixed."

Alexandra raised her hand. "I know a system for finding amazing talent on the cheap. It will also help with your retention rates. Can I show you?"

CAPABILITY - Moneyball Talent

"By all means." Matt stepped away from his computer.

Alexandra sat down and started to type. "This is called a Moneyball approach. There are trainloads of people who are talented but have some skin-deep flaw that causes them to be rejected from the system. Those are the people we're looking for."

Matt was skeptical. "The underdogs and misfits?"

"Yes. We want undervalued, underappreciated people with potential. The barnyard horse with the heart of a champion."

Matt scratched the back of his neck. "Well, everyone loves an underdog, but the truth is, they're one in a million."

Alexandra grinned and shook her head. "They're *everywhere*. Most people just never give them a chance."

Matt wasn't convinced. "Well, how do *you* know which horse to bet on?"

"There are a few hallmarks of undervalued talent. First of all, look past anything superficial. They're quirky. They talk a little bit funny. Maybe they're shy."

"Or they have terrible fashion sense," Jeffrey joked, eying Alexandra's orange GooCrew jumpsuit.

She laughed. "Right. None of those things matter. What matters is whether they can do what our company needs them to do. Can they do it brilliantly, and will they love doing it?"

> For a fun introduction to Moneyball Talent, I highly recommend watching the movie Moneyball (2011), based on the book *Moneyball: The Art of Winning an Unfair Game*, by Michael Lewis. It's the inspiring true story of a baseball team general manager who bet his career on a team full of bargain-bin players.

"What kinds of problems do you overlook?" Matt asked, leaning in to watch.

"A friend of mine had clinical depression for five years," Alexandra said. "By the time she got treatment, she had a massive employment gap on her resume. Whip smart, perfect GPA, hard worker, willing to commit. But they'd throw her resume away every time. Ignore gaps. Ignore job-hopping. Ignore tattoos. *If you see the other indicators you're looking for,* ignore a terrible GPA, lack of diploma, and jail time if your industry will legally allow it."

Matt stared at her in shock. "You're saying I should ignore problems *that* serious?"

"*Yes.* Who cares where they've been? People who have faced unemployment as a painful, uphill battle will be fiercely loyal. They'll be reliable, diligent workers. You'll get better results from them."

Matt looked torn. "Let's say I agree. How on earth am I supposed to sort through resumes if the people I usually reject are the ones we might want?"

Alexandra "Forget resumes. You need to value *potential* over *experience.* It's easy for people with experience to rest on their laurels. Experience is the past. Potential is the future. Use a skills-based system to sort your applicants instead."

Matt reached for his filing cabinet. "Okay. Well, let me check what applications we have on file."

Alexandra turned around. "That's a terrible first step," she said, surprised. "We haven't defined the job yet."

Matt laughed and waved his hand dismissively. "No, you don't understand. I only keep applications of people that seemed promising. Like when someone feels like a great fit for us. When I have an opening, I try to slip them in first."

"That's an extremely dangerous way to select workers."

Matt hesitated, folder in hand. "Why? It saves a lot of time."

"If you start to favor any applicant before you've defined the job, you'll end up writing the job description to match the person you like," Alexandra explained. "Not only is that bad for coming up with solid employees... subtle discrimination can start to creep in."

"Ahhh..." Matt suddenly looked at the folder in his hand like it was a snake. "Of course. I should have seen that. So defining the job is the first step..."

Right. What are the actual duties, skills, and attributes we will need?"

They brainstormed for a few minutes and came up with a solid list: Skills to repair, maintain, and troubleshoot industrial equipment. Specifically, they needed someone who understood motors, water pumps, and pneumatics. They also needed to be able to read and follow engineering notations on blueprints and operations manuals.

Alexandra explained that the interview process was simple. "We're going to craft two sets of interview questions. The first interview is ten questions. These ten questions assess job-specific skills. The second set only contains five questions, which measure cultural compatibility. Both kinds of questions are designed the same way. We're looking for very simple questions that will showcase understanding or betray ignorance."

"How do you do that?"

"It's easy." Alexandra turned to Tickerman. "What's a small question about our equipment that any decent maintenance engineer would know, but someone without proper training wouldn't have a clue?"

Tickerman smiled mischievously. "What's the most common reason for positraction breaking on a forklift, and how would you fix it?"

Alexandra turned back to Matt. "Do you know the answer?"

Matt shook his head. "No idea."

"Jeff?"

Jeffrey grinned. "Forklifts almost never have a positraction system. But on vehicles that *do*, visually inspecting the damaged ring, pinion gears, and bearings will usually show what's wrong. Most likely causes are lubrication failure, placing unequal load on the tires, or normal wear. If the bearing is the problem, you can sometimes diagnose it before you even open it up, because pitted bearings are noisy. Shall I go on?"

"That's plenty." Alexandra grinned at Matt. "See? You can do this with any field. If you're hiring a web programmer, ask how they would write code to prevent a cross-browser attack. Most applicants fail that question, *even though* they can go online while answering questions and learn."

"But that's cheating," Matt said.

Amused, Alexandra looked at him. "No, it's not. That's how life works these days. If someone lacks the skills, but they demonstrate an ability to learn rapidly enough that they can keep their head above water with everyone else, why not give them a shot? Even if they're learning from search engines, is the answer accurate? Is it thorough? Does it hit all the main points, and if applied, would it do the job? No one has everything memorized."

Matt and Jeffrey shifted uncomfortably and looked at each other.

Alexandra laughed. "Look, technology changes rapidly. Within 5 or 10 years of hiring someone, *everything* they learned in college will be outdated. Which person would you rather have on your team? Someone who graduated college but is totally dependent on lectures to learn; or a self-taught, passionate nerd who loves to browse tutorials online and can pick up any skill you need in six hours?"

Tickerman interrupted. "I know which person *I'd* rather train."

Jeffrey objected. "I think you're oversimplifying there. Not everything can be learned quickly. You wouldn't hire a brain surgeon just because they can list all the parts of the brain."

"Right," Alexandra agreed. "That's why it's important to ask the *right* question. For example, writing is a difficult skill for many people. It takes years to get good at it. If you do a grammar test, most people can find what's wrong and fix it. But can they write a coherent letter? Last time I hired an admin, only 1 in 15 applicants had that basic skill."

"So we design a question like this for each skill we need?" Matt clarified.

"Yup. At least, hit on the main points."

Tickerman raised his hand. "You mentioned a second set of questions?"

Alexandra turned back to the computer. "Ah, yes. There are three things you need in *every* employee: Intelligence, Initiative, and Teachability. That's what the other questions measure. If they have those three things, they can do almost anything. And Initiative can be trained. So look for either initiative or the capacity for initiative."

Matt pulled out a notepad to take notes with. "How do you measure initiative in a questionnaire?"

Alexandra thought for a moment before responding. "I like to say, 'Tell us about a time when you showed ownership or initiative, but you weren't technically the owner. I also ask them if they have any entrepreneurial experience. Anybody that has genuinely tried to start their own business has some degree of initiative. Whether they succeeded or not doesn't matter, as long as they can tell me what they learned."

> THERE ARE THREE THINGS YOU NEED IN EVERY EMPLOYEE: INTELLIGENCE, INITIATIVE, & TEACHABILITY

"Okay." Matt scribbled on his pad. "What about Teachability?"

"Have you ever heard of a Fermi estimate?"

Matt shook his head. "I don't think so."

Alexandra quickly explained the concept. "A Fermi estimate is a way to find the answer to a bizarre question about an unfamiliar situation, using rough estimates of things you *are* familiar with. So if I ask how many scuba divers live in Los Angeles, and you don't know, you can still guess. I know that about 300 million people live in the US, so the population of Los Angeles is probably more than 2 million, but not more than 15 million. I'll guess 10. Then I guess what percentage of people in LA like to scuba dive. More than the average person, but not everybody. Probably one in 20 have done it, and one in 50 scuba dives regularly.... If you keep using wild guesses like this, the high and low estimates start to balance each other out. The final answer usually comes close. Does that make sense to you?"

"Cool," Matt said, looking up. "That makes sense."

"Great. If I were interviewing you, I would explain this concept, and then throw a bizarre question at you. How many baseballs are manufactured each year in the U.S.? How many piano tuners live in Chicago? How many buckets of paint would it take to paint the whole earth?"

Matt stopped, starting the math in his head.

Alexandra smiled, waving at him to not worry about it. "Getting the right answer doesn't matter. We're interested in the process. Can they understand the concept of Fermi estimates that I just taught them? How well can they apply it? This measures both teachability and intelligence. Intelligence means capacity to learn something new. Teachability means willingness to be taught."

Matt reviewed his notes. "You mentioned five questions, though. What are the others?"

"The second interview should also quickly assess cultural compatibility, to make sure the person we're bringing on board is capable of thriving in a Hands-Off Leadership environment. Some people chafe at the idea of mutual respect because they know they're too aggressive. Others wither when you put them in charge of themselves."

Matt was appalled. "Seriously?"

"Sad, but true," Alexandra said with a nod. "When hiring programmers, my last team found that some cultures we were tempted to hire from had a *terrible* track record of waiting for orders. They couldn't think creatively. That's the kiss of death for a programmer. Our chief programmer came up with a quick question to tell the difference."

"What was it?"

"You're working on a project. Which is the most important thing for you to work on: a) what the boss has told you to do, or b) something else extremely important that you've noticed needs to be done?"

"Uh..." Matt stopped, struggling to answer.

"Again, we don't care about the answer," Alexandra went on, enjoying Matt's reaction. "What you're looking for is the way they *arrive* at the answer. The wrong candidates will say, 'Oh my gosh, you *always* do what the boss tells you.' "

Matt relaxed a little, appreciating her perspective. "What do the right candidates say?"

Alexandra smiled mischievously. "People who are willing to think will feel uncomfortable with the question. They'll feel tension between the two options, and they'll strike an appropriate balance.

CAPABILITY - Moneyball Talent

Something like, 'Depending on what it is, I may finish what the boss told me to do first, but if it's an immediate threat to the company, I need to handle it *now*.' Those are the people you want to hire."

Matt came back to Alexandra the next day and eagerly handed her his laptop. "Here's the application I designed so far," he said. "What do you think?"

Alexandra peered at it and started to scroll. "Is this an automated job application system?"

"Of course. Why?"

Alexandra deflated a little, reticent to correct too much at once. "Automated systems can't spot Moneyball talent. The algorithms use keywords to favor experience and cannot see potential. They cherry-pick the obvious, brilliant people, and you'll be forced to pay top dollar for them."

"We have *so* many applications coming in, for too many positions," Matt objected. "I can't possibly review them all."

"It's okay," Alexandra reassured him. "There are several ways to sort through the stack. For starters, automatically discard any application that's incomplete."

"I don't want to do that." Matt resisted, shaking his head. "We might miss good applicants."

Alexandra raised an eyebrow. "Do you want to hire people who can't or won't follow directions?"

Matt caved a little. "No. I suppose not."

"Then don't." Alexandra said with a smile. "Next step, make the application hard. It's like a demand curve. As the application gets harder, fewer people will apply. Make the application as hard as you need in order to restrict the number of applications to a point where you can handle the influx."

Matt stared sadly at the computer screen. "I feel bad for the people we'll still reject. If everyone made their applications super hard, some people would never find a job."

"That's very thoughtful of you. Hard doesn't mean time-consuming, though," she pointed out. "There are lots of ways to make something hard. My coaching team was recently looking for a marketer. So we asked applicants to make a 2-minute video and post it on YouTube."

"Was that related to the job position?"

"We needed to measure computer skills. Right away, they had to know how to post something on YouTube, or how to learn. They needed enough technical skill to operate a camera and computer. We could also see how professional they were. We got some amazing videos and some pretty dismal ones. With that *one* requirement, we filtered out a huge slew of applicants that otherwise would have sent us resumes."

"Huh," Matt mused. "I would have assumed a non-traditional application like that would annoy people."

"It does annoy some," she said, shrugging. "But Moneyball talent will be *motivated* by that kind of application. They *know* their resume keeps getting rejected from the system. When you give them a chance to showcase their skills in a way that might be listened to, they get excited."

Alexandra kept clicking through. "Your questions look solid, though.... Do you ask about salary anywhere?"

Matt shuddered. "Everybody hates that question."

"Yup. So ask it in a different way. Normally people say, 'Tell us the salary you want,' and the first person to mention a number loses. That's traditional negotiation."

Matt laughed darkly. "So true."

"Instead, break it up into three questions, so we can get a spectrum. First, how much do you need to earn to survive? Second, what salary are you hoping for? Third, what are your salary goals two years from now?"

Matt straightened. "Interesting! Any company that hires someone at their survival level is a dumb company, unless they're strapped for cash and they're offering some kind of additional incentive."

"Exactly," Alexandra said, delighted that he understood. "Seeing that range allows us to communicate honestly. If they have two kids with medical needs and can't survive at under $100,000 a year, that exceeds our budget. We can say, 'Brilliant application. This exceeds our budget, but we're going to recommend you to somebody who might be looking for you. Wish we could hire you, but we can't pay you anywhere close to that much. We're so sorry.' No need for either of us to spend any more time there."

"Ooohh..."

"We *do* want to ask about salary, to be sure our needs are aligned. Asking the question this way makes it safe to answer and satisfies the need for mutual purpose."

Matt grinned. "I love that."

"The rest of this looks wonderful, though." Alexandra handed the laptop back. "Post that job application, and I think we'll find a winner."

"Question..." Matt said. "What should I do with all these stacks of resumes I've already requested for other openings?"

"Send the interview questions to *all* of them," she told him. "Don't even look at the resumes. Just use their contact information. We know they're all interested, so give them all a chance."

"Even the terrible resumes?"

"Even those. We don't care if they can write the best resume. We're not hiring them to write. We're hiring them to fix machines."

"But a crisp resume shows attention to detail," Matt reminded her.

Alexandra hemmed and hawed a little. "Eh.... In reality, writing and engineering are completely different skill sets. They use different parts of the brain. If you need an engineer who pays attention to detail, then give them an *engineering* challenge that requires attention to detail. I mean, painting the Mona Lisa requires attention to detail, too, but if you search for the best engineer by looking at painting skills..." Alexandra started to laugh. "...you'll probably get a lousy engineer."

Matt laughed and threw his hands in the air. "Okay, you win."

"This system does work," Alexandra reassured him. "You just have to be patient with it, because it takes a while, especially in a tight job market, to find the right people."

Matt threw together a page on their website and blew the trumpet on job forums. Because they'd set up hurdles for applicants to jump through, they didn't get many applicants at first.

In fact, they didn't get any.

Matt started to grow nervous. He dragged himself to Jeffrey's office.

"Hey, Mr. Jackson, we're agile, right? It's been almost two weeks, and *nobody* has applied. I feel like we've made this application too hard."

Jeffrey sagged and made a note for himself. "Let me talk to Alexandra about it. I'll get back to you tomorrow."

But the next day, three applications were sitting in Matt's inbox. When Jeffrey and Alexandra arrived to discuss the job opening, Matt beamed at them.

"Guys, guys! You need to see this application. It's *gorgeous*."

Alexandra and Jeffrey rushed to read over his shoulder.

"This guy went to MIT," Matt gushed. "He wants to become an engineering manager, but he needs more hands-on experience. He works part time at a small business nearby and is looking for another part-time gig."

"Wow! That's perfect."

Jeffrey skimmed the technical questions. "His answers look like works of art. The depth of understanding... The conciseness, and yet the brilliant, intricate completeness of his answers is astonishing."

Jeffrey turned to Alexandra, confused. "I don't understand. Why the sudden flow of applicants *now*?"

Matt answered for her. "Well, the reason people weren't applying, it turns out, was because it *was* working. People were going out and learning about GooCrew like we asked them to. They were reading the things we asked them to read. And they were assembling the small projects we asked for. We don't have many applicants, but they're knocking it out of the park."

Alexandra smiled, delighted at their success. "That's how it should work. The people who come, look, and can't cut it self-select and drop out of the process."

CAPABILITY - Moneyball Talent

Matt spun around in his chair. "Surprisingly, his desired salary is lower than our budget. What should we do?"

"We have options," Alexandra replied. "If you're planning on paying someone $20/hr, and they come hoping for $15, it allows you to do something cool. You're going to hire them at $15."

Matt blanched. "How is that cool?"

Alexandra's eyed twinkled. "Because *then* you're going to *quickly* give them opportunities to earn raises to what you were planning on spending on them in the first place. They'll feel like the most amazing person in the world. It also helps them in the future, because they can say on their resume, 'I did so well, they gave me a 25% raise in six months.' "

Matt lit up. "Oh, wow!"

"In other words, this is a non-selfish way of working with people, being generous in taking care of them."

"I love that," Jeffrey said.

Matt turned back to his computer. "I'm going to set up an interview."

SUMMARY

- One unexpected thing that reinforces bad leadership is traditional hiring. You strengthen a Hands-Off Leadership culture by hiring people who will thrive in it.

- Instead of hiring for experience, look for undervalued, underappreciated people with potential.

- Look for applicants with intelligence, initiative, and teachability. People with these attributes can master almost anything.

WEEK SIX

ACTION: Transform Your Hiring Process

Change your hiring process to the Moneyball standard. Add this procedure to your Company Handbook:

- *Decide what skills and attributes are really needed. Keep it short.*
- *Do not wade through resumes anymore.*
- *Create self-sorting interview questions that reveal their initiative, skill level, and potential.*
- *Give applicants a tiny chunk of work and see how they handle it.*
- *Ask the 3-part salary question described in the chapter.*
- *Post your first position on your website for people to start self-recruiting.*
- *Once they pass the online interview, begin internal, face-to-face interviews as usual. Focus on increasingly difficult skills questions and watch for indicators that they will support a Hands-Off Leadership culture.*

CAPABILITY – Moneyball Talent

LEADERSHIP SCORECARD

NAME: Jeffrey Jackson

MY OVERALL SCORE: 2.4

WEEK SIX

4	**STEP AWAY** SUPPORT To Unleash Excellence	- Arnold asked for a raise (initiative) - Matt drove the new hiring process to find a great new person
3	**STEP BACK** COACH To Inspire Ownership	- Included Arnold's supervisor in Turnaround discussion. Facilitated but let supervisor provide most feedback - Brainstormed new hiring questions with Matt to measure initiative, etc. - Invited Clara to run weekly team meeting and coached her
2	**STEP BESIDE** TRAIN To Build Capability	- Gave $5 to Tickerman, apologized
1	**STEP UP** TELL To Ensure Clarity	
0	**STEP IN** TAKE OVER To Create Stability	- Pushed Tickerman away during flooding emergency (should have stepped Beside or Back unless out of control) - Pushed Alexandra away during flood emergency

LEVEL FOUR:
FOCUS

Where everyone starts to have too many good ideas

MPAs
MOST PROFITABLE ACTIVITIES

Soon, new employees trickled in. Tickerman got along famously with his new partner. Even during breaks, they were inseparable. The bay workers affectionately dubbed them Tick and Tock.

In the office, Clara recruited an intern. He hated coffee. It was just as well, because everyone in the department seemed to need coffee a little less.

For a few weeks, things ran beautifully.

Then the sheriff came.

When Jeffrey got the news, he was running numbers.

Alexandra wandered into the room after a morning walk-through of the departments. Jeffrey stared at his computer screen helplessly.

"Wow, you look glum," she said, sitting down next to him. "What's going on?"

"You remember how Heart wanted me to fix excess overtime?"

"Yes."

Jeffrey glowered at his computer. "No matter what we've tried—training better, hiring extra help—actual overtime charged for the most recent payroll period is still too high."

"By how much?"

Jeffrey scooted his laptop across the desk so she could see. "We've been at 20%. It only went down to 15."

Just then, Clara stomped in. "We've been served."

Jeffrey stood. "*What!?*"

Clara handed him an envelope. "The community is suing over odor control. They think we stink."

"You kind of do," Alexandra admitted. "I don't notice it as much now that I've been here a while. But I wouldn't want to live downwind of you."

"Maybe it's just the lake," Jeffrey said hopefully.

Clara gave Jeffrey a sidelong look. "You know better."

Jeffrey exhaled, feeling overwhelmed. "What can we do?"

"The sheriff recommends resolving it before we're taken to court," Clara answered. "If we can 'significantly reduce' the problem, the local HOAs are willing to drop their case."

Jeffrey called his team in for a meeting. "Guys, we've just received a citation for foul odor. The community complained."

Aaron objected immediately. "I'd love to fix it, but there's no way. We're broke, exhausted, and overcommitted. We just replaced most of the pipes in the bay. While the incinerator was down, we fell massively behind. The process team just rearranged entire floor, which we're getting used to. We're also swimming in dying machinery. If we have extra cash floating around, please buy new forklift batteries, not air freshener."

"This isn't optional," Jeffrey sighed.

Aaron folded his arms. "Then whatever treatment, installation, or extra processing you have in mind is going to cost more overtime."

FOCUS - Most Profitable Activities

Jeffrey grimaced and looked around for an ally. "Roxanne, what are your thoughts?"

Roxanne hesitated. "Well, there are two layers to this problem. The first is to fix whatever buildup is causing odor. The second is to resolve whatever process problem is causing build-up. And Aaron's right; both steps will involve some labor."

Jeffrey slapped a printout on the table in frustration. "These are our hours from the last two months. We're 22% over budget on payroll *every week*. If you need more time to fix the odor issue, fine, but total hours *have* to drop. You need to abandon 15% of your workload somehow."

Aaron smiled cheerfully. "Sure. Which waste shipments would you like me to not process?"

Jeffrey turned to Alexandra. "Help."

Alexandra had been leaning back in her chair, watching. Now she dove in with an appetite.

"Your needs aren't mutually exclusive," she said. "But you need focus. Razor sharp focus. You are all showing initiative, pitching in, working hard. And we're starting to have a wonderful problem. You guys are having too many good ideas."

Everyone laughed.

"No, I'm serious," Alexandra continued. "Over the last couple weeks, I've listened to each of you bring multiple brilliant ideas to Jeffrey during 1-on-1's. It's amazing to watch. But the downside is that you will always have more amazing ideas than you have time for. New ideas are also more fun, so if you're not careful, they can come at the expense of your core duties."

"That's fair," Roxanne agreed sadly.

"Jeffrey is right," Alexandra continued. "You need to shave 15-20% off your workload. Preferably a little more. You should always have enough wiggle room to handle a crisis like this."

Roxanne, Clara, and Aaron all glanced at each other in a look of shared pain.

"How?" Clara finally asked.

"Let me tell you a story. Right before I became a consultant, I worked as a Director of Sales. But I also had a handful of secretarial duties because it was a small office. The boss wanted everyone to pitch in."

Everyone nodded. The story was familiar enough.

"One day," Alexandra continued, "he asked me to replace a dead light bulb in the bathroom. A week went by, two weeks, three weeks…. And I didn't do it. He got increasingly frustrated with me."

The team started to look confused.

"Why didn't you just change the stupid light bulb?" Bob asked.

"Because I was responsible for producing bids on multimillion dollar contracts," she explained slowly. "I was working 60 or 70 hours most weeks. I hadn't replaced the light bulb because frankly, I had to choose. I could respond to a sales email, or fix the bathroom. The bathroom was functional, so I didn't worry about it. "

Bob nodded. "Fair enough."

Alexandra glanced at Clara. "Unfortunately, my boss thought I was trying to avoid work. He called me into his office one day for our 1-on-1, and he had this list of *every* little thing he'd ever assigned me. He went over it one thing at a time. It was a guilt fest. It was stressful. And he started doing it *every week*."

"Oh, gosh," Clara muttered under her breath.

"So I said, 'Look, these are all the things I *like* doing. I like emptying trash, believe it or not. I like sweeping. I like closing $100,000 contracts. I like programming, coaching, writing sales copy. I like fixing broken printers. I like creating leaders. I like designing letterhead.' "

Alexandra took a deep breath. "Then I said, 'But I can't do all those. To do *all* of those things, I'd have to clone myself twice over. So the question becomes: *with a limited company resource of only one me, where should I be focusing my energy?*' " Alexandra looked around. "Does that principle make sense?"

"Yeah," Clara replied. "It's a capacity thing."

"Yes," Alexandra reinforced. "You have limited capacity. So what actions can you focus on to give the greatest return to your company? Those things are your Most Profitable Activities, or MPAs."

"Makes sense," Clara said.

FOCUS – Most Profitable Activities

"Great. Let's apply this principle." Alexandra leaned back in her chair. "Clara, your primary responsibility is to produce our legal compliance publication. Your assistants do data mining, but you're the licensed professional who pulls it all together at the end. You're the only person who can do that. How much would it cost to replace you, doing *that* work?"

Clara hesitated. "Well, with my level of experience and expertise... If you could even find somebody to replace me, it'd be $600 an hour, at least."

"Great, $600. That's your MPA. You don't have marketing experience, do you?"

"No."

Alexandra raised her eyebrows. "I heard you're interested in creating email campaigns, lobbying for legislation that's both responsible and economically favorable."

Clara brightened. "That's correct."

"How much would it cost us to hire someone else to send those email campaigns?"

"Mmm... $20 an hour," Clara said, starting to sag a little.

Delicately, Alexandra delivered the fatal blow. "Does it make any sense for us to have a $600/hr person doing $20/hr work?"

Clara withered. "No, I guess not. It just sounded like fun... I was excited to do it."

Alexandra nodded. "Back to you, Jeff."

"Thanks for helping us get past that road block, Alex," Jeffrey told her. He looked at Clara, who seemed discouraged, and tried to think of what to say next. His mind felt blank. He grasped at the principles Alexandra had taught them, and suddenly remembered mutual empathy.

Jeffrey smiled encouragingly at Clara. "I feel your pain there. There are lots of things that are fun, and good. But we're strapped to the gills. You're used to working crazy hours, but it's not good for you. Now that we've loosened the pressure by hiring help, do you want to swamp yourself again with non-vital projects?"

Clara laughed, relaxing. "No, I don't."

WEEK EIGHT

"Good," Jeffrey said with a smile. "We need you fresh. And we like you happy."

Jeffrey turned and wrote on their whiteboard.

MPAs = Most Profitable Activities
KPIs = Key Performance Indicators

"Even the most disciplined employees get distracted," Jeffrey said. "So we need Key Performance Indicators to measure our MPAs. We're already meeting regularly. Reporting on MPAs might be a more effective way of checking into team meetings. From now on, say, 'My KPI's are XYZ, and these are my stats for the week.' How do you all feel about that?"

Matt raised his hand. "What makes for a good KPI?"

"Something we can measure. Something that keeps us focused on what matters most in our zones. For example, 'How many barrels do we process per day? What's our turnover?' Those are KPIs."

WHAT WE MEASURE IMPROVES

"Jeffrey's concern about overtime doesn't only apply to us," Bob challenged. "How can we get the people we supervise to focus, too? Especially when we're not supposed to boss them around."

Jeffrey nodded, grateful for the question. "The principle is simple: *What we measure improves*. If they know you're going to ask about KPIs, they'll start preparing for that question. Whatever you keep asking about is what they'll focus on. This is how you influence change as a leader. Focus happens by *asking*, not by telling."

Roxanne leaned forward. "So we should assess KPI's during 1-on-1's, too?"

"Absolutely," Jeffrey replied. "You're already doing an assessment, so you need to make sure you're asking about the *right things*. Whatever we measure will improve, so whatever we measure better match MPAs. If they don't, we're *asking* them to *not* focus on the thing we need most from them."

FOCUS - Most Profitable Activities

Aaron laughed. "Ask about light bulbs; they'll focus on light bulbs—at the expense of million-dollar contracts."

"Exactly."

Roxanne frowned. "I thought 1-on-1's were friendly mentoring sessions."

"Good. That's the goal," Jeffrey assured her. "We do *need* numbers. But I don't *only* ask for numbers like a soulless robot."

Roxanne nodded.

"Remember mutual empathy," Alexandra suggested. "When you track KPI's, people will fall short sometimes. So be prepared to listen and encourage. Ask questions, coach, and train as needed. Encouragement is especially important. No matter how nice we are, we can't just correct people all the time."

Bob grimaced. "When I'm struggling with something, I *hate* it when people come up to me and say, Good job, Bob! You should feel good about yourself! You're super-duper!"

Jeffrey laughed. "For sure. *That kind* of feedback, I call praise, and it's destructive. It leaves both the speaker and the people who hear it feeling slightly sleazy because there's no real data."

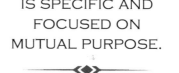

PRAISE IS GENERAL AND FOCUSED ON PERSONALITIES.

ENCOURAGEMENT IS SPECIFIC AND FOCUSED ON MUTUAL PURPOSE.

Bob was intrigued. "What kind of data do we want to give?"

"Encouragement. Praise is general and focused on personalities. Encouragement is specific and focused on mutual purposes. There is a difference between saying, 'You're smart,' which is a personality compliment and saying 'I was impressed with the way you paid attention to those details. You're really owning this. Thank you.' That's encouragement."

"I love that," Matt said.

Jeffrey smiled. "Don't praise people for just following orders, either. If our goal is to create leaders, we can't just reward *the tasks*. Encourage behavior that matches principles of great leadership. Like this:"

Jeffrey turned towards Clara. "Clara, I love the *initiative* you showed on the Zone 3 project."

Clara blushed happily.

Jeffrey turned to Bob. "Or I can say, 'Bob, thank you for being *accountable* when we realized there was a problem with Methuselah. Your example in humility inspired your team to be accountable, too. They are more responsive to all of us, and we've noticed. We're looking forward to Methuselah 2.0."

Bob blinked. "You're saying thank you? Or just giving an example?"

"No, I really mean it." Jeffrey insisted. "Thank you for being a great leader to your team. It impacts all of us."

Bob sat stunned in his chair, too surprised to even respond.

Watching him, Jeffrey remembered the thank you note still sitting in his own suit jacket. He understood Bob's silence. It was possible no one had ever told Bob thank you before. Wanting to let Bob savor that feeling without embarrassing him, Jeffrey moved on.

"So, team," Jeffrey said, smiling. "We have a problem: GooCrew needs someone to scrub and someone to identify the source of odor. Whose MPAs are these?"

Aaron sat quietly, afraid to answer, but Roxanne lit up.

"Air scrubbing isn't an MPA for any of us," she pointed out. "Let's look for a specialist."

Jeffrey nodded. "That's a great point. Thank you for championing that. Who could source the odor for us?"

"You know," Aaron suddenly realized. "Tick and Tock would probably love the challenge. Fixing things is their MPA."

"Perfect. Do they have the right kind of expertise?" Jeffrey asked.

"They have noses," Aaron laughed, "but they do lack chemical understanding. We have a lab technician downstairs, though. Together, I bet they could find the source."

FOCUS – Most Profitable Activities

> **SUMMARY**
>
> - Once workers start taking initiative, they start having too many good ideas. Stay focused by identifying MPAs.
>
> - MPAs (Most Profitable Activities) are work activities that give the greatest return for the time spent.
>
> - KPIs (Key Performance Indicators) are simple measures of MPAs.
>
> - Give encouragement that reinforces the principles of Hands-Off Leadership.

ACTION: Discover Your Team MPAs

Add "MPA Exercise" to your next team meeting agenda. Have everyone identify the activities they spend the most time doing. Then put estimated $/hr values for the company to hire each action out. Star each person's top two items. These are your MPAs.

Now add these MPAs to your Zone Chart. Flag each one with an asterisk. Make sure everyone can see them.

Finally, choose KPIs to match your MPAs. Certify: "How do we know this is a good KPI?" Review KPIs each week during 1-on-1's.

MULTIPURPOSING

LET YOUR DRAGONS SLAY EACH OTHER

Within a few days, Jeffrey realized MPAs weren't enough. People were *trying* to focus. Jeffrey's team was suddenly aware of their MPAs, but the important things always seemed to be at the mercy of the urgent things. Frustration was starting to build because people couldn't even *get* to their MPAs.

After discussing the problem with Alexandra, Jeffrey called another meeting.

When everyone entered the conference room, most of the table was covered with blank sticky notes. A fresh marker sat at each seat. Alexandra sat at the back of the room, watching silently.

Jeffrey stood mysteriously at the table and didn't answer questions until everyone was present. "Okay team, you've been working hard to focus, but everything is working against you. Since you want to focus on your MPAs, it's time to remove the lightbulb tasks that are cluttering your task list. Ready? Everyone grab a marker."

They did. Clara looked especially excited.

"We need to see all the tasks, threats, and opportunities we're facing right now," Jeffrey said. "Put each burning issue on a red sticky note. Red includes problems we don't yet have an answer for. Green is for golden opportunities that we've been wanting to seize. Things like Roxanne's contracting idea. Yellow are for projects we're currently working on that take your time. Ready? Go."

They burst into chatter. For the next ten minutes, they brainstormed.

Eventually, Bob stepped back with a look of satisfaction. "I think that just about covers it. Now what?"

"Now we let your dragons slay each other," Jeffrey said, grinning. "Go ahead and take a seat. This will take a few minutes to explain."

They pulled out their chairs. Jeffrey kept his marker close.

"There's an old legend about two armies," he said. "They had a big battle, and the smaller army beat the larger army. The larger army surrendered. Suddenly, this small army had *massive* numbers of prisoners. They were hard to guard. They didn't have a place to put them."

Jeffrey wrote "Loose prisoners are dangerous" on a red sticky note. Then he wrote "24/7 guard duty" on a yellow one.

"They retreated to their home city with prisoners in tow. The battle had been fought over this city, which was lush and beautiful. However, it was also extremely vulnerable, because it didn't have city walls."

Taking a green sticky note, Jeffrey wrote, "City walls."

"Why are you putting that on a green sticky note?" Roxanne interjected. "That's a problem."

"Because city walls are a luxury," Jeffrey explained. "It could be red, too. It doesn't matter which sticky note they're on. You'll see why in a minute."

"Okay." Roxanne settled back into her seat with a shrug.

"At some point, one of the underdogs looked around and said, 'Wait a minute. These three problems are the solution! Why not let the prisoners build us a city wall? It's easier to guard them when they're working, it creates the prison, and it protects our city from future invasion."

"Is that ethical?" Clara asked.

Jeffrey nodded. "This was thousands of years ago. In the days of tribal wars, for a small army just trying to protect their families, it served them well. When the prisoners had fortified their city to the point that the small army was safe forever, they let the prisoners go."

"Huh," Clara said softly, surprised and touched.

"It's the principle that matters." Jeffrey stacked the three sticky notes together and held them up. "Do you see how the burning issue, the resource drain, and the wish list item all came together to form a solution? They had three dragons, and instead of trying to tackle each one individually, they put them to work against each other."

Matt laughed. "Wow, that's brilliant."

Jeffrey grinned. "This is called multipurposing."

"You mean multitasking?"

Jeffrey shook his head. "No. Multitasking is just *switch-tasking*. You pick one thing up and work on it, then put it down before it's finished to keep something else from boiling over. Very inefficient. This is different. Multi*purposing* means feeding three birds with one seed."

> Great leaders find connections, even between things that look like opposites. This skill is sometimes called *integrative thinking*. To learn more, read *The Seasoned Executive's Decision-Making Style*, a Harvard Business Review article by Brousseau, Driver, Hourihan, and Larsson.

Jeffrey gestured to their tableful of problems. "These kinds of solutions swirl around us all the time. But they're hard to see, because they usually look like total opposites."

Aaron leaned on the table, surveying their workload eagerly. "So you want us to look and see which items we can pair up."

MULTIPURPOSING MEANS FEEDING THREE BIRDS WITH ONE SEED

"Exactly. The principle is 'Three wins and it's in.' Three or more of anything is a match. It can be three reds, two greens and a red, two yellows and a green. If you can find one project that resolve three different, unrelated things—speeds them up, improves, increases, resolves, etc.—then it's a good candidate to focus on."

They didn't need further prodding. Everyone jumped to their feet and started looking for connections.

"What about making maps, transporting waste, and debugging Methuselah?" Bob asked.

"Those are different steps of the same project, not separate things," replied Aaron. "Let's relabel everything to 'processing waste,' and put all those vital steps together."

"Well, it's processing *Heart's* waste. Other waste is a different project."

"True. Good catch."

Jeffrey folded his arms and surveyed the pile. "That's a lot of tasks. Let's start with the obvious ones. Are there any other tasks you see that we cannot ignore without failing our zone or running afoul of the law?"

"Yeah," Roxanne said. "We haven't fixed that odor yet."

Everyone sagged as Jeffrey moved *Odor Problem* to the whiteboard.

"Do we *have* to?" Bob sighed. "The HOAs are a bunch of oversensitive ninnies."

"Yeah, we got used to the smell, and we're a *lot* closer," Aaron complained. "That will chew up more of our inadequate budget."

CREATIVITY
IS JUST
CONNECTING
THINGS.

– STEVE JOBS

"Those are problems, but it doesn't mean we reject it," Jeffrey reminded them. "We're here to look for connections. Does the odor problem connect to anything else on here?"

"I suppose... We do need an influx of cash before we can install the equipment that will prevent odor from recurring," Aaron realized. "Before we're

FOCUS – Let Your Dragons Slay Each Other

even *capable* of responding to that legal threat, we need cash from somewhere."

"Roxanne's proposal..." Aaron mused. "That's about contracting out our services, right? That's a source of cash."

"Eventually," Roxanne said, embarrassed. "It would be cool, but it chews up too many resources up front. We should probably let it go."

As Matt went to put it in the bin, Bob suddenly looked up. "No, wait! That connects everything we've been working on."

"What do you mean?" Roxanne asked.

Bob grew excited. "You specifically asked me to include a feature that lets you run calculations on the data. We're almost done coding that feature. That's just one thing."

Bob looked around the table and started snatching up sticky notes. "Look at everything we've slaved for these past couple months. Process improvement, Methuselah 2.0... Then we have these problems over here: Aaron's equipment needs, unused trucker bandwidth. These yellow notes, too... Clara is *already* spending her time zoning things out, Roxanne *already* has transportation routes mapped. If you include Rocky's proposal..." Bob took the sticky note from Aaron, added it to the pile, and held them up. "That's eight sticky notes."

Jeffrey moved Bob's stack of sticky notes to the very top, circled it, and wrote:

Project Idea: Prepare to Scale

———<◆>———

An hour later, after intense discussion, the GooCrew team had a core set of projects. Some of them connected 4 or 5 deep. Everyone was smiling, and ready for a break.

Together, they taped the sticky notes to the whiteboard. Jeffrey circled them with a marker and wrote *Active Projects.* Then he glanced back at the team.

"What do we do with all the others?" Clara asked, gesturing to the leftovers. Scattered all around them were the misfits. Tasks, projects, and problems in one's and two's.

WEEK EIGHT

211

Jeffrey smiled. "We'll get to that. For now, everyone needs a break. There are sandwiches in the break room. Help yourselves. We'll reconvene in an hour."

> **SUMMARY**
>
> - "Multipurposing" means meeting more than one need with a single solution. It is *not* multitasking.
> - Improve focus by making connections to combine projects, ideas, and problems into single solutions.
> - If something meets three critical needs at once, it's usually a good idea to do it.

ACTION: Do the Multipurposing Exercise

Throw all your current problems and opportunities together on the table using sticky notes. Post them where you can leave them up for a week or more. Now start looking for connections like Jeffrey's team did. Remember "three wins and it's in." What connections did you make? Don't take these sticky notes down yet—you will need them in the next chapter.

SAYING NO

...TO A THOUSAND THINGS

When they returned from their break, four short boxes sat on the table.

"Here comes the painful part," Jeffrey warned. "It's time to shoot some of these pet projects."

This drew a cry of alarm from around the circle.

"This is why we came," Jeffrey reminded them, pointing at the table. "You needed to cut the fat and lose 20% of your workload. That's the fat."

"That's more than 20%," Clara objected.

Aaron looked over the remaining items, suddenly anxious. "I'm *not* comfortable just setting all these aside and not doing any of them."

"Good. You shouldn't. I'm just going to make it easier to say no. This next part was Alexandra's idea, so I've asked her to introduce it."

Alexandra took the floor and gestured to the boxes. "Meet my friends: Bernie, Parker, Harry Potter, and Humpty Dumpty.'

They laughed.

WEEK EIGHT

"Explain," prodded Matt.

"When you have work in progress, it's like a kitty cat," Alexandra quipped. "One kitty is an asset, but when you have 100 you get chaos. So before committing to something, ask yourself, 'How does this make life better for us and our customers?' When you have too much going on, you reach a point where adding something new doesn't make things better."

Alexandra picked up one of the sticky notes. "These problems aren't equally important. Some you're going to trash, some you want to hold on to and see if they mature. These are four tools you can use to say no when saying no is painful. First, we have the burn box."

Alexandra took a marker and wrote "burn box" on the first box. "Have you ever dejunked your home," she said, "and thrown out some special tool because you haven't used it in years, only to need it desperately a week later?"

Bob snorted. "Story of my life."

"That's why some people are pack rats. It's hard to let go of things when you aren't sure if you'll need it or not." Alexandra tapped the burn box. "The burn box helps you strike a balance between pack rat and dejunking things you really do need."

"How's it work?"

"When you think you *probably* don't need something anymore, but you're not *quite* sure, you put it in the burn box. Then you ignore it. Add other things as they come up. By the time the burn box is full, the things on the bottom probably don't matter anymore. If you haven't pulled them back out by now, chances are high you'll never need them."

"So you empty the bin?" Roxanne guessed.

"No." Alexandra grinned and held up a finger. "You only trash the bottom half."

Matt's jaw dropped. "Cool!"

Alexandra smiled. "This works wonders for reducing stress. Keep a box under your desk that you can toss things in: paperwork, tools, coupons, business cards, etc. You decide how often you feel like dumping."

"What about for bulkier items like computer parts and old monitors?" Bob asked.

She shrugged. "Have two bins and rotate which is on top."

Alexandra gestured to the table. "Now, you guys decide. Which of these do you think are *probably* okay to discard? Remember, we can pull them back out at any time if it becomes important."

After the team agreed which items were safe to toss, Alexandra moved to the second box. On this one, she wrote, *Parking List*.

"What goes in there?" Aaron asked.

"Things that are important, but don't align with other needs yet. This is also where you put things you'd love to do and are saving for later. A 'someday maybe' list."

"We're *not* going to act on them," she continued. "because they aren't emergencies yet. But we want visibility. So we'll keep them next to the whiteboard, and wait until we find connections where they mesh brilliantly."

Clara and Aaron started picking through the sticky notes and putting important ones in the parking list box.

"It's a trove of ideas you can draw from at any time," Alexandra summarized. "Every couple of months, you can check to see if there's anything you want to revive. As items age, it will become obvious whether they ought to be moved up to active projects or down to the burn box."

Everyone around the circle quickly added the items they cared about to the box.

"I still want to hear about Harry Potter and Humpty Dumpty," Matt laughed.

Alexandra smiled and moved to box number three. She drew a lightning bolt for fun and then wrote *Intentionally Ignore*.

"There are more *important* things to do," she said, "than you will ever be humanly capable of. And sometimes, to give yourself permission to focus on the

> INNOVATION IS SAYING NO TO A THOUSAND THINGS.
>
> – STEVE JOBS

crucial few, you have to choose which responsibilities you are going to willfully ignore...

"J.K. Rowling gets credit for this idea. She said, 'People ask me all the time, 'How did you do it? How did you write a book and raise a kid at the same time?' Truth is, I didn't do housework for two years. I am not supermom. And living in, um, squalor.... That was the answer.' "[14]

Everyone laughed.

Alexandra leaned forward. "No, seriously. This is a powerful idea."

"How is it different from the parking list?" Matt asked.

"The parking list helps us set aside big new ideas. This is different. This is a more permanent list of responsibilities you will always have. These are things you *should* do, and are going to ignore anyway to make room for things you love more. J. K. Rowling *should* have kept a clean house. That's generally very important. But something infinitely more precious was at stake. She couldn't have Harry Potter *and* a clean house. So she chose."

"What's on your list?"

"Lightbulbs."

While they laughed, Alexandra pulled up a list on her phone.

"Since you asked nicely... My work list includes networking events, formatting documents so they look nice, solo lunch breaks, formal sales pitches. I replace long email replies with phone calls. Having a personal list is important too. My personal list says fashion, dishes, birthday cards. Each of those was an important burden that I felt strongly about but had to let go of to find balance. I mean, I still wear clothes, but never curl my hair. Does that make sense?"

"How do you avoid dishes?" Clara wondered.

Alexandra laughed. "Paper plates. I *hate* paper plates. But I love having an extra three hours every week. I still do about one load a week, but that's it. When I look at the few unwashed dish-

---

[14] From transcript of an interview with J.K. Rowling: (28 December 2001) *Harry Potter and Me* [BBC Christmas Special, British Version].

es in the sink, they don't bother me anymore. I feel a wonderful sense of liberation and satisfaction because I *know what I'm getting instead.*"

Clara frowned. "Eh... I still think that's kind of gross."

Alexandra turned gentle eyes toward Clara.

FOUR WAYS TO SAY NO

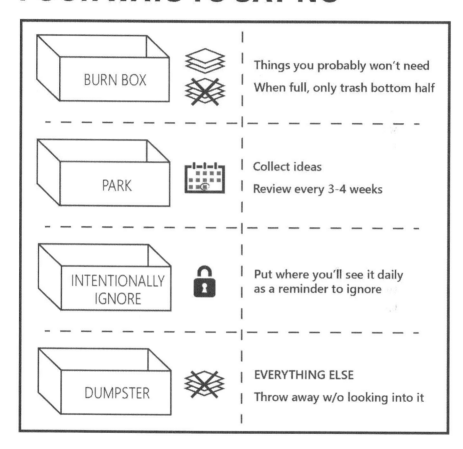

"I believe everyone has something in life they are meant to do," Alexandra said quietly. "Their own personal Harry Potter. But there are always things begging for our attention, burned out lightbulbs accusing us of being irresponsible. You don't have to ignore your dishes, Clara. Look for the duties that drain *you*, and remember that you are worth more than that pile of dirty whatever-it-is. Divert your resources away from things you only do so others won't judge you. Invest in what you really believe in."

Alexandra tapped on the box. "That's all this box is here for. It gives you permission to do what makes you happy. Both personally and as a team."

"Huh." Matt reached over, grabbed a few sticky notes, and tossed them in the box. "Speaking of things we only do so others won't judge us... We don't need to repaint our parking lot. That's silly."

Jeffrey glanced at his watch.

"I'll have to leave soon," he said. "Can you quickly explain the last box?"

"Sure," Alexandra said brightly. She wrote *The Dumpster* on the final box, and then took *all* the remaining sticky notes and put them inside, face down.

Aaron started to laugh nervously. "Wait, what are you doing?"

Alexandra flashed a mischievous grin. "When I was a teenager, my parents made me clean out the garage. I wasn't happy about it. They rented a dumpster and told me to get to work."

She chuckled and shook her head. "I remember looking around and thinking. *This is all junk.* I looked at the garage... I looked at the dumpster... and the solution was obvious. After separating out the few things that mattered, I took *everything* else and threw it away."

"No way!" Aaron gasped.

Matt laughed hysterically.

Alexandra nodded. "When I told my father I was done, he came to see. The moment he saw the garage, his jaw dropped. I saw him about to panic, so I said, 'If you can name anything I threw away, I will personally jump in that dumpster and pull it back out.' "

Roxanne eyed the box. "Well, I can remember some of the things you put in there, but I don't particularly care about any of them."

Alexandra grinned. "Exactly. Once you've pulled out what matters, the rest *doesn't* matter."

Bob frowned. "I don't know... that seems wasteful to me."

"Oh, it wasn't a waste. We found something very important during that purge."

"What?"

FOCUS - ...To a Thousand Things

"A box full of C-4 plastic explosives and dynamite. Enough to literally blow up the block. A bomb disposal team came to remove them. It was very exciting."[15]

The room went dead silent.

"Um," Jeffrey finally asked. "Why did you have explosives in your garage?"

"They were left over from one of my father's early business ventures," she explained. "Here's the point: Simplicity is a powerful way to manage risk. Sometimes there are dangers lurking that you can't see until you clear away the junk."

> **SUMMARY**
>
> - When examining open projects and tasks, ask, "How does this make life better for us and our customers?"
>
> - Use burn boxes, parking lists, intentionally ignore lists, and dumpsters to make it easier to say no.

ACTION: Implement Simplicity

AS A TEAM: Assemble a tiger team to decide which projects to set aside so you can focus on what matters most.

PERSONALLY: Pick one of the tools in this chapter and Implement it. If you choose burn box, find a box and a convenient place for it. Under your desk is usually fine. If you choose the Intentionally Ignore list, take 5 minutes, brainstorm what you want to ignore, and put it where you'll see it daily. For the first few weeks, your list will change quite a bit. That's normal.

---

[15] This is a true story from my childhood. In the early 1960's, my father did research on mining methods. When the research was done, they had various explosives left over—TNT, dynamite, blasting caps, Primacord, and 6 large blocks of C-4. The box lay forgotten in our garage for a decade.

ACTION: Implement a Quick Business Case (QBC)

Just saying "no" isn't enough. You also need to stop saying "yes" to the wrong new things. The Quick Business Case lets you self-certify before bringing an idea to the team. This is what Roxanne did on p. 81.

Put together a QBC template with questions like these:

- What's the problem? What's your solution?
- How does this support our thematic goal? Is it a distraction?
- What will it cost in time, money, and other resources?
- What's the impact if we ignore it?
- What are the risks? What are the benefits?
- Who will build it? Who has to manage and support it afterward?
- What are the potential profits? Can you prove it with Actual Data?

It should only take 10 minutes to fill out. If that feels like too much work, the idea is *obviously* not important enough to pursue.

Make the QBC available to everyone in the company, from janitors to executives. Everyone should be using it before presenting new ideas to the team, including the CEO.

FOCUS - ...To a Thousand Things

LEADERSHIP SCORECARD

NAME: Jeffrey Jackson

MY OVERALL SCORE: 2.7

4	**STEP AWAY** SUPPORT To Unleash Excellence	- Bob identified new master goal: Prepare to Scale - Team ran with their own solutions on odor control crisis, temporary fix in place
3	**STEP BACK** COACH To Inspire Ownership	- Invited Alexandra to run meeting to present her "boxes" Focus idea - Challenged team to solve odor problem
2	**STEP BESIDE** TRAIN To Build Capability	- Trained MPA exercise with team - Trained team on Multipurposing
1	**STEP UP** TELL To Ensure Clarity	- Held team accountable to 20% workload reduction. Established boundary and then Stepped Back so they could choose specifics
0	**STEP IN** TAKE OVER To Create Stability	

WEEK EIGHT

221

LEVEL FIVE
===

VISION

Aligning Action

MISSION

EVERY SHIP NEEDS A COMPASS

"What's GooCrew's mission statement?"

"I dunno. It's on a plaque downstairs."

"Right. But what does it say?"

Jeffrey set down the stack of papers he was reading and turned to Alexandra. "Does it matter? It's just mumbo jumbo to make the big people feel good."

"If you don't know your mission, how do you know where you're headed?"

Jeffrey swiveled in his chair. "What we have to do will never change. Not even if we bedazzle our work with fancy words and a pretty logo. We're garbage collectors, Alexandra. We're in the ground *below* garbage collectors. We're like cockroaches or dung beetles. People hand their worst trash to us, and we make it disappear."

Alexandra pointed at him. "*Exactly*. Did you know your workers are embarrassed to work here?"

Jeffrey paused. He blinked. "Oh."

"I'm not suggesting we cover cockroaches with glitter. You're not demigods of Olympus come the save the world. But you're not cockroaches either. You perform a *very* important service that helps keep our planet clean and safe. Why not help your workers take pride in the work they do?

"How?"

"I think your mission statement is a good place to start."

Jeffrey grimaced. "I don't have the time."

Alexandra laughed. "No, don't decide from your throne. Who are the stakeholders here?"

The intercom sputtered into life. Jeffrey's voice echoed across the loading bay and every building across GooCrew's campus.

"Hey team," Jeffrey said. "We are updating the GooCrew mission statement for this region. If you want to help pick something fun and inspiring, come to the conference room tomorrow at 4:30. We'd love your input. *Anyone* who cares is welcome."

The next evening, Jeffrey muttered to himself as he locked his office door. Alexandra had insisted he attend the meeting, but he wasn't thrilled about it. He had a dozen matters more pressing and was frankly annoyed. At least there would be pizza.

On his way to the meeting, Jeffrey found a postal worker wandering through the halls, poking her head through one doorway, then wandering to the next door. She looked lost.

"Can I help you?" Jeffrey asked.

The woman spun around. She stared at Jeffrey's expensive suit and grew flustered. "I um, I came for the meeting? About the mission thing."

Jeffrey blinked. "But you don't... work here. How did you even find out about it?"

She reddened. "I'm sorry! I was in the lobby... They said anyone who cared... Oh, I knew it was silly. I'll just go."

"No, wait." Flabbergasted, Jeffrey stopped her before she could walk away. "I'm curious. Why do you care?"

VISION – Every Ship Needs a Compass

She hesitated. "Well... I've been delivering mail here for 22 years. Both my children worked here to save money for college. I was delivering mail yesterday when somebody made the announcement—that's how I heard about it. And thought, maybe *I* care."

She stared at the floor, preparing to leave again. "Plus it just sounded like fun. Didn't figure anyone would rightly ask me t'be part of something like that again. I don't know what I was thinking."

Jeffrey stared at her. Here he was—the manager with power to hire or fire, the one who held jobs of several dozen people in the palm of his hand—bored out of his mind. Did the *mother* of *old* employees care more about GooCrew than he did?

Embarrassment hit him like a clothesline, and he felt his priorities shift.

"Stakeholders.... I'll be darned." Jeffrey beckoned to her, starting to smile. "You're in exactly the right place. Come with me."

Altogether, thirteen people showed up. Some wore suits, others wore coveralls. They were delighted to find stacks of pizza waiting for them.

Jeffrey presented the postal worker as their guest of honor.

"Everyone, this is Elsa. She's here to represent our community. They should have a voice too. Give her a round of applause."

Elsa bumbled happily to a corner in the back and sat down. She was too embarrassed to take any pizza, but Tickerman loaded a plate up and passed it her way.

Alexandra had removed the plaque from the lobby. She passed it around. "Here's the mission statement you've been using."

It read,

> *Provide superior service, innovation, quality, and commitment while adhering to the laws of the jurisdictions in which the company operates, and at all times observing the highest ethical standards.*

It was followed by four paragraphs of vauge niceties. She passed it around.

"This is one of the worst mission statements I've ever seen... and so are all the others," she quipped. "Don't feel bad. This is pretty typical. But, wow... Can you smell the fear?"

Someone raised their hand. "If this is terrible, what are we looking for in a new mission statement?"

"First of all, it has to be *short*. No more than 12 words. Easy to remember. And it needs to give us a vivid, actionable picture of our reason for existing. It should inspire us. Why bother cleaning up trash before you chuck it? What is the heart and soul of what you're trying to do?"

She wrote on the board:

- *Short (12 words or less)*
- *Inspiring and Actionable*
- *Vivid*
- *Points us back to main responsibilities when we get off track*

Tickerman was skeptical. "How does a mission statement steer you when you get off track?"

Alexandra grabbed a marker and started writing on the whiteboard. "These are examples of brilliant mission statements."

- *Never wait on hold again.*
- *Organize the world's information.*
- *Transportation as reliable as running water, everywhere for everyone.*

"Compare these to our checklist," Alexandra said. "You could ask yourself at any time, 'Are we doing this?' These examples provide clarity. Before you ask the sales manager of million-dollar contracts to change the bathroom light bulb, you can say, 'Let's think about this light bulb... Does it help us achieve our mission? Sometimes the light bulb *does* matter. But you should be asking."

Jeffrey broke everyone up into groups of three and had them brainstorm ideas. Vigorous discussion filled all corners of the room. After a few minutes, when they appeared to be slowing down, Alexandra called them back into the main circle.

"Alright, what are your favorite ideas from each group?"

VISION - Every Ship Needs a Compass

- *Exceptional waste disposal that protects, preserves, and improves the environment.*
- *Do more to prevent lawsuits and build good feelings with the community than 100 lawyers.*
- *Provide waste management services that protect the environment and utilize recycling methods wherever possible, in order to contribute to a safe and healthy planet for current and future generations.*
- *To ensure community health, environmental quality, and economic vitality.*
- *Trash treatment that doesn't stink.*

Everyone laughed at the last suggestion. Aaron and Tickerman gave each other a high five.

"Good job, guys. Some of these are really vivid." Alexandra said, stepping back from the board. "We're not going for perfect. Which of these are going in the right direction, and what do we like?"

People shouted out their favorite phrases, and Alexandra circled them.

"I *love* the economic vitality idea," Jeffrey said.

"We have some common threads there. Safe and healthy, building good feelings, community health. Those all flow together."

- *Exceptional waste disposal that protects, preserves, and improves the environment.*
- *Do more to prevent lawsuits and build good feelings with the community than 100 lawyers.*
- *Provide waste management services that protect the environment and utilize recycling methods wherever possible, in order to contribute to a safe and healthy planet for current and future generations.*
- *To ensure community health, environmental quality, and economic vitality.*
- *Trash treatment that doesn't stink.*

"We're not going to include the 'doesn't stink' one?" Bob asked, disappointed.

229

"It wasn't serious," Aaron laughed. "We just thought it was funny."

"Fun is good," Alexandra said, adding a smiley face next to it. "Fun is vivid. Fun is memorable. Fun is inspiring and easier to be proud of."

"I *love* the idea of something fun," Jeffrey said, starting to enjoy the discussion.

Matt raised his hand.

"I think we shouldn't ignore the lawsuits idea," he said. "I know the way it's phrased, it sounds ominous, but there's a lot of mistrust in our community. We ought to be mindful of those relationships, not just our minimum legal obligation."

Alexandra turned to Elsa. "What do you think, Elsa? What role do *you* see us playing in your community?"

Elsa stood, smiling and flattered by all the attention.

"Well," she said thoughtfully, "this is my favorite mail stop. It's so pretty here by the lake. I rearranged my route so you could be my last stop, and then I take a walk along the trail. Some people say that the lake has gotten worse since GooCrew came. They blame you for the fish dying."

"Wait, there are fish die-offs?" Jeffrey asked, surprised. He shared a look of shock and concern with Alexandra.

Elsa nodded. "It's not your fault though. It's the farmers. Fertilizer runs off the farms and into the water. Makes the algae real happy, and that kills the fish. I see 'em belly-up sometimes when I go walking."

Next to Elsa, Tickerman's jaw dropped.

"Fertilizer," he muttered. "Of *course*." Tickerman waved to Elsa to keep going, and then slipped out of the room.

Elsa shook herself, embarrassed to have gotten off track.

"But anyways, the role I see *you* play… You pour good, clean water back into the lake. Seems to me that you balance out what the farmers do. You try to balance what the factories do, too. People blame you 'cause you're willing to touch things they'd rather not think about. They think if you're willing to touch stuff that's dirty, that maybe *you're* dirty. But I know better. You have a hard job. You're last ones standing, the superhero at the end of the line of thoughtless people. I think you make the world more beautiful."

She sat down.

There was a long pause, and then everyone burst into applause.

Jeffrey looked at Alexandra. "Well, there you go. How about, *Making the world more beautiful every day?*"

Alexandra grinned. She added it to the list on the board.

Making the world more beautiful every day.

"I like it. Let's compare it to our checklist. Does it meet the crucial qualities of a good mission statement? Is it short and vivid? Is it inspiring? Is it sufficiently actionable?"

Clara hesitated. "I feel like that's too vague. It doesn't say anything about environment responsibility."

Arnold Fitzherbert, who was sitting next to Bob, spoke up.

"No, I think it does," Arnold said thoughtfully. "When people hand us toxic waste, they expect us to hide it away somewhere that we don't have to look at it. And sometimes we have no other choice. But when that *is* part of the process, we sort of know that we're hurting the planet. This mission statement inspires me to not just use the cleanest methods for today, but to actively look for ways we can improve our processes."

Clara was unconvinced. "It doesn't say all that. It just says beautiful. You can slap a flower on top of a landfill. That's beautiful. But it doesn't reverse generations of irresponsible dumping that poisons groundwater and makes people sick."

"Well, sick children aren't beautiful," Fitzherbert replied with a shrug. "In my mind, *beautiful* doesn't just mean *pretty for today*. I imagine a clean, safe, grassy park where my children can run barefoot."

Clara sat back in her chair, impressed. "Okay... I'll buy in. If that's what beautiful means to us, I can get behind that."

Matt laughed. "Wow, that puts the odor problem we're facing in a whole new light. Suddenly instead of feeling annoyed and frustrated, I'm looking forward to fixing it."

"That's the power of a great mission statement." Alexandra looked around. "Does it feel fun to you guys?"

They nodded.

"Does it inspire you? Particularly those of you who work on the ground level?"

They smiled and nodded.

"It doesn't include economic vitality…" Alexandra mused.

Jeffrey shrugged. "That's the job of *every* business. I don't feel bad leaving it out."

"Okay," Alexandra said with a shrug. "By show of hands, how many of you are at least 70% happy with this mission statement?"

Buy-in was unanimous. Judging by their smiles, they were more than 70% happy.

Alexandra capped her marker with a smile and tossed it to Jeffrey.

"That was fast," he said in surprise.

Alexandra chuckled. "I tried to tell you."

"What can we do to remind ourselves of this mission every day?" Jeffrey asked.

One of the bay workers laughed. "Our front entrance is depressing. It's all concrete and gravel. What if we landscaped it a bit?"

The idea was immediately popular.

Jeffrey watched everyone getting excited. Instead of pointing out the problem, he asked a question. "I *love* the idea. What's our budget?"

Matt sagged. "Oh. There is no budget."

"It's not automatically impossible," Jeffrey said with a smile. "How could we make it less expensive?"

Without skipping a beat, Elsa said, "I have some big yellow bushes in my yard. I can bring you cuttings."

Everyone in the room got excited. They tossed ideas out.

"You can buy a giant bucket of wildflower seeds for next to nothing."

"My brother owns a nursey, and I get a discount there."

"Oh! Let's make a sign with our mission statement on it!"

Alexandra grinned. "These are great ideas. How can we coordinate all these resources so it looks professional?"

Jeffrey smiled. "We could allocate a *little* money. Is there Moneyball talent we could tap into?"

VISION - Every Ship Needs a Compass

Matt lit up. "Let's line up a student landscaping project at the nearest college. With clippings, a bucket of seeds, and $100, I bet *somebody* can make something awesome."

Fitzherbert raised his hand. "Hey, can I recommend another thing?"

"Go for it," Jeffrey said.

Fitzherbert pulled at his orange jumpsuit. "Can we *please* change the color of our uniforms? If you want us to feel pride in our work, you probably shouldn't dress us like prison inmates."

A cheer rose from every bay worker in the room.

Jeffrey laughed. "Yeah, I always wondered why GooCrew did that. What color would you prefer?"

"Green!"

Jeffrey groaned playfully. "But that's so cliché."

Arnold chuckled. "If it's a choice between orange and cliché, I will take cliché *any* day. Who else thinks green is a good color?"

Jeffrey was outvoted. He laughed and took a note. "I'll talk to the person who orders uniforms."

Matt raised his hand. "Can I ask a question before we conclude?"

"Go for it," Jeffrey said.

"Not to be a killjoy, but this won't change anything unless we live it," Matt pointed out. "I never noticed that plaque in the lobby before. I doubt I'd notice another. What'll be the difference this time?"

Alexandra grinned. "Eureka! *That* is the golden question."

"Is it?"

"Yes. It's easy. You know how you already do weekly performance reviews during 1-on-1's based on your worker's KPIs?"

"Yes."

"Tomorrow, we'll break down our mission statement into phases called Thematic Goals. Thematic Goals are the next practical phase of achieving our mission. All *you* have to do is make sure each worker's KPIs contribute to the Thematic Goal, which should automatically be tied to our mission."

Matt's eyes lit up. "That makes sense. I could probably do the same thing with our annual performance review."

"Absolutely," Alexandra agreed. "Just ask, 'Hey Joe, What's your role? Which parts of your role contribute to our mission?' Then Joe

WEEK NINE

picks the three KPIs that contribute most to our mission, and he gives himself a grade for each. A to F, with examples."

Alexandra tapped her marker on the board, where their mission was written. "The net result of that is focus. Everything is focused on our vision. Suddenly it's clear how mission, strategy, and thematic goal impact their work—where in the past, it had no impact at all."

> **SUMMARY**
>
> - Great mission statements are short, inspiring, actionable, vivid, and focused on your main purpose.
> - Ask regularly: "How does this help us achieve our mission?"
> - Once you have a great mission statement, reinforce it by using it in performance reviews, awards, meeting templates, etc.
> - KPIs support the current thematic goal (introduced in the next chapter), which supports the mission.

ACTION: Assess and Upgrade Your Mission Statement

Follow the example in this chapter and review your own mission statement. Is it brief? Inspiring? Actionable? Vivid? Pointing the way? Invite the people who care and upgrade it as shown in this chapter. It's very important to get feedback and buy-in from the key stakeholders, champions, owners, and subject matter experts.

DEPARTMENTS: If your company mission statement isn't great, you can have your own as long as it directly supports the company mission. If your new one is good enough, you may even inspire a revised mission statement at the top.

THEMATIC GOAL

THE KEY TO HYPERFOCUS

The next morning, Jeffrey called an All-Hands Meeting to announce the new mission statement. They met in the bay, because it was the only place large enough to hold everyone, and it had a whiteboard. Some office staff and bay workers stood on the ground, while others watched from crowded catwalks.

The moment Jeffrey walked into the bay, he could feel their apathy—they were already bored to death, falling asleep on their feet, dreading the next ten minutes.

Thinking quickly, Jeffrey changed his mind about writing on the whiteboard and turned to face his workers. "8 weeks ago, we changed the forklift speeds," he began. He looked around. "What is it now? Does anyone know?"

"10!" shouted a driver.

"Cool," Jeffrey said. "Who likes 10? Let's give Hans and his process team a round of applause for their amazing work."

The workers woke up enough to cheer a little for Hans.

"Six weeks ago," Jeffrey continued, "we gave them power to shape this workplace. A *limited* amount of power. We gave the process team one vision—pick any speed and make it safe. Whatever they decided, we trusted. They rearranged this bay. When the process needs tweaking, *they* choose how they want to tweak it."

Jeffrey looked up at the people on the catwalks. "These aren't supervisors or shift managers. They're just like you. And they aren't getting shot down, bossed around, or shown up. They choose. Who else wants freedom like that?"

The waste handlers shifted on their feet and looked at each other. They were afraid to answer in case the question was rhetorical, but the sleepy look in their eyes was replaced by hunger.

Jeffrey made eye contact with a handful of them. "Today we're giving away more power. A lot of it. Just like we did with the process team, we're going to give you a vision and let you run with it."

He turned back to the whiteboard and picked up his marker. "Imagine a boat. They've got a *vision*. They've got a great vision."

In the style of an adventure map, Jeffrey drew a boat. Then he added a large "X" on the other side of the board and drew a straight line from the boat to the X.

"They know exactly where they're headed. Their compass is pointed straight. The whole time. Their goal is the *only* place they look. Regardless of reefs, or other ships, or islands that might be nearby where they could replenish their supplies..."

He quickly added sharks directly in their path, a pirate ship that was about to intercept them, and an island off to the side that was loaded with coconuts. He reinforced the line oblivious to them all.

VISION - The Key to Hyperfocus

The workers chuckled.

Jeffrey smiled with them. "Right, that's obviously dumb." He erased the path with his thumb, then redrew it to navigate the obstacles appropriately.

"Instead of choosing an inflexible vision, we're embracing a method called Active Waiting Strategy. Golden opportunities open quickly and close quickly," Jeffrey explained. "They're hard to see a long way off. Sudden threats arrive just as fast, and they must be addressed. Active Waiting means we watch for changes on the horizon."

Jeffrey pointed to the island full of coconuts.

"The day may come when we stop *everything* and switch direction to seize a golden opportunity that has suddenly fallen into our laps. We're telling you this so you don't think the company is unfocused—or that we're facing a crisis—if we suddenly switch to a new thematic goal. It's part of agility. It's called *pivoting*."

Over the big X, Jeffrey wrote:

Making the world more beautiful every day.

"This is our new mission statement," Jeffrey explained. "This is our vision. To keep it from being useless, we need a long-term strategy for living that mission. A good strategy has three parts."

On the board, he wrote:

> Now
> Next
> End Game

Jeffrey capped his marker. "If we want to make the world more beautiful as a waste treatment company, then there's a natural progression of responsibility. First, we *start by identifying the ways we're making it less beautiful.* After that, we can *start helping other people not make it uglier.* Finally, we *start making it nice."*

Jeffrey gestured to the board.

"For example, right now one of the ways that we're making the world uglier is by releasing foul odors. We've temporarily treated the problem. To prevent it from happening again, we need to install some new equipment... which requires cash. We've sent a proposal in requesting permission to sell our services to third parties. Until we hear back, we have one focus for the whole company, for every team, every department: Prepare to Scale."

Jeffrey wrote PREPARE TO SCALE in big letters and circled it. "This is called a thematic goal. The thematic goal is the practical next phase of achieving the mission. Scaling means adding new clients. Basically, be ready to handle more waste, in the same hours, with the same equipment."

He knew this could be a sore point for the crew.

"The point isn't to squeeze more work out of everybody," he assured them. "The point is to work smarter. To spend *less* energy. If we find a better rhythm, we can add paying clients. Paying clients mean we can take better care of *you*. Profit also means we have resources to make the world more beautiful, instead of just hauling trash. We want to leave the earth better than we found it."

This seemed to resonate with everyone. They were looking at each other, talking quietly, nodding.

Jeffrey paused for a moment, then asked what most managers would consider a dangerous question.

VISION - The Key to Hyperfocus

"Do any of you have questions or concerns about this thematic goal?"

One woman immediately raised her hand. She looked distressed. Jeffrey called on her.

"Does this mean we might lose our jobs?" she asked.

Laying people off was so far from Jeffrey's mind that the question caught him off guard and he almost laughed. He stopped himself just in time.

"Of course not," he said, shocked. "What makes you think that?"

Unconvinced, the woman frowned. "Change, efficiency, profit... In my experience, those words mean technology is coming. I don't know technology."

Jeffrey's gut instinct was to assure her technology wasn't going to be replacing anything. They were impoverished, after all. But he stopped to think for a moment before replying. If affordable superior technology were available, would they take advantage of it? Absolutely. They weren't there yet, but he didn't want to tie his hands with a foolish promise. Her fears were real and fair.

"I hear your concern," Jeffrey assured her, looking her in the eyes. "The answer is quite the opposite. We're going to invest in you. Our goal is to create leaders. You know waste processing better than anyone. If we need to take advantage of technology, we're going to provide world-class training so you can master it. Basically, this is a promotion for you."

Her expression relaxed. She nodded and melted back into the crowd. Jeffrey looked around.

"We're not just talking about knowledge promotions here," Jeffrey clarified. "Think about *your* workflow. If you could change anything, what would it be?"

Jeffrey pointed to their thematic goal. "Specifically, imagine scaling your duty. What's in your way? What do you need? What stupid rules need to change so scaling is possible in your area?"

An older gentleman with a salt and pepper beard lit up. "Like the old forklift speed?" he asked.

> The concept of thematic goals comes from Patrick Lencioni's books *The Advantage* and *The Four Obsessions of an Extraordinary Executive.* Both are valuable and delightful reads.
>
> The purpose of Active Waiting is to keep you agile in spite of your thematic goal. To learn more about Active Waiting, see the article *Strategy as Active Waiting* by Donald Sull (Harvard Business Review, Sept 2005).

"Exactly," Jeffrey said. "Like the old forklift speed. Starting now, you have authority in your zones. You want something to change? Change it."

A burly man in the back spoke up without raising his hand.

"What are the limitations? You're obviously not giving us unlimited power."

Jeffrey set his marker down. "After this meeting, your immediate supervisors will do an exercise with you to help you identify your Most Profitable Activities and define your zones. Within your zone, you don't need approval. Just seek buy-in from stakeholders—not because you have to get *permission*, but because you're becoming leaders. And great leaders don't steamroll the people around them."

Jeffrey pointed to the four corners of the bay.

"I mentioned principles. You will notice new posters here in the bay. Over the past month, we've collected principles about how we do things at GooCrew. We've posted them around the bay to remind us all to use these principles to guide our actions."

The workers craned their necks, looking around for the nearest posters.

"Go ahead and find the poster closest to your work station. Your supervisors will meet you there."

As the meeting disbanded, Tick and Tock approached Jeffrey.

"Mr. Jackson!" Tock said. "Speaking of making the world more beautiful, we know why our pipes corroded."

Jeffrey perked up. "You do?"

Tickerman nodded. "We use lake water to cool the incinerator, right? Yesterday, Elsa got me thinking when she mentioned fertilizer runoff."

"So we tested the pH of the lake," Tock pitched in.

"It's acidic!" Tickerman explained. "And when it's acidic enough to kill fish, it also causes sudden, severe corrosion in the pipes."

"Wow!" Jeffrey's eyes widened. "So even though we've installed new pipes..."

"We haven't solved the problem," Tickerman concluded. "We have to help the lake or our pipes will break again."

SUMMARY

- Active waiting strategy means watching for golden opportunities and sudden threats—and quickly responding as they arise.

- A thematic goal is the next phase of achieving the mission and usually lasts 6-9 months.

- The current thematic goal should be communicated and reinforced through KPIs, weekly agenda items, and performance reviews at all levels.

ACTION: Choose a Thematic Goal

STEP ONE: Identify a current ideal thematic goal for your organization, or clarify/validate the current one. It should be reachable in 6-9 months. Involve any stakeholders who care, including directors, the executive team, and other key stakeholders.

STEP TWO: Ask everyone to synchronize their personal and team KPIs, weekly meeting agenda items, and performance reviews with your new thematic goal.

ACTIVE WAITING STRATEGY

NEVER LET A GOOD CRISIS GO TO WASTE

Aaron called an emergency meeting. He was furious.

"The lifting arm is dying. Based on the wear we're seeing, we have exactly 13 days before it gives out completely. We can no longer repair the machine. Unfortunately, Heart is blocking equipment requests and we don't know why."

"Can we cope with just the forklifts?"

"No," Aaron said flatly.

"Did you explain the severity of the problem?"

"I did."

"What did they say?"

Aaron scowled. "Same answer they've given for months: 'Make it work.' Then they hung up on me."

Jeffrey stood up and walked to their parking list. The wall was littered with dozens of sticky notes, which Jeffrey studied carefully.

"Roxanne," he asked, "What's the status on selling our services?"

Aaron waved his arms. "How does that help? That requires *more* equipment expenditure."

"Yes, but it's also a potential *source* of revenue. I'm just looking for connections."

Roxanne frowned. "I have seven preliminary contracts in hand. They've committed to subscribe if we acquire the equipment. But I've been hounding headquarters for months. I don't think they're ever coming around."

>
>
> THE PLACE WHERE THE BIGGEST PROBLEMS AND BIGGEST OPPORTUNITIES CONNECT IS YOUR SOLUTION

"You said the equipment we need would pay for itself quickly. What was that number again?"

"8 months."

"Add the cost of the equipment Aaron needs. What's the break-even point if we do that?"

Roxanne opened up her laptop.

Alexandra joined Jeffrey at the board while Roxanne crunched numbers. "What are you thinking?" she asked.

Jeffrey hesitated. "I don't know. I'm grasping at straws, honestly. We're so close to that influx of cash... Maybe that's just wishful thinking. The equipment it would require is a luxury we don't have. If Heart gave us the money, we'd need to spend it on Aaron's repairs first."

Alexandra frowned and looked at the sticky notes. "It's tempting to say 'Don't worry about that right now,' but the place where the biggest problems and biggest opportunities connect is your solution. What else is on the board?"

Jeffrey lifted some of the sticky notes to read others underneath. "Efficiency suggestions, route changes, lobbying, community outreach ... Lots of good ideas. But I don't see a bridge."

Roxanne raised her hand. "It more than triples the time, sir. 26 months."

Jeffrey ran his hand through his hair. "That's still amazing."

Aaron snorted. "Too bad we have no way to access that income *now*."

"Don't assume you can't," Alexandra suggested. "Say 'we can *if...*' If what? Under what circumstances *could* we access that income now?"

Aaron sighed in irritation. "I don't know!"

"Apply constraints. How would we do it if Heart Manufacturing never gave us any additional funding? If Heart didn't even exist. Realize the world is our oyster. There are all kinds of resources, people you can partner with. How can you tap into that?"

> Adam Morgan shows you simple questions with a profound impact on innovation. We recommend reading *A Beautiful Constraint: How to Transform Your Limitations into Advantages, and Why It's Everyone's Business*. Chapters 4 and 5 are particularly useful.

"Hold on..." Matt rubbed his chin. "We have seven companies waiting, desperate for our services? That's not a risk, that's a gold mine. It just needs somebody to fund it."

"Exactly," Alexandra said. "Who would be interested in funding it?"

"What about the bank?" Bob suggested. "With a business plan, a spreadsheet of the vital equipment, and contracts in hand—*all* of which we have—we can get a loan from the bank independent of the parent company."

Dead silence.

Matt swallowed hard. "Are we really talking about going behind everyone's back to take out a loan on our own? They'll think we're going rogue."

Jeffrey laughed nervously. "Do we even have the power to do this? Legally?"

Clara hesitated. "You could take a business plan to the bank and apply for the line of credit... You just wouldn't be able to sign off on it. We'd need Khalil for that."

245

"Sounds like a winner to me," Alexandra said with a grin.

Jeffrey exhaled nervously. "Alex, I trust you a lot. But this is delicate territory. I think this is a bad idea. It feels like we're overstepping our bounds."

"Initiative always does," Alexandra replied coolly. "It doesn't mean it's bad. You're not suggesting anarchy or grasping for power. You have a serious emergency here. Heart has ignored your pleas for help. Are you just going to stand around and let GooCrew die?"

"Of course not," Jeffrey snapped.

"So step up! Do CPR on this patient. You have *everything* you need. Literally the only thing holding you back is the fear that overstepping your bounds is unethical. You know what's unethical? Standing back and doing nothing. Letting a catastrophe domino down on you, even though you can see exactly what's coming and you have time to prevent it."

Jeffrey felt the weight of the problem settle on his shoulders. She was right, and he hated it. Terror and adrenaline raced through him. He took a breath.

Then Jeffrey turned to his team. "If we do this, we do it together. Do any of you see a better way?"

No one spoke.

"People get fired for far less," Jeffrey added, rubbing his eyes wearily. "So I want more than 70% buy-in this time. Are you all 90% okay with this plan?"

"Boss," Bob said affectionately, "don't worry so much. We've got this."

The whole team sat Mr. Khalil down.

Aaron cleared his throat. "Are you aware that Heart Manufacturing has repeatedly refused our pleas for vital equipment upgrades?"

Khalil nodded.

"Can you do anything about it?" Aaron asked.

"Unfortunately, no." Khalil folded his hands, his face unreadable. "They're being extremely firm about budgets this year. There's been too much waste in the past. They've asked us to think creatively."

"In that case..." Aaron stepped back.

Roxanne set a short stack of papers in front of Mr. Khalil. "We are five days away from being unable to operate because of exhausted equipment," she said. "Our solution is to contract out our services. We have contracts in hand. The bank has guaranteed a line of credit against these contracts so we can buy equipment. We just need you to sign off on it."

It took several seconds for Mr. Khalil to process her words. When he did, Khalil reeled. Then he yelled.

"What in the *world*? I didn't give you permission to do this!"

"That's correct, sir," Jeffrey pitched in, with greater calm than he felt. "We're not asking for your permission. We're simply letting you know what we need to do to keep going. Please don't veto it."

Mr. Khalil looked around the room, in silent shock. His eyes fell on Alexandra, who was standing off to the side. He stared at her long and hard.

Alexandra met his gaze, both with confidence and empathy. She sidled over to him and dropped her voice.

"This probably looks really scary."

"You think?" Khalil said, trying to hold back his anger. "Did you incite this?"

"Sir, they just found a solution to a critical problem *without* using company resources. They're doing it quickly. While billing fewer hours, they're expanding into the marketplace to bring in additional resources... and you didn't have to get involved."

Khalil's mouth snapped shut.

"Invite them to certify their plan," Alexandra suggested.

"What's certifying?"

"You ask questions. They prove they've covered all the bases. Questions like, 'Have you considered this? What about that?' "

Mr. Khalil thought about it for a moment. Then he turned to Clara.

"What about compliance? Are we within regulations? Would this exceed capacity? How does Legal feel about it?"

Clara gave a crisp nod. "I sat down with two of my associates and read our regulations from beginning to end, comparing all seven contracts with legal requirements, including limits for on-site waste. This plan has a green light from me."

"Are you sure?"

"That question will only yield an emotional answer," Alexandra pointed out softly. "A more powerful question is 'how sure are you?' That allows you to get a percentage and see their thought processes. Nothing's 100%."[16]

"Alright," Mr. Khalil said, softening a little as he addressed Clara. "How sure are you?"

"We're as confident about these new contracts as we've been about the other hazardous waste we process. These companies are as safe a bet as Heart."

"Mmm..." Khalil nodded, pondering. Then he looked sternly at Aaron. "I thought you guys were having problems with transportation getting backed up. I got complaints from the factories about it. What's changed?"

Aaron smiled. "Sir, we set up a process team to vet our workflow. They standardized our processing patterns and rearranged our bay. We shaved 40% off our processing time, and I have the reports to prove it."

"We're updating the software too," Bob added. "Already, waste gets cycled and processed on time. If something gets misplaced, we notice the problem immediately. The system will scale."

"Will this interfere with servicing Heart in any way?"

"No," Roxanne said. "And we *know* that because Heart's flow of waste is predictable. With Bob's new software, we can even see the pattern for satellite accumulation purges. We've scheduled all new pick-ups and processing to happen during our lulls."

"What other ways could it fail?"

"We'd be in trouble if we lost our contracts," Roxanne admitted. "But the principle is, *never put more than 40% of your eggs in one basket.*

---

[16] The question "How sure are you?" comes from David Marquet, and is part of the certifying process he pioneered.

We have seven contracts, none of which constitute more than 30% of our projected income. It's unlikely that any of them will fall through because we have a semi-monopoly right now. There's no one else in a 6-hour radius who processes hazardous waste. But if we fail to respond, competition will emerge, and we'll lose the opportunity."

Mr. Khalil nodded. He narrowed his eyes, his voice stern. "What if something unforeseen happens and it fails anyway? Assume Heart won't bail you out. What are the consequences?"

With this, Aaron smiled. "The big fallback—if something unforeseen happens: All we've done is used a line of credit to buy equipment which secures that line of credit. That equipment is *essential* for the safe ongoing operation of this facility *anyway*, and Heart needs this facility operating, even if we don't take on any additional clients."

Mr. Khalil rubbed his chin, considering the spreadsheet in front of him. "You don't have to buy as much equipment. Or you could get cheaper versions."

Aaron looked nauseated by the thought. "Yes, sir, but then we're just maintaining. We can't go anywhere. We're just treading water, trying to keep from drowning. It's very hard to motivate people to tread water and just keep swimming in one place. It's *easy* to motivate them to swim somewhere cool."

"Besides," Roxanne pointed out, "if we don't *expand*, we can't *profit* from the purchase, which means we can't pay the bank back. The bank won't grant the loan without independent income."

Khalil caved. He smiled, shivered, and shook his head.

"You guys are insane. I applaud your courage." He pulled a pen from his suit coat and took a deep breath. "Clara, you're a notary, right?"

At the end of the meeting, Mr. Khalil pulled Alexandra aside. "I just wanted to check in with you on Jeffrey's progress," he whispered. "I'm concerned."

"Why?"

"I noticed in the meeting that Jeffrey didn't do much of the talking."

Alexandra laughed and laughed.

"Don't get me wrong," Khalil added, "I'm impressed with this initiative. I'm just worried Jeffrey has given up and is letting everyone else do the work."

Alexandra smiled warmly. "Jeffrey's problem, when we first teamed up, was that he was too dominant. He steamrolled everyone with his opinions. His workers were demoralized. They had to be horsewhipped into action. What you see now is months of hard work and humility on Jeffrey's part. Jeffrey is a massive success. You have nothing to worry about."

"Are you—" Khalil stopped, then smiled. "*How* sure are you?"

"Let's put it this way: Is Jeffrey going to have to babysit this initiative? More importantly, will it continue to live after he's gone?"

Mr. Khalil lapsed into silent thought.

Alexandra touched his arm gently and smiled. "Jeffrey *developed* these leaders. Inspired them to work together. Enabled them with resources, encouragement, and expertise. You *wanted* this. Creating leaders instead of followers was on his scorecard. Don't mistake Jeffrey's quietude for weakness. This is what great leadership looks like."

SUMMARY

- Constraints can stimulate creative solutions.
- Instead of saying, "we can't" say "we can if..."
- Look for resources outside your organization that you can tap into. The world is your resource.
- Great leaders create teams who take the lead.

ACTION: Implement Active Waiting

Implement the Active Waiting Strategy. First, discuss it with your team. Clearly communicate the principle of pivoting, and why pivoting isn't lack of focus.

This means you now welcome anyone pointing out sudden threats or golden opportunities. Then "scan the horizon"—list all your current looming threats and golden opportunities. What storm clouds are gathering that need to be watched? What windows are opening that may need to be seized? Use the Quick Business Case tool to quickly decide if each one is worth addressing.

NEVERBOSS - Crenshaw

LEADERSHIP SCORECARD

NAME: Jeffrey Jackson

MY OVERALL SCORE: 2.9

4	**STEP AWAY** SUPPORT To Unleash Excellence	- Elsa came to Mission meeting - Team arranged everything for bank proposal: Roxanne led, Clara volunteered as her champion. Team included me at the right time - Team took the lead presenting solution to Khalil
3	**STEP BACK** COACH To Inspire Ownership	- Invited people to Mission meeting - Asked questions to identify solution to lifting arm crisis - Coached mission team by asking questions about landscaping
2	**STEP BESIDE** TRAIN To Build Capability	- Company-wide principles training - Presented company's new vision and corresponding Thematic Goal
1	**STEP UP** TELL To Ensure Clarity	- Authorized workers to make decisions in their zones
0	**STEP IN** TAKE OVER To Create Stability	

LEVEL SIX:

RESULTS

Forgetting yourself, especially during triumph

THE FINISH LINE
───────────

HOW TO AVOID SUCCEEDING TO DEATH

J effery rushed through the bay area, clutching a rolled-up paper in his hand.

Shiny new equipment stood in sharp contrast to the grimy, jimmy-rigged, rusting pieces still in use. As Jeffrey paced and searched from aisle to aisle, he felt a twinge of pride for the process team that stood up to him and insisted they rearrange the bay. It wasn't just faster for the bay workers. It was easier to walk around in general, and Jeffrey no longer felt like he was constantly in danger of getting run over.

Arnold Fitzherbert drove by, grinning stupidly as he navigated small boxes with one of their upgraded forklifts. Tick and Tock tinkered together nearby, bantering while they wrestled a sluice gate wheel that had jammed.

"Hey," Jeffrey called, "has anyone seen Roxanne? She's not in her office."

"Nope. Sorry, sir!"

Jeffrey hurried past the whiteboard, where daily average unloading times were posted. Internal inspectors scurried the other direction to the pre-screen point they'd set up. In all directions, progress and positivity prevailed. But Jeffrey could not find Roxanne anywhere.

He tapped the rolled-up report against his leg and decided to check outside on the off chance that she was talking with truckers.

He almost collided with her as he walked through the door.

"Roxanne!"

Jeffrey noticed immediately that Roxanne had swapped her formal office attire for a green plaid shirt and jeans. Her hair was in braids. It suited her. She looked happy.

He gave her a stern look. "I've been looking for you everywhere."

"I'm so sorry," she said breathlessly. She had clearly been running. "I was just walking with Elsa around the lake during my lunch break. I didn't realize it would take so—"

Roxanne finally noticed the look on Jeffrey's face. "What's wrong?" she asked. "Am I in trouble?"

Jeffrey allowed a little bit of a growl in his voice. "Yes. Big trouble. For the first time in GooCrew history.... we're in the black."

Roxanne froze, and then lit up. *"Really?"*

Jeffrey whacked her gently with the report and handed it to her. "We're the first district to *ever* be in the black."

Roxanne unrolled the financial reports, skimmed them, and started to laugh. They laughed together for a full minute, savoring the hard-won moment.

"Heart Manufacturing is going to have a heart attack when they see this," Roxanne gushed. "They won't believe it."

"Do *not* announce this to anyone yet," Jeffrey warned her. "Accounting is going through numbers meticulously. We're expecting an audit because it's so unlikely. Before we announce anything, we want to make sure first that we've really, really done it."

Roxanne nodded. "I understand."

Jeffrey grinned. "*But*, either way, this is still a *massive* success. The exact numbers are still in debate, but we've certainly never pulled in this much money, this rapidly. This is even after the down payment on our new equipment."

"Wow," she breathed. "I can't believe you did this in three weeks."[17]

"Can't believe *we* did this," Jeffrey corrected. "Have you forgotten that this was your idea?"

Roxanne looked delighted, but she shook her head. "Never would have happened if you hadn't asked."

Next, they quietly told the executive team.

After they celebrated, Alexandra told them a story. "Did you guys know that Kodak invented the digital camera decades before it came to the market?"

"Seriously?"

"Yes. They invented it in 1975, then sat on the technology. They were afraid to release it because they were making so much money with film. They had big investments there and didn't want to interrupt the market. Bad move. Digital cameras became popular anyway, and Kodak got left behind. They bankrupted in 2013 after selling off 800 patents."

Matt cocked his head. "Why are you telling us this?"

"Because now that you're sitting on a cash cow, I want to teach you how to avoid a pitfall that commonly comes next: succeeding to death."

As they laughed, Alexandra drew a simple timeline on the board. It only had one point—Now, which divided the past and future.

"You've worked *really* hard to be here," she said, pointing to the middle. "You've used a lot of strategies to get to this point. What most people don't know is that what happens next...."

She circled the future half several times.

---

[17] Based on real situations. Using these principles, one company made a crisis turnaround in 11 days. Another went from impending equipment repossession to non-distressed acquisition in under 3 weeks.

"...is just as important, and requires as much planning as what you did in the past."

Aaron coughed politely. "I don't see what the big deal is. We already set up our mission statement and strategy. We just move to the next step, right?"

"Yes and no. Usually, each step requires several rounds of thematic goals before you have truly fulfilled that step. You've barely begun step one."

"That's true... We have several things we need to fix, starting with that odor."

"So are you ready to pick a new thematic goal?"

Clara raised her hand. "Not to rain on your parade, but we only *just* hit this target. We're not rolling in the dough yet. Wouldn't it be wise to pad the bank account, continue updating equipment, and stabilize a little before we go rushing off to save the world?"

Alexandra nodded vigorously. "Absolutely. Sometimes you want to keep pursuing the current cash cow. But you want to decide in advance what your new finish line will be. How long do you want to pursue this cash cow for? When will you know you're ready to do something else?"

Alexandra leaned down and erased half the timeline. "Kodak didn't have a vision of their next step. When it came and they were still milking their cow, they were afraid to move forward. Making money is great. But that's not your purpose. Money is just the resource you gather so that you can fulfill your bigger purpose."

Alexandra added the future line back in, and then drew a checkered flag at the end. "We didn't address this last time, but from now on, you should. Whenever you choose a new goal, you *also* need to define your finish line. Write it down, and when you hit it, reassess."

She put her marker away and sat down. Then she waited.

Roxanne was the first to speak. "Well, we've hit our finish line, so let's assess. What worked? What did we do well? What could have gone better? What's the next step toward fulfilling our mission? Is our strategy still valid? What's our next finish line?"

On the final days of Jeffrey's temporary placement, Jeffrey stood by a pile of boxes in the yard, calling out names.

"Stockton, Peterson, Haddad!"

Three bay workers approached, and Jeffrey handed them new green uniforms. They ran off eagerly to change. Thanks to Roxanne, no deliveries were scheduled for the next two hours. The whole team was gathering outside to take a group picture.

Jeffrey pulled one of the uniforms out of the box and held it up. The secretary who had ordered them had done a wonderful job. He'd been afraid of a nauseating color, but they were classy. Vibrant enough to meet safety standards, but still stylish. On the back, they were embroidered with the new mission statement.

"Hey..." Jeffrey glanced at the secretary. "Do I get one?"

"We got polos for the office workers," she said. "No more white collars and blue collars. We're all green collars now."

He grinned. "Did you get one for Elsa?"

The secretary smiled. "She's already wearing it."

Once everyone was dressed, they gathered in front of the building. For being freshly landscaped, there were an impressive number of blooms. A sturdy wooden placard had been installed: *"Making the world more beautiful every day."* They insisted that Elsa stand next to the sign. Even Mr. Khalil came to be in the picture. He wore a green tie in their honor.

Once they had everyone lined up and the camera on the tripod was ready to go, Jeffrey stood by the tripod to address the crew.

"We lied to you," Jeffrey began.

They laughed.

"We didn't just want to take a picture. We have a special announcement to make. Thanks to you—your hard work, initiative, and willingness to speak up for what you believe in—we are the first district *ever*, since GooCrew was founded over 40 years ago, to be cash flow positive."

Jaws started to drop, but it wasn't quite sinking in.

Jeffrey laughed. "Guys, we're *profitable*."

That did it.

Pandemonium broke loose. They cheered and danced and hugged each other, laughing the whole time.

Jeffrey leaned over to hit the camera's 10-second timer. "*Now* we take a picture."

After the picture, they gave the workers time to mingle. A few workers ran to get refreshments that were waiting in the break room.

Mr. Khalil was delighted to be there, but he seemed a little scatterbrained. Jeffrey saw him staring out at the lake absent-mindedly.

"I'm so glad you could make it," Jeffrey said as he approached. "Did you get a chance to tour the bay?"

"I did." Khalil turned with a smile and surveyed the happy crowd around him. "Jeffrey, the fact that *any* region can be profitable changes *everything* for *every* region. I'm sorry I was so cold when you started here. Can you put together a report on how to replicate this program?"

"Of course. I'd love to."

As they broke open light refreshments, Jeffrey sidled up to Alexandra, holding something behind his back. "Hey, I got you something."

"Really?" Alexandra's face lit up. She seemed surprised and genuinely delighted.

Jeffrey shrugged. "It's no big deal. Hold out your hands."

As she did so, Jeffrey handed her the biggest, fattest rainbow-sprinkle cupcake she'd ever seen. A blue candle in the middle burned merrily.

"Happy birthday!"

"It's not..." Alexandra's stopped in confusion. Then her eyes filled with recognition.

Arnold Fitzgerald saw, and gasped with delight. "I didn't know it was your birthday." He called out, "Hey everyone! It's Alexandra's birthday!"

"Nooooooo...." Alexandra objected uselessly, caught red-handed with the fluffy cupcake.

RESULTS - How to Avoid Succeeding to Death

Elsa took her by the arm and dragged her to the center of the party as everyone started to sing. "It's okay, sweetie. Don't be shy."

Alexandra glared at Jeffrey. "I will *so* get you back."

Jeffrey walked off laughing.

He moved to the back of the party to help Matt open a second set of mysterious boxes. They'd been resting near the uniform boxes, but contained a different surprise. As they discreetly unpacked them, a shiny black car rolled up the gravel driveway and rolled to a stop. Most people were too busy singing "Happy Birthday" to notice.

Matt and Jeffrey watched the car in confusion. They weren't expecting anyone else.

A tall, bald man stepped out. He looked around and buttoned his jacket.

Jeffrey nudged Matt. "Who's that?"

Matt sagged a little. "Vanderman."

SUMMARY

- Define a finish line for each thematic goal, so you know when to set a new one.

ACTION: Define your Finish Line

Set a standard that tells you when you've reached your current thematic goal and are ready to switch. Remember: The thematic goal is the practical next phase of achieving the mission. So once you succeed here, what's your next step?

GIVING CREDIT
───────────
WHERE HANDS-OFF LEADERSHIP GETS TESTED

Jeffrey felt his heart skip a beat. This was it. His time was over.

Mr. Vanderman looked around in curiosity, buttoning his suit jacket. Jeffrey scraped together all his training in sportsmanship and put on a smile.

"Mr. Vanderman, welcome. I thought you wouldn't be here until next week."

Vanderman smiled. "Well, Khalil said you were putting on a party. I hope I'm not intruding."

Jeffrey tried to swat away the sadness welling up inside. He chuckled. "I suppose my reign of terror had to come to an end sometime."

Vanderman laughed.

Alexandra escaped somehow from the well-wishers. "Jeffrey, they're gathering everyone for the awards." Then she turned to Vanderman with a bright smile and offered her hand. "Hi, I'm Alexandra. I don't believe we've met."

Jeffrey slipped away, grateful for the excuse.

As Jeffrey had a rushed, distracted conversation with Matt about awards, he watched Alexandra from the corner of his eye. She laughed with Vanderman, introduced him to the new employees, and escorted him to a front-row seat. Vanderman looked like he was having fun. As Alexandra sat next to him and whispered quiet explanations about the event, Jeffrey felt his protectiveness easing up.

Alex is on our side, he thought. *If she's guiding him, everything will be okay.*

"What are the principles for giving credit?" Jeffrey asked.

They assumed it was rhetorical. He was supposed to be giving a speech, after all. He scanned the crowd. "Bob, who gets the credit?"

"The boss gets the credit," Bob quipped.

Everyone laughed.

Jeffrey smiled at the joke. "Good, I'm glad you all know that's not how we do things anymore."

Jeffrey looked down at the ground, staring at the lush green grass between his shoes, wondering what he wanted to leave them with. This was the last time he'd get to talk with most of them.

He looked up.

"Most of you don't know this, but when I came here, I was a failure. A total reject. Mr. Heart and Mr. Khalil *personally* showed up to an intervention meeting and put me on probation. That's how bad things were."

This revelation was met with surprise from all quarters. Based on their reactions, Alexandra hadn't shared this news with anyone.

"*I* thought I was amazing. I thought *I* deserved all the credit for the good things that happened on my watch. So this transfer was a huge slap in the face."

Jeffrey stuffed his hands in his pockets, embarrassed. "Can you imagine if I tried to take credit here? The thought is *so* absurd, it's uncomfortable.

"Back at headquarters, they don't understand yet. They think I'm awesome. They're sending me to Florida so I can do this again…

They don't understand that a leader is only as powerful as the people they lead. And the people they lead are only as powerful as the leader allows them to be. For us to be great, I have to step back."

Jeffrey smiled at his teammates.

"Bob wrote the code. Roxanne dreamt of profit and made *all* our sales. Aaron's team rearranged the bay. Matt patiently retrained our entire staff. Clara pulled all-nighters to keep us out of jail. All of you! On the front lines, you came up with a hundred solutions and turned them into reality."

Jeffrey shook his head, honestly confused. "Yet an outsider tries to give me all the credit. Isn't that strange?"

Jeffrey lapsed into silence again, thinking, feeling. He wanted to leave them empowered enough that no leader could ever take advantage of them again.

He looked up with sudden conviction. "When things go wrong, people tend to blame the leaders, which is fair. But they blame us for the wrong thing. They say, 'Why didn't you step in? How could you let this happen? You should have intervened.' ...But that's not the answer at all. What they *should* say..."

Jeffrey turned to Mr. Khalil with a quiet smile.

"...what I hope they learn to say, is... 'Why are you trying to control this? Why aren't you stepping back? Let your people lead.' "

Jeffrey smiled and stared at the ground again. He had more he wanted to say, but his throat was growing tight, and if he kept going, he was afraid he'd cry.

"Thank you for being my friends and my champions. Not just professionally, but *personally*... I owe you everything. Thank you."

As they applauded, Jeffrey cleared his throat and unveiled a small stack of plaques.

"It's time to honor some of our teammates who went above and beyond the call of duty, starting with Hans – Team Lead, for volunteering in an intimidating situation, standing up to the boss on behalf of your team."

Hans sprinted up to the front and accepted his plaque. It wasn't fancy, but Hans held it with tremendous pride.

Jeffrey picked up the next plaque. "Bob – for championing and designing Methuselah 2.0."

The award after Bob's had been carefully timed.

ARE YOU TRYING TO CONTROL THIS?

WHY AREN'T YOU STEPPING BACK?

"Aaron – for demonstrating extraordinary leadership through the twin forces of persistence and humility."

As Aaron came to collect his plaque, he made eye contact with Jeffrey. They smiled knowingly at each other as they shook hands. Aaron seemed satisfied.

"Before you go, Aaron," Jeffrey said, loud enough for everyone to hear. "You've been working here on a interim basis, haven't you?"

Aaron's eyes grew big. "Yessir."

"I think it's about time we made your job official." Jeffrey looked at the crowd. "Don't you?"

The bay workers broke into riotous applause. Several people jumped to their feet, chanting Aaron's name. Aaron returned to his seat, laughing, amidst a sea of whistling and back-pats.

After burning through a few dozen plaques, Jeffrey gave the last one to Elsa.

Jeffrey glanced at the empty tablecloth, then checked his watch. "Well, folks, I think that's it. Thanks for—"

"Wait!" Matt shouted from the back. "We forgot one!"

Matt rushed forward from the back, carrying one of the small boxes the plaques had been shipped in.

Jeffrey laughed as Matt set it down on the table.

"That's embarrassing. Who'd we forget?" Jeffrey opened the box, and confusion washed across his face. Inside, there was an old dented doorknob instead of a plaque.

A doorknob? He stared at it for several seconds.

Then it dawned on him.

RESULTS - Where Hands-Off Leadership Gets Tested

The doorknob was embedded to a base, like a trophy. The base was a rich, dark wood, glazed to a shine. There was an inscription.

"To Jeffrey Ja—" Jeffrey stopped in shock, reread the inscription, and looked up. "You guys got something for *me*?"

Laughing, Matt put an arm around Jeffrey and turned to address the crew.

"What Jeffrey said is true, but incomplete," Matt explained. "Who gets the credit? *Everyone* gets the credit: the workers for owning and driving it, the team for supporting it... and the boss for creating leaders."

Matt held up the trophy and read the inscription for everyone to hear. "To Jeffrey Jackson – Mentor and Friend, for setting us free."

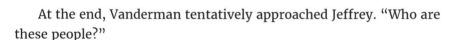

At the end, Vanderman tentatively approached Jeffrey. "Who are these people?"

Jeffrey laughed.

"No, I mean it," Vanderman said, looking around in confusion. "I don't know what you've done with my team. They're *smiling*. They're bragging about each other instead of themselves. Roxanne looks radiant, Clara's scowl is gone. And Bob! Even Bob is happy."

Vanderman took a troubled breath, then hesitated. He had something to say, but it was hard to admit, even to himself. "Honestly, Jeffrey... I'm afraid to take back my position. Afraid I'll break it somehow. I don't know how to lead like you do."

Jeffrey felt a stab of hope. Part of him wanted to stay, more than anything. But it wasn't the best path. These workers would be fine without him. To stay now might cause them to lean on him too much. He knew where he was needed.

Jeffrey looked across the lawn, where Alexandra was deep in discussion with a bay worker.

Jeffrey turned back to Vanderman and smiled.

"It's okay. They'll teach you."

> **SUMMARY**
>
> - Instead of asking, "Why didn't you step in?" we should ask, "Are you stepping back? Are you letting your people lead?"
>
> - In great organizations, everyone gets the credit—the workers for owning and driving it, the team for supporting it, and the boss for building leaders.

ACTION: Commend Someone Else

Congratulations! You've just met a major objective. REMEMBER, now more than ever, that you are not the center of the universe. You didn't make this happen. Your workers did.

By "commend," we don't just mean go to their office and give them a pat on the back.

What honors are YOU being offered because of this project? Have you been invited to interview for a newspaper, magazine, or TV show? Who do you think is most responsible for how this success played out? Invite them along or suggest that they might be a better person to interview.

IDENTIFY AN HONOR that you are privy to as a result of this success, and pass it on or share it with someone else who you think deserves it. Find some meaningful way to reward them AND publicly honor them for the work they've done.

Are there other teams or people who deserve a thank you? What would they most appreciate? What is most useful or would benefit them most in their future?

RESULTS – Where Hands-Off Leadership Gets Tested

LEADERSHIP SCORECARD

NAME: Jeffrey Jackson

MY OVERALL SCORE: 3.5

4	**STEP AWAY** SUPPORT To Unleash Excellence	- All hands implemented the new plan, adapting their zones as needed and reporting back regularly - Profitability in 3 weeks (!!!), driven by everyone together - Team gave credit and encouragement unprompted (saw lots of this among teammates. I appreciated being included, too.) - Team is prepared to take initiative under Vanderman
3	**STEP BACK** COACH To Inspire Ownership	- Brainstormed Finish Line with team and charted a course together
2	**STEP BESIDE** TRAIN To Build Capability	- Discussed Hands-Off Leadership basics with Vanderman and gave him a tour of new bay prior to management hand-off
1	**STEP UP** TELL To Ensure Clarity	
0	**STEP IN** TAKE OVER To Create Stability	

WEEK THIRTEEN

NEVERBOSS - Crenshaw

TURNAROUND SCORECARD

NAME: _Jeffrey Jackson_

SELF Grade = [A]   BOSS Grade = [A]

STANDARD: *"An ideal employee in this position..."*	METRICS: *"We will know these standards are met when..."*	
CULTURE Creates leaders instead of followers. Builds relationships with co-workers.	- Workers take initiative	A+
	- Workers say meetings are exciting and effective	A+
CLARITY Admits when wrong and allows team members to hold him accountable, regardless of title or rank. Doesn't overrule reasonable decisions made by workers.	- Workers are comfortable speaking up and feel heard	A
	- All workers know their areas of responsibility and have authority over them	A+
CAPABILITY When a worker is underperforming, trains instead of taking over. Retains and improves employee talent.	- Improve employee turnover by at least 5% *Zero Turnover!*	A-
	Keep practicing coaching instead of giving answers	B+
FOCUS Worker MPAs and KPIs are established. Workers are reporting KPIs.	- Overtime needs to drop to less than 5%	B+
	Overtime dropped by half. Plans in place to reach target.	B+
VISION Responds to sudden threats and golden opportunities. Team works in a unified direction towards a shared master goal.	- Factories serviced on time, never forced to halt operations	A
	- Allocates budget carefully and maintains adequate emergency reserves *Team's emergency response is A+*	A+
RESULTS Team meets commitments and standards. Gives meaningful commendations to workers.	- No fines *Had to pay fine for smell*	A-
	- Master goal is on target to be met *Master goal met!*	A
	- Workers feel they have received credit for their work *Credit for work!*	

RESULTS – Where Hands-Off Leadership Gets Tested

Dear Mr. Heart,

The trial period on our leadership experiment has concluded. Jeffrey's most recent scorecards are attached for you to review.

You will notice Jeffrey's turnaround scores are all at or above the minimum standard we set for him. There is still work to do. However, I feel very comfortable recommending him for another management position. His progress has been exemplary and he is continuing to grow. I believe his next team will thrive.

Thank you for this opportunity. It has been a pleasure to work with your bright and enthusiastic employees. I look forward to discussing next steps with you at our Thursday meeting.

A Hamilton

Alexandra Hamilton

INTO THE FIRE

Jeffrey Jackson loved his job.

Just as Vanderman was returning to his post, Jeffrey and Alexandra were invited to Heart Manufacturing headquarters. Jeffrey knew he'd passed with flying colors. He assumed this meeting would discuss the cash-positive system their region created, and consider how to roll it out to the rest of the districts. He had a full report in a folder under his arm and a slide presentation on his thumb drive. He'd never felt more prepared in his life.

He checked his watch again. *Early. Good.*

When Jeffrey and Alexandra arrived, they were admitted to a shiny glass room. This was *the* conference room. Mr. Heart greeted them personally at the door.

Jeffrey felt a flood a warmth for this man he barely knew. Mr. Heart was a powerful man, but he was growing old. His hair was more white than gray, and today he seemed unsteady on his feet.

"Mr. Heart!" Jeffrey shook hands, surprised at Heart's strength. "I wanted to thank you for giving me a second chance." Jeffrey paused and swallowed. "I didn't know until later that you were the only person who wanted me to stay."

Mr. Heart lit up and laughed quietly. "I don't like to give up."

"Something we have in common, I think." Jeffrey smiled. "Sir, I don't know why you picked me to test Alexandra's leadership style, but it's changed my life forever."

Heart looked Jeffrey in the eyes. "Your success couldn't have come at a better time. Find yourself a seat. We'll be starting soon."

More people wandered in. Mostly people in thousand-dollar suits.

Jeffrey leaned over to Alexandra, a little confused. "Where are the other regional managers?"

Alexandra whispered back. "They aren't here?"

"No." Jeffrey shook his head. "That's Tom Jennings. He leads production design for the factories. Sarah Suthers, Chief Engineer, is sitting next to him. Then there's Heart's head of HR, their CFO, and legal counsel... and a handful of other people I've never seen before. I don't see any GooCrew faces."

Alexandra shrugged.

The massive conference table held 20 seats. When all of them were filled, Heart's entire executive team filed into the room, and they shut the doors.

Everyone looked expectantly at Mr. Heart.

Mr. Heart took a deep breath. "Friends and loyal employees... Heart Manufacturing is about to go bankrupt."

Jeffrey felt his heart skip a beat.

"We're massively short on money to pay our obligations," Heart admitted flatly. "After months of trying to avoid this outcome, my team and I have exhausted all the avenues we can see. We have no idea what to do."

Mr. Heart had desperation in his eyes as he looked around the table. "We've cherry-picked you to be in this room because you're the very best people we have. You have three days to look for a solution. In the end, if you see no way out, I will accept your conclusion, and we will close our doors."

The weight of what he was saying finally registered. Jaws began to drop.

Mr. Heart sagged. "To be clear, this isn't the bailout kind of bankruptcy. Your people... our people... will all lose their jobs."

Into The Fire

The engineer was angry. "How could you wait until the last moment to bring us in?" she asked. "You want us to prevent bankruptcy in *three days?*"

"Look, I feel horrible," Mr. Heart snapped. "I never created this company to get rich. I wanted to create jobs—good, safe factory work that paid a living wage—"

Mr. Heart took a sharp breath, trying to keep his emotions under control. "As you prioritize financial burdens," he added in a softer voice, "please be kind to our workers. If you need to choose between laying people off or cutting hours, cut hours. Our workers are number one."

With that, Heart went silent, unable to say more. He gave a brusque nod to his CFO, who stepped forward and set a stack of folders on the edge of the table. "These are our most recent financial statements." The CFO said. "Good luck."

Then Mr. Heart fled the room. The executive board followed him without a word.

As the door clicked shut, the room filled with suffocating silence.

Eventually, someone coughed.

"How did we get here?" a sales manager asked in a tight, flabbergasted voice. "I know *my* department isn't the problem. We always meet our targets."

"My region had record output last quarter," said a production head.

"Just because you earned your Christmas bonus doesn't mean you're profitable," snapped an accountant. "That's *exactly* our problem. You guys only care about yourselves. You never think about the big picture."

The argument quickly dissolved into chaos.

Jeffrey felt like the wind had been knocked out of him. *Heart Manufacturing, bankrupt?* The thought was inconceivable. But then he thought back over the past few years. All the equipment upgrades that kept getting declined, the increasingly tighter budgets, the obsessive irritation over fines and overtime costs. In retrospect, it was obvious. How had he missed it?

At some point, Jeffrey noticed Alexandra. She sat calmly in her chair, musing over the news but not startled.

His eyes narrowed. "You knew?"

She nodded grudgingly. "Sort of... Heart called a few days ago. Didn't tell me what the problem was. Just that something was wrong and he was about to let a lot of people down. I suggested he pull the key stakeholders together, be honest with them, and ask for their help... I guess that's what this is."

For about 20 minutes, people panicked. They accused each other of recklessness, selfishness, and stupidity. They even suggested embezzlement.

Jeffrey and Alexandra watched the whole affair carefully.

Finally, Jeffrey grimaced. "This isn't working."

"We need buy-in," she replied. "What's something you all have in common?"

Jeffrey thought for a moment, then reached out and knocked on the table. No one noticed. So Jeffrey slammed a hand down, hard.

The loud bang startled everyone into silence. They turned and stared.

"Before we settle into painful negotiations," Jeffrey said, "there's one question we should answer."

"What?" asked an annoyed lawyer.

"Is this company even worth saving?" Jeffrey raised his hand high in the air. "By raise of hands, how many of you love Heart Manufacturing and want to see it live past today?"

The question startled them. For a moment, no one responded.

But slowly, one by one, people joined in until every hand in the room was up.

People looked at each other. The pain in their eyes relaxed a little.

"I'm scared, too," Jeffrey admitted. "But this isn't a game of Clue. Heart didn't gather us to look for a murderer."

They laughed a little.

"We're the people who give him hope," Jeffrey pointed out. "If anyone can turn this around, he believes it's us. We're not enemies.

We're allies. Even if we have different ways of doing things, everyone here has been doing their best to help this company succeed."

They were still deeply shaken, but the anger started to evaporate.

Jeffrey invited everyone to sit back down, and he passed around the financial statement folders.

"Let's look at the hand we've been dealt." Jeffrey picked up his folder and opened it.

For three days, they barely slept. People brought food from time to time, and everyone took turns stealing troubled naps in the corners and nearby rooms. At night, theirs was the only light on in the building. The meeting never stopped.

Tens of thousands of jobs were on the line. The accountant on their team crunched numbers over and over. More than once as they struggled to make things fit, Jeffrey thought of Arnold, who was still working graveyard shifts, praying for a two-dollar raise.

On the third day, they emerged. At the team's request, Jeffrey presented their plan. Jeffrey's suit was wrinkled, and he had bags under his eyes, but he had never felt better about himself.

"We have 130 changes," Jeffrey announced, passing out copies of their plan to Mr. Heart and the executive board.

The CFO whistled.

"30% of those changes will require massive concessions from the unions," Jeffrey admitted. "We'd like to save those changes until the end. We believe by implementing the other 70% first, we can demonstrate that we care about the union personnel."

Jeffrey looked around at his ragged team. They were exhausted, but everyone was excited about their plan. "We all agree that we want to bear as much of the burden up top as possible, before taking a penny away from our loyal blue-collar employees. Everyone here has agreed to a pay cut."

Heart nodded. "I hope you included me in that count."

Jeffrey relaxed a little. "We did take the liberty of recommending one, sir. You'll find the numbers on page 3."

Heart looked at the page. He signed his initials next to it and traded papers with his CFO. "Effective immediately."

The CFO glanced at the sheet, then at Jeffrey's team. Unexpectedly, the CFO also made an adjustment to the sheet, initialed it, and then passed it to the next executive. Wordlessly, all the executives reduced their salaries.

Jeffrey's team took heart.

For the next half hour, Jeffrey quickly summarized the controversial parts of the new budget. Mr. Heart listened carefully to every word as Jeffrey laid out their plan.

"It won't be easy… But it fits, sir," Jeffrey concluded.

Mr. Heart laughed once, choking in relief. He leaned forward, eagerly reviewing the numbers in front of him.

"This plan is brilliant. How do you recommend we proceed?"[18]

---

[18] This final chapter is based on an emergency meeting held by Lufthansa Airlines in 1992. By 2000, Lufthansa not only recouped their losses—they broke their previous profit records.

GLOSSARY OF TOOLS & RESOURCES

Now that you see the big picture, we have summarized the crucial elements of a Hands-Off Leadership culture for your reference. These tools and resources are arranged chronologically, as they appear in this book.

CRITICAL ELEMENTS

Hands-Off Leadership Definition & Roadmap (p. viii)

A clear description of Hands-Off Leadership, its benefits, and the steps for implementing it. "Empowerment" is a popular concept with many variations (some of which are unhealthy). By defining Hands-Off Leadership, you clarify the vision and inspire your team. The Roadmap helps you eliminate uncertainty and build buy-in by making the path clear.

List of Feeling, Thinking, Acting Questions (p. 18, 29, 37)

Questions to spur feeling, thinking, and initiative. Helps you inspire ownership and break out of controlling leadership. We give you specific examples, so it's easier to think on your feet.

Step Up, Step Beside, Step Away (p. 45)

Leadership Steps that make it easier to see the impact you have on your team. Gives you room to intervene when necessary, and holds you accountable when you are intervening too much.

Principles of Buy-In and Agility (p. 58)

Tools for winning universal support quickly. HOL requires stepping back and allowing teams to decide. Without buy-in and agility, decisions will be slow and painful. With them, decisions get made in record time, and everyone feels heard.

Fast Flex Meeting Structure (p. 69)

Pain-free, team-run meetings you'll look forward to attending. Your meetings are the best measure of the health of your team or company. If your meetings are painful or dull, something is wrong.

1-on-1's (p. 73)

Weekly meetings between leaders and direct reports. Tackle and review issues together without interrupting regular work. Your best training, coaching, and early intervention opportunity.

Rules of Engagement (p. 88)

Standards that create universal safety, so information flows freely. Makes it safe for everyone to say what is on their mind. Without this, groupthink or silence can emerge, and people will not feel safe holding each other accountable.

Open Floor Policy (p. 99)

"If you have a problem with someone, talk with them directly. We'll keep it safe." Addresses a very common problem—people don't like to confront each other directly. They'd rather use a grapevine. Requiring candor (while ensuring safety and resolution) improves trust and accountability among team members.

Leadership Roles (p. 113)

A clear definition of the different leadership and team roles, each with unique responsibilities and authority. Without this, confusion is unavoidable. Once these duties are clear, everyone naturally works and thinks on the same page.

Zones Chart (p. 116)

Clear division of responsibilities, so everyone knows who is accountable for what. Used instead of (or with) a traditional org chart, this communicates zone ownership. Also, identifies allies people can turn to and prevents turf wars.

Decision-Making Authority (p. 129)

Reserving the right to "make the call" when the situation requires it. Prevents bottlenecks when teams get gridlocked. Also, a crucial guardrail that allows you to intervene without violating your promise to be hands-off.

Guiding Principles (p. 132 and 137)

Time-tested truths that inspire and guide action. Principles sound like common sense rules, but they are also backed with Actual Data. They act as guardrails—naturally aligning everyone's work and making initiative safe for both bosses and workers.

Accountability (p. 143)

Everyone is accountable to everyone else, regardless of title or rank. People also answer directly to their teams and managers. Empowers anyone to raise the issue when something is wrong.

Turnaround Scorecard & Safe Intervention Process (p. 159)

A fast, fair way to save the people who can do better. Some of your employees will struggle. You also need a generous but firm strategy for approaching employees who aren't improving.

Certifying Competence (p. 166)

A simple method for verifying decisions or skill. It's unwise to give full power to people who don't understand their jobs. "Certifying" builds learning and confidence without killing initiative.

Actionable Mission Statement (p. 228)

An inspiring, shared agreement about where you are headed, so people know the big picture. Naturally focuses initiative.

Active Waiting Strategy (p. 237)

A tool for responding to golden opportunities or sudden threats. Without this, almost any organization can become nearsighted and not respond to changing market conditions.

Thematic Goal (p. 238)

Hyper-focus for the entire company over the next 6-9 months. Unifies short-term vision. Empowers Hands-Off Leadership organizations to move efficiently in unison, without silos and turf wars.

Well-Defined Finish Line (p. 258)

Communicate where you're headed and when you've arrived. This prepares everyone to switch the moment you're ready for something new. Prevents stagnation and "succeeding to death."

SUPPORTING TOOLS

The following tools are also introduced in *Neverboss* and make it easier to navigate common situations. Like the Critical Elements, these are arranged in the order they appear.

Glossary of Tools & Resources - Supporting Tools

"Redefining Pride" Exercise (p. 44)

An activity that prepares you to take pride in others' accomplishments. Redefining pride establishes your new purpose as a leader and prepares you to celebrate your team's initiative. Otherwise, when you give up power, you might feel useless and tempted to take back the reins.

Leadership Scorecard (p. 46)

A tool to measure how often you intervene. Old habits die hard. To break them, you need visibility. A scorecard gives you an objective way to measure progress together and see what areas could improve.

eGROW Coaching Method (p. 54)

A simple tool that inspires ownership, initiative, and innovation. Coaching is essential to HOL. eGROW helps anyone coach effectively without formal training, so they can start to build leaders around them immediately.

Initiative Scorecards (p. 71)

A two-minute tool for measuring employee empowerment. Encourages initiative while giving visibility on what is being worked on, without adding busy work. It also communicates the HOL vision to everyone and provides metrics on progress.

Efficient Communication Channels (p. 122)

This tool filters communication by urgency. Hands-Off Leadership teams move faster. To maintain visibility, everyone needs fast communication channels that get the right information to the right people at the right time.

Quality-of-Decision Training (p. 131)

Shared standards for making good decisions. People usually make decisions based on personal instinct, with bad results. This simple training prepares people for greater autonomy. It helps them communicate their choices, prepares them to accept each other's choices, and lays the foundation for accountability.

"Daily Intents" Check-Ins (p. 148)

A simple tool for reporting back and staying in sync. A fast way for teams to coordinate and help each other. Increases transparency and creates effortless accountability, reducing the need for supervisor intervention.

Moneyball Recruiting (p. 181)

A super-efficient hiring strategy that screens for initiative, intelligence, and teachability. One unexpected thing that reinforces bad leadership is traditional hiring. You strengthen your Hands-Off Leadership culture by hiring people who will thrive in it.

Most Profitable Activities Chart (MPAs) (p. 200)

A quick way to see everyone's MPAs. An MPA Chart is a vital boundary that keeps your organization productive. It helps excited employees focus their attention. Without this, you'll have squirrel syndrome—too many people chasing too many tasks.

Initial Cleansing Exercise (p. 208)

A fast activity that gives overloaded workers power to combine and prune responsibilities. Helps people focus when they have more freedom. Supports Multipurposing and Four Ways to Say No.

Multipurposing (p. 209)

Resolving multiple problems and opportunities with a single solution. This skill helps everyone think like a CEO, making optimal decisions and selecting ideal opportunities.

Four Ways to Say No (p. 217)

Four memorable tools that make it easier to say no: *Burn Box, Parking List, Intentionally Ignore,* and *Dumpster.* Great leaders say no—a lot. These tools help maintain focus when everyone starts having too many good ideas.

Glossary of Tools & Resources - Supporting Tools

Quick Business Case (QBC) (p. 220)

A vetting protocol for new ideas. Creates fast standards for saying yes or no. Trains everyone to filter their own suggestions and think like business owners. The result is better ideas, faster.

"Commend Someone Else" Exercise (p. 268)

An exercise to build a rewarding new habit of commending others. It's tempting to take credit for work your team did. Giving credit reinforces equality, personal ownership, and motivation at all levels. And it feels wonderful.

About the Author

Kevin Crenshaw is a culture turnaround expert, rapid turnaround CEO, and leadership trainer. He draws on more than 35 years of leadership and consulting experience—transforming leaders and firms in dozens of industries around the world. As a speaker, coach, and leader, he loves stories and principles that inspire hearts, reach minds, and unleash lasting change. He is currently the approachable CEO of Priacta, Inc.

Before branching off as a 6x+ entrepreneur, Kevin earned his BS in Physics and worked as a space shuttle & satellite technician. (His fingerprints are in space.) He and his wife, Midge, are parents of 10 highly entrepreneurial children.

About the Owner of Story

Laura Shanae Crenshaw is a senior in Business Entrepreneurship at Arizona State University. A passionate writer, she created Jeffrey and his world from 100 hours of interviews and real-life stories. Her recommendations and tireless initiative helped distill the Neverboss model into its simplest form.

Made in the USA
Coppell, TX
14 September 2021